NOWVILLE

NOWVILLE

THE UNTOLD HISTORY OF NASHVILLE'S CONTEMPORARY ART SCENE

JOE NOLAN

VANDERBILT UNIVERSITY PRESS

Nashville, Tennessee

Library of Congress Cataloging-in-Publication Data

Names: Nolan, Joe, 1970- author.
Title: Nowville : the untold history of Nashville's contemporary art
    scene / Joe Nolan.
Description: Nashville, Tennessee : Vanderbilt University Press, [2024] |
    Includes index.
Identifiers: LCCN 2024017630 (print) | LCCN 2024017631 (ebook) | ISBN
    9780826507396 (paperback) | ISBN 9780826507402 (epub) | ISBN
    9780826507419 (pdf)
Subjects: LCSH: Art and society--Tennessee--Nashville--History--20th
    century. | Art and society--Tennessee--Nashville--History--21st century.
    | Artists--Tennessee--Nashville--Interviews. | Nashville
    (Tenn.)--Intellectual life--20th century. | Nashville
    (Tenn.)--Intellectual life--21st century.
Classification: LCC N72.S6 N65 2024 (print) | LCC N72.S6 (ebook) | DDC
    701/.030976855--dc23/eng/20240722
LC record available at https://lccn.loc.gov/2024017630
LC ebook record available at https://lccn.loc.gov/2024017631

To Antonia

CONTENTS

THE CAST

DAVID ONRI ANDERSON is an artist and curator. David exhibits his multimedia paintings internationally. He's the cofounder of Mild Climate gallery and founder of The Electric Shed exhibition space in his backyard in South Nashville.

https://davidonrianderson.com/home.html

CELENE AUBRY is a designer and printmaker, as well as the associate director and manager of Nashville's iconic Hatch Show Print.

https://www.hatchshowprint.com

KELLY BONADIES is a developer, curator, and artist. Kelly is a talented painter whose Bonadies Urban Development has transformed several North Nashville properties to house galleries, studios, artisanal small businesses, and more.

https://www.budbuilds.com/kelly-bonadies

OMARI BOOKER is a multimedia artist. Omari's paintings range from portraits and personal narratives to works that use symbols and allegory to address social issues.

https://omaribooker.com

JARED BRENNAN is a musician, designer, archivist, curator, and gallerist. Jared created the Historic High custom vintage fashion brand. He's also the founder of the Brikolaj boutique/gallery/performance space at The Arcade.

https://www.instagram.com/_brikolaj_

LANDRY BUTLER is a visual artist, spoken word performer, and musician. He is a founding member of the Untitled Artists group.

https://www.landrybutler.com/about

CHRIS CAMPBELL is an artist and curator. She is the founder of Ruby Green gallery.

https://rubygreengallery.blogspot.com

DANE CARDER is an artist, curator, and gallerist. Dane's paintings are steeped in Southern history, and his Threesquared Gallery and Dane Carder Studio helped to define the Wedgewood-Houston arts district.

https://danecarder.com

MATT CHRISTY is an artist, educator, and writer. Matt is a prolific multimedia artist as well as a novelist, art critic, and professor.

https://www.theredarrowgallery.com/artist/matt-christy

KATIE CONNOLLY is a collage and assemblage artist. Katie makes use of materials and techniques traditionally associated with craft making. She's a cofounder of the Yart Sale happenings.

https://www.instagram.com/katie_dazey

JEFF DANLEY is an artist. Jeff's meticulous portraits paint their subjects into surreal narratives. He was a studio artist at The Fugitive Art Center.

https://www.cumberlandgallery.com/jeff-danley-page

JAYJIT DASGUPTA is a film and television writer/director/producer as well as a visual artist and a poet. Jay spearheaded the "Salon" art house-party scene in Nashville.

https://www.jayjitdasgupta.com

PATRICK DEGUIRA is an artist, curator, and educator. Patrick's conceptual art practice includes a wide range of materials and techniques. He was a board member of the Fugitive Art Center.

https://www.patrickdeguira.com

AMANDA DILLINGHAM is an artist, educator, and filmmaker. She's a cofounder of the Secret Show series.

https://gsfta.com/arts-programs/filmmaking

CHRIS DOUBLER is an artist and gallery designer. Chris's multimedia art practice includes printmaking and music synthesis. He's the cofounder of Apollo Art Services.

https://www.apolloartservices.com

SAM DUNSON is an artist and educator. Sam is known for his signature painting style, and his practice also includes experimental animation and sculpture.

https://www.samueldunson.com

ROBERT DURHAM is a painter and educator. Bob's masterful, uncanny portraits often cast his fellow artists in scenes ranging from irreverent to disturbing. Bob was one of the original studio artists at The Fugitive Art Center.

https://www.cumberlandgallery.com/robert-durham-page

SARA ESTES is an artist, curator, and writer. Sara was the curator of Threesquared Gallery in the Chestnut building. Her art and culture writing has appeared in local, regional, and national outlets.

https://copytiger.com/about

MARLOS E'VAN is an artist and educator. Marlos is a multimedia artist whose sometimes-satirical art practice spans from painting to filmmaking. He's a cofounder of the McGruder Social Practice Artist Residency at the McGruder Center in North Nashville.

https://www.marlosevan.com

RICHARD FEASTER is an artist and curator. Richard's large abstract paintings combine techniques in formalist explorations of materials.

https://zeitgeist-art.com/richardfeaster

CARY GIBSON is an artist and curator. Cary's wide-ranging art intersects with her spiritual practice and her social activism. She's a former artist-in-residence at the Downtown Presbyterian Church.

https://www.instagram.com/carygibsonart

BETH GILMORE is an artist, curator, and gallerist. Beth's multimedia art practice is informed by her love of history. She's a former artist-in-residence at the Downtown Presbyterian Church and the cofounder of Twist Art Gallery, which helped to launch the original Downtown Art Crawl.

http://www.bethgilmore.com

J. TODD Greene is a prolific artist and musician. His *Paw Paw Sermons* exhibition at J&J's Market & Cafe was a sold-out affair that helped to put Nashville's alternative art spaces scene on the map. Todd was also the second-ever artist-in-residence at the Downtown Presbyterian Church.

https://www.jtoddgreene.com

ANDY HARDING is an artist. Andy's otherworldly sculptures combine natural materials with cosmic concepts. He was in the first generation of the Downtown Presbyterian Church's artists-in-residence program.

https://www.andyhardingart.com

KRISTI HARGROVE is an artist and educator. Kristi's art practice explores the overlap of sculpture and drawing. As an educator she was instrumental in transforming Watkins Institute into an accredited college, and in developing Nashville's first and only MFA program.

https://kristihargrove.com/home.html

BRADY HASTON is an artist and educator. Brady's drawings and paintings reflect the historical, geographical, and personal narratives he pulls from his local environment in Nashville. He has mentored a generation of artists as an associate professor at Watkins College of Art.

https://bradyhaston.com/home.html

DUSTIN HEDRICK is an artist and curator. Dustin is best known for his painter's tape mural installations. He's also the founder of Channel to Channel gallery.

http://dhedrick.com

JOHN HILLEY was the pastor at the Downtown Presbyterian Church when he helped to launch their storied artists-in-residence program in 1994.

http://patmosllc.com/the-team

RYAN HOGAN is an artist and futurist. Ryan's sculptures and performances combine an unlikely mix of sci-fi conceptualizing and gooey, sticky physicality. In Ryan's Nowville, it's always tomorrow.

https://ryanphogan.com

DANIEL HOLLAND is an artist. Daniel is known for his large, abstract, multimedia paintings. He was one of the artists who occupied a studio space at the Chestnut building.

https://www.danielhollandart.com/bio

JIM HOOBLER is a historian and curator. Jim was senior curator of art and architecture at the Tennessee State Museum. He's also the church historian of the Downtown Presbyterian Church.

https://www.amazon.com/This-Used-Nashville-Jim-Hoobler/dp/1681063425

MARK HOSFORD is an artist and educator. Mark has exhibited his printmaking, drawing, and animation internationally. He's an associate professor and the chair of the department of art at Vanderbilt University.

https://sugarboypress.com

LAURA HUTSON HUNTER is a writer and curator. Laura is an independent curator and the arts editor of the *Nashville Scene*.

https://laurahutsonhunter.com

COURTNEY ADAIR JOHNSON is an artist, educator, and curator. Johnson's art is rooted in environmental and social themes and makes use of reused and recycled materials in her work. She's a cofounder of the McGruder Social Practice Artist Residency at the McGruder Center in North Nashville.

https://www.courtneyadairjohnson.com

VERONICA KAVASS is an art critic and book author. She helped to define The Packing Plant as a contemporary art destination as the first curator to display creative work in the building before it was renovated and remodeled.

https://www.instagram.com/veronk11

M KELLEY is an artist, curator, writer, and educator. M is a champion of handmade art and publishing, and a prominent member of Nashville's printmaking community.

https://linktr.ee/studiomnivorous

SUSAN KNOWLES is an art historian, curator, and writer. Susan is an independent curator and one of the first art writers for the *Nashville Scene*.

https://www.linkedin.com/in/susan-knowles-44a80b12

DANIEL LAI is an artist and curator. Daniel founded the Dangenart Gallery at The Arcade and helped to launch the original Downtown Art Crawl.

https://www.artbydaniellai.com/about-the-artist

RON LAMBERT is an artist and educator. Ron's videos and sculpture often push at the boundaries of what contemporary art can be. He was a professor at Watkins College of Art and a founding member of the COOP artists collective.

https://www.instagram.com/ronlambertart

ALEX LOCKWOOD is an artist and gallerist. Alex is known for his colorful, large-scale, figurative sculptures made from recycled materials. He's the founder of Elephant art gallery in North Nashville.

https://alockwood.com

DAVID MADDOX is a musician and writer. David is an avant-garde jazz saxophone player who became an influential art critic at the *Nashville Scene* during the first wave of Nashville's contemporary art renaissance.

https://perambulating.blogspot.com

JULIA MARTIN is an artist, curator, and gallerist. Julia's whimsical painted portraits and narrative scenes feature the same loose, intuitive style she brings to programming her namesake gallery.

https://www.juliamartingallery.com

JONATHAN MARX is a writer and editor. Jonathan was the *Nashville Scene*'s first culture editor. He was instrumental in making a space for local contemporary art in the pages of the city's alt weekly.

https://www.instagram.com/jonathanmarx

MICHAEL J. MCBRIDE is an artist, curator, and educator. Michael is a painter and illustrator and an instructor at Tennessee State University. Michael cofounded Atelier 427 with James Threalkill, and the pair are recognized as creative godfathers of today's North Nashville muralist movement.

https://linktr.ee/michaeljmcbrideart

BRYCE MCCLOUD is a printmaker whose varied production spans commercial art, traditional printing, and conceptual community-based projects.

https://www.isleofprinting.com

JERRY DALE MCFADDEN is a musician, curator, and gallerist. Jerry Dale is a keyboardist and member of The Mavericks. He's also the cofounder of The Attic Gallery (TAG)—one of the creative spaces that launched Nashville's original Downtown Art Crawl.

https://www.instagram.com/jerrydalemcfadden

ARMON MEANS is an artist, curator, educator, and motorcycle enthusiast. Armon is a photographer, a lecturer, and studio technician at Watkins College of Art at Belmont University.

https://www.armonmeans.com

RICHARD S. MITCHELL is an artist and curator. Richard's conceptual, multimedia art often explores and challenges viewer's perceptions. Richard played key roles in the development of both the Untitled Artists group and The Fugitive Art Center.

http://www.urchard.com

ELISHEBA MROZIK is an artist and creative community organizer. Elisheba is a pioneering North ("Norf") Nashville mural artist and the owner/operator of One Drop Ink Tattoo Parlour and Gallery. She's also a cofounder of the Jefferson Street Art Crawl and the North Nashville Creative Coalition.

https://www.queenbeeink.com

ADRIENNE OUTLAW is an artist, curator, and writer. Adrienne's known for her socially engaged multimedia sculpture. She's the founder of Seed Space gallery.

https://linktr.ee/adrienne_outlaw

LESLEY PATTERSON-MARX is an artist and educator. Lesley is a multimedia artist whose creative practice spans textile art, printmaking, and book art. She was on the board of the Fugitive Art Center and a founding member of the Platetone Printshop.

https://lesleypattersonmarx.com/home.html

GREG POND is an artist, curator, and educator. Greg's multimedia sculpture installations, films, and writing reflect on everything from pop culture to politics, from architecture to the natural environment. He's the cofounder of The Fugitive Art Center along with Bryan Hunter.

https://gregpond.net/about

JAIME RAYBIN is an artist and curator. Jaime's multimedia work marries her attention to detail to offbeat cultural and scientific observations. She cofounded the Off the Wall artist collective.

https://jaimeraybin.com/pages/bio.html

KIT REUTHER is a self-taught painter, sculptor, and a veteran of the Chestnut building's art studio community.

https://www.kitreuther.com

DAVID RIBAR is an artist, curator, educator, and writer. David is a Belmont University professor emeritus and one of the *Nashville Scene*'s first art critics.

https://david-ribar.squarespace.com

JACK TUTTLE SNELL RYAN is an artist and educator. Jack's art explores culture through sound, drawing, and sculpture. He played key, early roles in the development of The Fugitive Art Center and the evolution of Watkins College of Art.

https://www.jacksnell-ryan.com/biocontact

HANS SCHMITT-MATZEN is an artist and curator. Hans is a painter and sculptor, a former board member of Fugitive Works, a founding member of the COOP artists collective, and an artist-in-residence at the Downtown Presbyterian Church.

https://www.hansschmittmatzen.com

JON SEWELL is a founder and publisher. Jon is the owner of The Packing Plant, which he transformed from a dilapidated meatpacking building into a creative center that's become the hub of the contemporary art scene in Nashville's Wedgewood-Houston neighborhood. Sewell is also the co-publisher of the *SALT Weekly* counterculture zine.

https://www.thepackingplant.com

JAMAAL SHEATS is an artist, educator, and curator. Jamaal exhibits his sculpture internationally. He's the director and curator of the Fisk University galleries, where he's also an assistant professor and an expert on the Alfred Stieglitz Collection.

https://www.jamaalsheats.com

JIM SHERRADEN is an artist, preservationist, and educator. Jim's celebrated printmaking is emblematic of Nashville's letterpress scene. He mentored a new generation of Nashville print artists during three decades as master printmaker and manager of Hatch Show Print.

https://jimsherraden.com

SHAUN SLIFER is an artist, curator, and educator. Shaun cofounded the Rule of Thirds house gallery in Nashville.

https://www.sslifer.net

TERRI SMITH is a curator, writer, and educator. Terri's groundbreaking contemporary art programming at the museum at Cheekwood Estate and Gardens helped to amplify the aesthetics of Nashville's underground art scene, connecting local trends and movements to national and international contemporary art conversations.

https://terricsmith.blogspot.com

NICK STOLLE is an artist. Nick's evolving creative practice spans a variety of mediums. His art combines offhand aesthetics with conceptual sophistication.

https://nickstolle.org

TERRY THACKER is an artist and educator. Terry is an abstract painter and an aesthetic philosopher who mentored a generation of Middle Tennessee artists as a beloved educator at various institutions.

https://www.cumberlandgallery.com/terry-thacker-page

JAMES THREALKILL is an artist and educator. James is known for his chromatic portrait painting and his tireless creative work with young people. He cofounded Atelier 427 at the Chestnut building, and he was special assistant for community affairs and arts in the office of the mayor of Nashville during Phil Bredesen's term.

https://jamesthrealkillarts.com/bio/james-threalkill

CAROLINE VINCENT is a curator and gallerist. Caroline is the cofounder of Twist Art Gallery, which helped to launch the original Downtown Art Crawl.

https://www.thecreativemanager.com

BEN VITUALLA is an artist, curator, educator, and gallerist. Ben is the founder of the pioneering community-art-based gallery Blend Studio.

https://blendstudio.wordpress.com/exhibits

THAXTON ABSHALOM WATERS is an artist, educator, curator, and gallerist. Thaxton helped to launch the North Nashville mural movement, and he's the founder of the Art History Class Lifestyle Lounge & Gallery.

https://www.instagram.com/arthistoryclassllg

CARLTON WILKINSON is an artist, educator, curator, and gallerist. Carlton is a photographer and a Nashville native. He's the founder of the In the Gallery art gallery in North Nashville and the Nashville African American Arts Association (N4A).

https://www.wilkinsonarts.com

HERB WILLIAMS is an artist and curator. Herb is best known for his Crayon sculptures, his street art, and his public projects. He was one of the first wave of artists to pass through the Downtown Presbyterian Church's artists-in-residence program.

https://www.herbwilliamsart.com

TOM WILLS is a painter and a film archivist. He's the founder of the Downtown Presbyterian Church's artists-in-residence program.

https://dpchurch.com/art/artist-residency

WOKE is an artist and curator. Woke is a native Nashvillian. He went to Tennessee State University before becoming a pioneering muralist who helped to spark the creative renewal of North ("Norf") Nashville.

https://wokethree.com

DONNA WOODLEY is an artist and curator. Donna Woodley's portraits and narrative scenes engage social issues with irreverence and humor. She's one of the artists associated with the creative revival in North Nashville.

https://www.donnawoodley.com

JANET DECKER YANEZ is an artist, curator, and gallerist. Janet's process-focused art makes use of recycled materials to engage with social issues. She's an artist-in-residence at the Downtown Presbyterian Church and the founder of Ground Floor Gallery + Studios.

https://www.instagram.com/janet_decker_yanez

BARBARA YONTZ is an artist and educator. Barbara is a sculptor and university instructor who was instrumental in developing the baccalaureate program at Watkins College of Art.

http://www.barbarayontz.net

LAIN YORK is an artist and curator. Lain's abstract multimedia paintings are unmistakable, and he's known as the "Mayor of Art Town" for his tireless connecting of artists, opportunities, and resources across the city's creative scene. If Nashville's contemporary art renaissance had a motto it would be "You should talk to Lain."

https://lainyork.com/news.html

PREFACE

NASHVILLE'S CONTEMPORARY ART RENAISSANCE was sparked by a number of artist-led projects beginning in the 1990s. Artist groups, co-ops, studio communities, and independent, experimental galleries emerged in neighborhoods like Hillsboro Village and Wedgewood-Houston. These bootstrap projects repurposed unused spaces, deployed DIY innovating, and passed that knowledge to successive generations of independent artists and curators who have always been the lifeblood of Nashville's art scene. But while it's easy to find information about Nashville's art institutions or its commercial galleries, it's difficult to trace the Nashville tradition of domestic art exhibitions or to identify the founding members of a fringe creative group that formed and dissolved before the internet.

This book collects the voices of the people who created Nashville's contemporary art renaissance. The decades-long movement reclaimed the city's unique modern art legacy and transformed it into a vibrant and expansive visual arts community in the twenty-first century. The real story, the true underground story of Nashville's contemporary art scene, doesn't exist in an accessible form. I know that story because I was at the first Glow Shows in the early days of the Untitled Artists Group, and I rarely missed a dance party at The Fugitive. And in my writing about visual art in Nashville, I've covered nearly two decades of exhibitions, installations, and pop-ups in art journals, papers, and platforms from *Nashville Scene* to *Art in America.*

The most important fruit of Nashville's contemporary art renaissance is the community itself. I decided that the best way to present the talented, smart, funny, and generous people that make it up was to let them speak in their own voices. Most of the oral histories I love are pop culture books. George Plimpton and Jean Stein co-wrote an unforgettable oral biography about Edie Sedgwick called *Edie: American Girl.* Plimpton was associated with the New Journalism authors, and techniques like immersive reporting and using extended interview quotes are emblematic of that movement's groundbreaking literary journalism. There's a great oral biography of Perry Farrell and Jane's Addiction by Brendan Mullen called *Whores.* I've also read a handful of books by Victor Bockris who has written several oral biographies about literary and music icons like William S. Burroughs, The Velvet Underground, and Keith Richards. Bockris worked for *Interview* magazine at Andy Warhol's Factory headquarters where he developed his flair for conversational writing by never preparing interview questions and treating his assignments like cocktail party conversations.

This book was created from eighty interviews with seventy-six artists, curators, founders, leaders, writers, and educators between January 2022 and October 2023. Most of the interviews were recorded during Zoom sessions that lasted approximately one hour. I transcribed the audio from each interview and edited the texts down to the essential, relevant quotes I thought I might make use of. These pieces of conversation were pasted into documents labeled for the various chapters of the book. Once I'd completed, transcribed, and edited all the interviews for a given chapter, I arranged all of those quotes into a particular order. That process always began with identifying a "protagonist" whose comments serve as the trunk from which the rest of the conversation branches. I aimed to make a text that flowed like a conversation while also providing a clear history of each chapter's main subject. Some of my comments in the book are transcribed from the interviews, but some are bits I added as I read and re-read these chapters. Most of my words are there to tie the conversation together or bridge gaps in information.

I wrote the book's first chapter as a brief historical backdrop illuminating Nashville's unique place in the development of modern art in America. I couldn't collect a chorus of eyewitnesses to events that occurred about one hundred years ago, so I filled in these broad strokes based on my interview with artist Jamaal Sheats, director and curator of galleries and assistant professor of art at Fisk University. The phrase "Nashville's contemporary art *renaissance*" became a refrain in the book because the art scene in today's Nashville is a revival of the city's modern art legacy. The people, places, and events in the first chapter of the book bring layers of context to the chapters that follow.

I hope the result reads like the collection of eyewitness accounts that it is, but also like a poetic collage of conversations, snipped apart and pasted back together again, into a whole that's greater than the sum of its parts. For me, the book feels like an art object—a bubble of blown glass populated by all these innovative, gritty, inspired, hilarious personalities. It's like a snow globe but when you shake it, it's Crayon sculptures and rhinestones. It's immersive, with all these funny, sad, brave, and crazy conversations to drop in on. *Nowville* was built to transport you, the reader, into the moldy creative studios, living room galleries, front yard art sales, and warehouse dance parties found in these pages. It's like a snow globe but when you shake it, it's chicken-fried performance art and cast iron cornbread. You'll smell the fumes and hear the animals in the walls. You'll feel the frigid galleries at The Arcade in the winter, and watch the fireworks over the old Nashville Sounds baseball stadium from the roof of the Chestnut building, on a sweltering Saturday night, in the summer, in the South. You'll meet face-to-face with the brilliant, profane, talented, and irreverent personalities who share their stories here, inside of this glass bubble. It's like a snow globe but when you shake it, it's wood type and neon.

Nashville's Modern Art Legacy

1930–1949

IT FELT LIKE WE WERE BUILDING Nashville's contemporary art infra-
structure from the ground up in the 1990s. That was back when the active
ranks of the city's independent contemporary art scene could all gather
at a single Untitled Artist Group opening reception. Nashville's few commercial galleries mostly dismissed local emerging artists, so we found
alternative spaces to show our work in and built the walls to hang it on.
Most local audiences and potential collectors were out of touch with the
bigger regional and national art conversations we were trying to engage
with at that time. So we published reviews and interviews and profiles
to shine a light on local artists, demonstrating how we were up to something different than the paintings of guitars and of Nashville's iconic sky-
line that they still sell in the tourist gift shops downtown. We made studio spaces in forgotten industrial buildings and curated in our living
rooms. We stapled-together our cultural commentaries at Kinkos, and
traded cash for canvases at front yard art sales.

It felt like we were pioneers in undiscovered territory, cutting a path
to some untouched destination. But that wasn't entirely true. Many of us
were unaware of Nashville's role in the early development of modern art
in America. The biggest reason for this blind spot was that we were trying
to create work and curate spaces and write criticism that was of our moment at the edge of the millennium. Local events from the World Wars-
era seemed like ancient history to feral young bohemians at the dawn of

the internet. Another reason for the blind spot is that Nashville's modern art legacy emerged from traditionally Black neighborhoods, and at a Historic Black College/University, during the decades of institutionalized racial segregation in the South. The Jim Crow era in Tennessee lasted from 1936 to 1955.

Nashville's modern art legacy is rooted in three events in the city's Edgehill and North Nashville neighborhoods, in the first half of the twentieth century: Aaron Douglas's founding of the Art Department at Fisk University in the 1930s; William Edmondson becoming the first Black artist to mount a solo exhibition at the Museum of Modern Art in 1937; and Georgia O'Keeffe's gifting of the Stieglitz Collection to Fisk University in 1949.

THE KING OF HARLEM

Aaron Douglas was a major figure of the Harlem Renaissance of the 1920s. Douglas's paintings reconnect the Black American experience to the Mother Continent with a signature style that marries African-inspired imagery to modernist aesthetics. That's the style Douglas deployed when he first visited Fisk University in 1930 to paint a series of murals in the Cravath Hall Library. The murals depict a panoramic epic of the African diaspora in the New World, simultaneously pointing back to the cradle of humanity and forward to the Afrofuturism of the 1970s.

Douglas's murals still provide creative inspiration for the artists on Fisk University's campus, but his deeper contributions to Nashville's modernist legacy were as an educator and a curator. Charles S. Johnson was the founder and editor of *Opportunity: A Journal for Negro Life*, the official publication of the National Urban League. Johnson was an influential publisher with an eye for creative talent. He was one of the architects of the Harlem Renaissance and a mentor to Douglas. Johnson joined the faculty of Fisk University in 1928 and became the school's first Black president in 1946. It was Johnson who invited Douglas to develop the university's art department in 1939. And with his support, Douglas went on to become chair of the art department before retiring in 1966.

Aaron Douglas was also a gifted curator. He mounted exhibitions by photographers Man Ray and Irving Penn in 1950 and '51, respectively. He also curated objects and exhibitions from institutions like the Brooklyn Museum of Art and the New York Historical Society for his displays in North Nashville. Douglas also continued and expanded Fisk University's

Spring Arts Festival which began in 1929. The annual event continues today.

Douglas and Johnson both saw the art department as a resource that could inform the knowledge in every field. And throughout his career at Fisk, Douglas engaged faculty and students from language arts to physics with the art department's resources, its galleries, and its museum quality modern art collection. Douglas and Johnson also invited the artists they connected with in New York to be teaching residents at Fisk. Abstract sculptor Martin Puryear and multidisciplinary artist Walter Williams came to town. Abstract printmaker Stephanie Pogue, ceramicist and photographer Earl Hooks, poet James Weldon Johnson, and more made the trip south. Douglas and Johnson connected Nashville directly to the crucible of modern art in America in the decade before Jackson Pollock painted the Guggenheim *Mural* (1943).

THE GIFT

American modern art pioneer Georgia O'Keeffe gifted one hundred and one works of art to Fisk University in November of 1949. The Stieglitz Collection was named for her late husband, the groundbreaking photographer and gallerist Alfred Stieglitz. The collection was also shared with the most prestigious art institutions in the country: the Metropolitan Museum of Art in New York, the Art Institute of Chicago, the National Gallery of Art in Washington, the Philadelphia Museum of Art, and the Library of Congress.

It speaks to O'Keeffe's eye as a curator that the school's collection constitutes a brilliant learning library of images. It tells the story of modern art's evolution on its journey from Europe to America. From Cézanne, Renoir and Picasso to Charles Demuth, Arthur Dove, Marsden Hartley, O'Keeffe, and Stieglitz. The HBCU's collection also includes a selection of African art and objects collected by Stieglitz that speak to the African influences in European modernism.

O'Keeffe told *New York Times Magazine*, "I think it is a good thing to do at this time and that it would please Stieglitz." In 2006, O'Keeffe's longtime assistant, Doris Bry, wrote a letter to Fisk's president clarifying that the gift was made in response to racial segregation in the South. And that it was meant to assure that the Black students at Fisk—and all the citizens of Nashville—would have access to a world class collection to study and learn about modern art.

The Stieglitz Collection is the only museum quality collection of modern art in Nashville. It's the crown jewel of our visual arts institutions and a precious reminder of Nashville's unique place in the story of the development of modern art in America.

GOD'S OWN ARTIST

William Edmondson was born in Davidson County, Nashville in 1874. His parents were formerly enslaved sharecroppers. Edmondson and his six brothers and sisters had no formal education, spending their days working alongside their parents on the Compton Plantation where they tended cattle and raised corn. In the summer, when the corn was high, Edmondson would get lost in the maze of waving rows. He'd look up at the blue sky in between the green stalks and imagine that the clouds he saw were angels, and that they were speaking to him.

Edmondson heard the voice again when he was sixty years old, in 1934. He was standing in the driveway of the house he'd purchased with his earnings as a hospital custodian in Nashville's Edgehill neighborhood. The voice told Edmondson to gather his tools and carve a tombstone, and he saw a vision of a tombstone design suspended in the clear afternoon sky. Edmondson often used a railroad spike as a chisel and he worked almost exclusively with the limestone he'd salvage from building demolitions. Edmondson took to sculpting and expanded his repertoire to include lawn ornaments and birdbaths and decorative works for gardens. He carved biblical characters, Black heroes, and everyday Nashvillians in his signature style—stout figures with round heads and small facial features. Edmondson started his career selling his sculptures from a makeshift display in his own front yard.

Many of Edmondson's Black neighbors in his segregated Edgehill neighborhood proudly displayed the sculptor's work on their own lawns and in their gardens. And when Peabody College professor, playwright, and member of the Fugitive Poets Sidney Hirsch happened by Edmondson's sculpture display, he introduced himself to the artist and became his biggest booster. Hirsch collected Edmondson's work and introduced him to Nashville's white bourgeoisie, who did the same. Nashville photographer Louise Dahl-Wolfe captured iconic images of Edmondson at work, but they were rejected by *Harper's Bazaar* due to owner William Randolph Hearst's bigoted opinions about Black art. But when Dahl-Wolfe showed her images to Alfred Barr, director of the Museum of

Modern Art, she got a different reaction. Native Nashvillian William Edmondson became the first Black artist to mount a solo exhibition at the museum in 1937.

FOUNDATION

In separate and particular ways, American modern art pioneers Aaron Douglas, Georgia O'Keeffe, and William Edmondson earned Nashville a remarkable place in the development of modern art in the United States: just one degree of separation from the hot house of mid-century New York City, and in a unique relationship with the African influences that informed modernism's European roots. In the chapters that follow you'll find the influences of Douglas, O'Keeffe, and Edmondson in the origin story of the contemporary art scene flourishing in Nashville today. They're in North Nashville's neighborhood murals and in the do-it-yourself ethos that's always defined the evolving edge of the city's visual arts community. They're in every one-night-only exhibition and every street corner art drop. They're in every wheatpasting poster barrage, every hand-stapled culture zine. They're in every front yard art sale and at every living room gallery talk. They're in the pages of coffee-stained sketchbooks and in the sweaty blur of every art gallery dance party. The vision of Aaron Douglas, the generosity of Georgia O'Keeffe, and the devotion of William Edmondson are still right here, today, in Nowville.

Untitled (Fools Rush In)

1992–Today

THE UNTITLED ARTISTS GROUP WAS the outlandish first flower of Nashville's contemporary art renaissance, which reclaimed the city's unique modern art legacy and translated it into a surging, twenty-first-century visual arts community. Other spaces, places, and people contributed before Untitled was born in the early 1990s, but nothing galvanized Nashville's independent, often self-taught, mostly nonprofessional artists' scene like Untitled. During a time when the city's few commercial galleries were focused on established artists, and an MFA was a required passport for entry into the city's art establishment, Untitled Artists stopped asking for permission. The group burned bridges across the city with their uncensored and uncurated pop-up displays. They sidestepped traditional gatekeepers, flouting professional expertise and hierarchical categorizing. The artists who "got it" joined Untitled in groundbreaking displays that paired rank amateurs alongside established creatives, academics, and gallery and museum professionals. Untitled organized the alternative art scene that sparked Nashville's contemporary art renaissance, and it was the boot camp where many of Nashville's early contemporary art leaders learned to ambush, evade, and survive at the edges.

LANDRY BUTLER: I was born in Memphis and my parents moved here in 1975. They dragged me here, and I tried to leave several times, but I keep getting sucked back in a black hole. So I kind of made peace with it. It's a good place to be. I've been here long enough to be a native, I guess. Art was something that I always wanted to do, but didn't have much of an outlet for. About my second year of college at Andrews University up in Southwest, Michigan, I started thinking that I could just make art myself. So, I came back to Nashville and tried to figure out what I was gonna do from here. I started doing design, and I started a band and a record label, and started making cassette tapes. I had a design client at the time that was a tape duplication place. And so I could make these copies of the tapes on demand, and I didn't have to stock any inventory or anything. That was fun. Saved me a lot of money.

JOE NOLAN: No Kinko's, no Untitled Art, no Nashville contemporary art renaissance.

LANDRY BUTLER: I got a job working at Kinko's, you know, to make money, because you need that too. And I ran into other artists who were doing similar things. I met up with Lynn and Laura—Laura Chenault and Lynn King. We all worked there. I met Neil Armstrong, Michael Durham. It was within that group when the whole idea of "Let's have a party and look at each other's work," came up, which is kinda what the Untitled concept was about. That Kinko's group sparked Untitled in 1992, maybe. The first show was there in an upstairs space at Multi-Bob, which was down there in Hillsboro Village. We had a space up there and everybody brought some art. We had some fabric artists, people that designed clothes, so there was a fashion show. I didn't have any visual art for that show so I read a poem or something like that. It was a good time and we had enough people interested that it just caught on.

JOE NOLAN: Multi-Bob was a restaurant and bar known for its pine nuts and crawfish pizza, its beaded curtains, its arched Moorish doorway adorned with marching elephant sculptures. The Multi-Bob name was a Church of the Subgenius reference.

RICHARD MITCHELL: I'm from Nashville. I had spent like eight years or nine years away from Nashville, but then I ended up coming back and I basically had to stay there because as my parents got older, I was taking care of them. I think it was in like 1992, Brian Robinson was telling me about this group of artists who had done a show. It was in Hillsboro Village, somewhere above one of those bars. And he asked me to go to this meeting because they were thinking about getting it going. And, obviously, if you're gonna do that, you need money. And he said I was the only trustworthy artist he knew. He thought that I could actually handle money without either stealing it or spending it on something. And I was hooked after that meeting because of the whole philosophy.

I was really hooked on the notion that anybody could join. Anybody could show artwork. So that was a big, important thing. Having the shows open to everyone.

LAIN YORK: After coming back from Knoxville in '89, from UT, I was working with Metro Arts Commission and Anne Brown's Summer Lights Festival, and I got introduced to the studio community through Susan Knowles. Very few of these artists were figuring into the galleries. Nobody really cared about that. It's a more grassroots thing. And everyone was figuring into these popup groups. I'm running around with this older crowd. It was great, but I was always the kid. A number of us going to the Visual Arts Alliance of Nashville meetings were anxious to show our work and that group moved very slowly. About that time I heard about Untitled and I went to the first meeting at Multi-Bob—that was in Hillsboro Village. People were throwing chairs at each other. It was fun. It was very LGBTQ and became a hub for that community. And that was Untitled 1.0.

JONATHAN MARX: People would be a little kind of critical and dismissive of Untitled because it was essentially like anything goes, but that's what made it so great in retrospect. You would go and like you would see complete and utter crap, and then you would see things that were brilliant sometimes. People weren't trying to meet a particular standard, they were just trying to be authentically themselves.

JOE NOLAN: The anarchy and irreverence made Untitled magnetic. Those shows were alchemical—there was shit and there was gold.

LANDRY BUTLER: I didn't know any real artists. I knew a couple of people that could draw or play music or something, but I didn't know any professional people. I didn't know anybody who would even consider that as a career. And then I came back to Nashville and started looking for those people and there's tons of us here. That was just a good time for everyone to get together and share information and ideas and stuff. You could work with people who were professional artists and they would show up at the Untitled shows and they would show their work. Alan LeQuire did a lot of stuff there. He participated in the early Untitled. And then you'd have students and you'd have just random people showing work.

LAIN YORK: They were planning for a show called *Heaven and Hell* that ended up in The Emperor's New Clothes [a vintage shop] on Lower Broad. They had the run of the upstairs and Untitled existed solely to put these shows on. So the artists are coming together and then it's like,

"Who can drive a truck?" "Who can hang a show?" "Does anybody have a cordless drill?" Pretty much the usual thing. There was no AC upstairs and the idea was to get these big blocks of ice and some fans. So I show up at the ice house over on Centennial Boulevard and it's July or maybe August and it's hot. And I'm in there literally with a two-man saw with this dude, sawing a big block of ice and getting ready for this show. And then it was shut down by the cops—it was everything you could possibly want! It was a total disaster. When I was driving back with all the blocks of dry ice. They got wet on the way on I-40, coming back into town. I'm in the Trooper and I got the windows rolled down. I'm this like Deep Purple show trying to get that shit loaded in before the exhibition. Of course, nobody showed up to help, but that was the Untitled experience.

LANDRY BUTLER: You get a chance to see what other people are doing, see how they do their thing. And it's nice to be able to show off what you've done, and having it in that context of other work, and being able to see how the stuff is hung or maybe they painted the edge of their canvas or something. And that's really fun because I like pulling ideas from other places, and if you're just starting out, you take it all in because it's all good.

LAIN YORK: Untitled's early pop-up venues were The Emperor's New Clothes, The Cannery [a music venue]. That was '92 or '93. Those were some of the venues that we were working and then the wheels came off, and the group went on hiatus for about six months. But then there was a meet-up with five of us in Rebecca Walk's kitchen. That became the *Phoenix* show. And that started Untitled 2.0, which took off so fast. The initial group addressed a need, but unfortunately it was so volatile. The principals left and it was probably a good thing because they would've killed each other. There was a core left and then all these new people showed up, and it was fantastic. Richard Mitchell and Barbara Harris really helped to stabilize the group. Barbara was there from the start and she was a very organized person. Richard happened to have a background in accounting. So these were artists, but at the same time they had unexpected executive skills in the midst of this hurricane of weird, mercurial, people. And that's really the beginning of Untitled 2.0.

RICHARD MITCHELL: I had majored in studio art in college. I was mostly a painter. I did a lot of painting, for better or worse, in the '80s. It was a good time to be a painter, but a lot of my stuff was real slop that I don't want anyone to ever see. Every now and then I look at something,

"Oh, that's not so bad after all." Anyway, I was a painter already and I was friends with Brian. I was dating Brian's best friend, Tim, and that's how I met Brian Robinson. He used to hang out with us, and he was an aspiring artist. He had an art gallery on Hillsboro Road [Robinson/ Willis Gallery]. His brother was running it and then his brother freaked out, and so Brian basically inherited it.

JOE NOLAN: Richard is the person I always associate with Untitled. He was smart and hilarious and he made people feel optimistic about creating their own opportunities. His art was part playful, part provocative, thought provoking.

RICHARD MITCHELL: The rich people in Nashville bought their artwork from Zimmerman Saturn Gallery. They were connected with all the big commercial galleries in New York—that was sort of their claim to fame. There was Carol Stein's gallery in Green Hills—Cumberland Gallery. That was a fairly legitimate gallery, but it was also very exclusive. It was really hard to get a show there. She didn't really do like emerging artist group shows or anything like that. Anne Brown opened The Arts Company in the late 1990s. She was kind of notorious in Nashville because she had strong opinions about things, and she was really ambitious. I always liked her, but some people found her hard to take in large quantities.

JOE NOLAN: Anne Brown started showing some new artists like Herb Williams, Todd Greene, and Tom Wills, but she couldn't show every young artist looking for an exhibition in Nashville. Untitled changed all of that without anybody's permission. Those artists wanted to make art and wanted people to see it.

LAIN YORK: At one of the early Untitled 2.0 shows we set up an internet link with an independent group in Boston that was doing a show the same night we did. And we broadcast their show at The Cannery with this crazy time lapse. And then we didn't have any video artists so I think we showed *Caddyshack* or something like that.

LANDRY BUTLER: We always tried to move around and not be in a gallery space—that was one of the ideas. We tried that one formula for the first show, and we just kept doing that, and iterating off of that, and making some small improvements as we went along. That's how we got the idea to build the walls on wheels. They're easy to roll around. You can put them wherever. They're easy to paint because you can just roll them outside and paint them. And at some point we got into the sponsorship stuff that came around. We had sponsorship for a while for some of those parties that we would do over in Marathon Village—these huge events with visual art, and Sideshow Benny would show up with his piercings and do a performance. Somebody pulled off a vodka martini sponsorship. That was great.

LAIN YORK: I think the group moved faster than a lot of people were comfortable with. We went from like twenty-five artists at The Cannery—this very nice controlled thing—to literally 250 artists at Marathon Village for Live and Active Culture in '96. That was the first big show. It was also the first time that we served alcohol. A representative from Absolut showed up and it's like, "Who is this guy? Where did he come from? How did he hear about us?" And he says, "I'm here to hook y'all up with all the martinis you can serve. How many people are you expecting?" We say, "two thousand?" And he's like, "We'll have martinis for two thousand people along with two thousand glass martini glasses that say 'Absolut.'" And here's Richard Mitchell at his finest. We wanted to show these venue operators, the city, and the business community that we could be responsible. And Richard started directing everybody: we bought an insurance policy, we bought permits, we scheduled visits from the fire marshal, we arranged for security. Every venue invited us back.

RICHARD MITCHELL: That was a big show we had with one of the vodka companies sponsoring us. You had to pay for the drinks, but the drinks were amazing. All these different kinds of vodka martinis. We had the police department patrolling. We had a fire marshal there, because that building was really scary. We did a lot of rewiring for our show. I helped build a stage. That was probably in '97, '98, something like that. At the time I was channeling Chuck Close and I was making big portraits.

LAIN YORK: The idea was to have these theme shows because the group existed to put shows on with no curator, no censorship, no juror—anyone who showed up and kicked in fifteen bucks was in the show. Very few of the Untitled people had formal backgrounds. It's not like there were many people with MFAs involved. But we had to figure out a way to ensure that people weren't just turning in the same piece each time. The themes were a device that we used to keep people making fresh work.

RICHARD MITCHELL: We always had a theme for every show that most of us would just ignore. But the show's always held together. It was sort of just like an inspirational theme. Except for the Glow Show which was obviously glowing stuff. The Sex Shows were pretty focused.

LAIN YORK: We had to be really organized at getting that stuff in, but also at getting stuff out. Usually about ten o'clock, maybe eleven, you're standing around with patrons and patrons are saying, "Wow, this is incredible. This is fun! How much longer is this going to be up?" It's like, "Fourteen minutes." Then fifty-two artists get busy: All unsold work goes right out the door. A crew starts taking the lighting rigs down. Another crew starts taking the walls apart. All of that stuff goes into a rented twenty-four-foot truck. And it sails right on down the street. You know, the whole shebang. And people are standing around with what's left of their wine going, "That was great." And then you're stopping off and grabbing a case of beer and unloading the truck. And then somebody's gotta take the truck back and it's 2:00 a.m. And you gotta go back and clean up the venue and turn the keys over by noon the next day. Untitled wasn't everybody's cup of tea because it was hard. But there was nothing else to do. And when it did work, and everybody pitched in, you didn't have to stay too late.

LANDRY BUTLER: We were promoting Untitled like a band. We'd make posters and then put them in all the coffeehouses and music venues. It got the word out. We created that name recognition, which kept the thing going for a long time. We did go through a couple of phases where there was nobody to step up. And so we didn't do shows for a while. But somebody would always come through and we could get it started again. And the people that had done it were great at being resources for the new people, because we wanted to pass that information on. They don't teach you business in art school. That's one of the things you have to figure out. The gallery process is part of that. The publicity process is part of that. So just having all of those people around to borrow and bounce ideas off of was really important for everybody.

LAIN YORK: So Sideshow Benny [Ben Wade] and this guy Jay worked for one of the digital printers. This is like the dawn of digital printing. All of a sudden we've got access to a lot of material, a lot of toys. So we made programs, lanyards, posters. Michael Ray Nott was coming in and designing these crazy posters. Michael was a big part of the Austin punk community. He did flyers for all the punk bands in his Austin days. And as things started going more digital, we had Richard Mitchell and a number of folks who were very tech savvy. They start putting digital databases together. As people are joining we're taking like Earthlink addresses, and we start putting this database together and publishing this newsletter. So there was like this really interesting timely tech push, and all of a sudden it's all going out digitally. We're printing newsletters and we're mailing them out to southern Kentucky, northern Alabama. And all of a sudden, all these people start showing up at meetings.

JOE NOLAN: Untitled revealed this visual creative underground across our whole region. The art industrial complex has dropped a lot of its exclusivity in the years since Untitled, but that group poked a hole in all of that pretense thirty years ago.

RICHARD MITCHELL: It worked for, I mean, I don't even know how long it worked. It worked for ten years, maybe, you know, nine years, something like that. I ended up going to grad school, so I left Nashville in 2001 and I think it had kind of petered out before that, you know. It kind of lost its momentum, which is normal for things like that. We were no institution or anything. We were just very loosely formed. People didn't know what to think of us.

LAIN YORK: Untitled had become a not-for-profit, and Barbara says she's got this money in this account, and what are we doing with the group? I bring three people to a meeting, and the former board members, and, like everybody brings somebody to the meeting just to see if there's any interest in reviving this. And that's when Casey Gill and her crew stepped in. And a couple of months later, there was the show in 2002 at that weird little building in the parking lot of the Cannery. It had a whole new life. That was Untitled 3.0, and that ran until, shit, 2010? Something like that. At least.

OMARI BOOKER: Untitled was cool. We did a show in Antioch in the old mall, Hickory Hollow Mall. It was a great space to have a piece and show it. And it was very open to all artists—radically. With Untitled you can have a piece and show, and let friends, family, community know, and also get to meet a lot of other artists too.

BETH GILMORE: We did all these things that you would never expect would be things you need to be doing. Having to work with all these different people we never would have interacted with, and having to just hang things up, and carrying walls into a bar and they're like, "What the hell is going on here? What are you guys doing?" And it all worked. It wasn't supposed to work.

SARA ESTES: It was really my very, very first entry into the Nashville art world. I was making paintings in my house and I think I was like working at Starbucks or as a server or something. I remember working on a lot of paintings for it. And I finally submitted like one that I was really happy with and they accepted it. And I remember going to the show and it was in a big space with all these temporary walls. And I invited a couple friends to it. It felt so cool to me that there were tons of people. I met Sam Callahan and Daniel Lai. I remember they kind of took me under their wings a little bit. They were just really nice because I felt like a nobody. I didn't know anything, and they treated me with a lot of respect. That was kind of my entry into the Nashville art scene. It was September of 2007.

LANDRY BUTLER: I met a lot of people that I'm still friends with through Untitled. I'm surprised it lasted as long as it did. I just found the poster the other day. They had the last one over on Davidson Street. I think it was like twenty-five years from when it started.

JOE NOLAN: The last Untitled Artists show was *Undone* in 2013. The group reformed in 2024.

BETH GILMORE: Untitled started everything. It started it all.

The Fugitive Kind

1998-2004

THE FUGITIVE ART CENTER EMERGED from the industrial district of Wedgewood-Houston at the end of the 1990s. The studio complex and gallery sparked a vision that the raw and ramshackle spaces in We-Ho might become the center of the city's contemporary art scene. The Fugitive was one of the first permanent locations for Nashville's DIY contemporary art community—a nomadic confederation subsisting on pop-up displays and kitchen sink art making. The Fugitive's studio spaces nurtured a squad of engaged artists and leaders, and its programming connected Nashville with artists, curators, galleries, and institutions across the US and beyond. The place and its curatorial collective were named for the Fugitive Poets, who published *The Fugitive* literary journal out of Vanderbilt University in Nashville in the 1920s. "Fugitive" is also an adjective used to describe art-making materials that are particularly changeable and impermanent over time.

GREG POND: I only came to Nashville for a girl, and she left me as soon as I got there. So I moved into Marathon Village. That was a disaster zone at that time. I didn't even have a bathroom. I walked out to take out my trash and I saw an eighteen-year-old with a pipe like standing over this sixty-year-old man. He stopped at that moment. It was a mess down there. It was just everything you do as an artist, just to try to survive.

JIM HOOBLER: A number of artists created studios in places like the Marathon automobile factory. Bruce Matthews used to have a studio in there back in the day, when that neighborhood was full of drug dealers and prostitutes. And Barry Walker [owner of Marathon Village] would walk in and out of the building with a gun because he was afraid he might be shot by a drug dealer or something. The artists have always had to be in sort of peripheral areas, just because, as they're starting out, they don't have a lot of income, so they have to be in the literally low-rent district.

GREG POND: There was an Untitled Art show that Lain York and Richard Mitchell had put together at Marathon Village just before I got there. So I landed there and then I was moving back and forth between Athens, Georgia and Nashville.

JIM HOOBLER: Marathon Motor Works was built in 1881 as the Nashville Cotton Mills with additions being added in 1885 and 1887. The building has a four story Italianate tower with coining curved window hoods and two bracketed corners. The factory had six hundred employees. The 1893 depression forced through organization into the Phoenix Cotton Mills, which lasted only until 1908. And then that's when the Southern Engine and Steam Boiler Company out of Jackson, Tennessee, decides to move to Nashville and they start the automobile factory in there.

GREG POND: I knew that I needed a community. I needed to have artists around. So I walked into Barry's office and said, "Where are these people? How do I find them?" So a few days later I walked in J. J.'s and met Lain and Richard, and Lain got me The Fugitive space.

JIM HOOBLER: Originally at the Houston Station building they were making jellies and jams and things like that on the ground floor. And then upstairs, they were sorting tobacco.

JOE NOLAN: Gene Sizemore and Terry Martin opened Martin-Wiley gallery in Hillsboro Village in the late 1970s. Sizemore's first name was Wiley and his friends called him "Coyote." They were ahead of their time because they were more focused on contemporary artists from the South. Their last show was a Red Grooms exhibition in 1978.

LAIN YORK: Terry Martin's family owned the Houston Station building that housed The Fugitive. We rented from Richard Hall who was running that space, effectively, for the Martin family. So the Martins were very invested in the contemporary art scene. Terry came in and looked at one of my shows, and said, "This is the worst shit I've ever seen in my life."

GREG POND: I lived in a trailer in the alley for a little while. I was sharing a trailer with this gay couple—we were all refugees from Marathon

Village. And then I lived in the building for a little while. But those were in many ways like the happiest days of my life. At the other end of that entire space was Tennessee Repertory Theater. I worked for them making sets and props. We started building gallery walls and then creating artist studios. Richard and Lain were wanting to do something more with the art scene, and then the people that I called started to show up.

BOB DURHAM: I was born in Gallatin, Tennessee, outside of Nashville. I graduated from Vanderbilt and I was going to be a writer. I went to Scotland and wrote a bunch of short stories—it really sucked. So I decided I would go to a technical school and learn to be an illustrator. I went up Northeast and right outside of New Haven and I lived right near the whole center of New Haven where Yale is and stuff. I went two years to a school called the Paier School of Art and then dropped out and started freelancing and had a nineteen-year profession up there. I got married up there and then that fell apart and I moved back home. And then I decided to stop doing the commercial art and try to do some stuff for galleries. It took me a year to get into any schools, but finally I went down to Georgia [University of Georgia in Athens] and Greg Pond and Terry Glispin and Jack Ryan were all down there. I got my MFA credentials and then Greg said he was moving to Nashville. By the time I got back here he had this whole thing going with The Fugitive.

GREG POND: I knew Bob Durham from grad school. Bob was from Nashville and he'd already come back. Bob helped me build. Bob and I did insane things in terms of trying to structure the floors in the back where I was sleeping. Donna Tauscher came into the group and told me that when she left for work I could just come over and use her shower every day. She lived just around the corner.

BOB DURHAM: I mean, it was horrible. That first year it was just me and Greg and Bryan Hunter—Terry Glispin came later. Everybody just shared an open space. I mean, there was no partitions or anything. So it was crazy, but it was pretty interesting. Greg was living off of nothing in a trailer in the back end of the place or something. And then Greg started getting more serious artists in there and it was pretty amazing. I was always shocked that we pulled it out of our ass.

GREG POND: Bryan was the anchor, seriously. He came up with The Fugitive name—he's a poet and he even wrote some poetry about that place. The night of the first exhibition that we had, he and I were sitting on the couch going "What are we going to call this place?" And we were like two hours before opening. When I met Bryan he was showing these really crazy paintings at Untitled shows. He also saved our asses financially many times over and negotiated to get us incorporated through nonprofit lawyers. Bryan and I were basically side-by-side establishing this and then we were supported by the board which included people like Lain York, Richard Mitchell, Carol Mode, Lesley Patterson-Marx, Jack Ryan, Terry Glispin, and his partner Megan.

JACK RYAN: Greg and I met at the University of Georgia. He was leaving the program before I did, with his masters. I actually drove him. He had an Oldsmobile from maybe the mid-'80s that I drove out for him. We packed his stuff and he moved to Marathon Village in Nashville while I was still a grad student. He invited me to exhibit at The Fugitive while I was a grad student in 1999. I went there and I slept on a cot in my exhibition space. It was an exciting city. In some ways it was more dangerous than New York City. I was an undergrad in New York during the late 1980s during the crack epidemic. So there were parts of Nashville that were actually kind of more dangerous. And there were all those massage parlors everywhere. I was amazed at this kind of vice that was so transparent and mysterious behind all those stores everywhere. And then there was the music scene and the artistic energy.

RICHARD MITCHELL: That area was completely derelict when we were hanging around there. There was some woodworking tool companies or something like that, but there was very little. A lot of the buildings were completely abandoned.

JACK RYAN: I remember Iwonka heard gunshots at some point. And she was also chased into the building by a pack of dogs. And when I was coming to The Fugitive and I saw the dogs, I would race in my car, jump out and get into the building before the pack of dogs arrived. And Iwonka was, I think Iwonka was literally chased, you know. Like a kind of more desperate situation with the dogs. When Bryan heard about Iwonka having problems exiting and entering he put up a camera above the door so you could look at the camera and see that there was no one out there about to jump you.

LESLEY PATTERSON-MARX: Even though it was so strange and musty it had a charm. Bob Durham and Jeff Danley had a studio there for a while and then I moved in with my friend, Margaret Pesek. And while we were there, the building got broken into by a gang. They spray painted and they busted the door. I don't recall any artwork being damaged, but that was scary. Margaret and I would be very careful when we were leaving there at night. One of us would poke our head out and look, and they eventually installed that camera at the front. I didn't have a cell phone at that point, you know, very few people did.

BETH GILMORE: There had been a break-in and they had a lot of trouble calling the police for help because they were like, "No, we're called *The Fugitive.*"

PATRICK DEGUIRA: The first night I ever went there, there was a guy getting a blow job. Right when I pulled my car up, this guy walks out with his pants down and a hard-on and he's got his hands up in the air because he thought I was the police. And then this woman walks out. He was one of the truck drivers from the old canning factory up there. There would be trucks parked all around The Fugitive and Chestnut building. They're just sitting there in these eighteen-wheelers. They're just waiting to load-up and meeting with these hookers. And then later there was like the headless hooker they found across from the Secret Show building. There was this shitty pizza place and there was a dumpster next to it. Matt Christy was there, Amanda Dillingham, Will Clen-Dening, Chris Doubler, I think all those guys were down there. I get a call and they're like, "Man, they found a prostitute across the street and her head had been cut off." It was insane. It was industrial wasteland back there. And there was this Confederate guy across from the old church, which now is some hipster coffee shop. This guy would hang a huge Confederate flag outside of his building all the time. He was like a militia guy, like kind of a doomsday prepper before they started making shows about them. He had two rottweilers he wouldn't keep on a leash and they would just run like crazy. Iwonka Waskowski almost got mauled by one. He was like this super racist, fucked-up, rebel Confederate asshole. So that guy was our enemy number one, you know? It was a weird place.

RICHARD MITCHELL: We started talking and Lain and I had done Untitled so well, so we just decided let's just have a show and see what happens. I did all the drywall. I had some help, but we had extra drywall from an Untitled show that I had purchased. I also dismantled the walls I'd built for this other show. I built all these walls for an Untitled show. I took them apart. Then I took them down to The Fugitive. It looked really nice, but the floors were just like terrible. I mean, they needed to be jacked up and braced and stuff, but they were safe. You didn't fall through them.

BOB DURHAM: We had studios probably about a year before we had the gallery, I think. And so this space and a lot of floorboards are missing. So I would get invasions of mosquitoes every day and I'd have to coat myself with mosquito repellent shit. And everywhere you went, there were places just falling in. So it was really nuts. Even when everything was up and running there was always stuff falling through.

JACK RYAN: I had a studio in the front. Iwonka had a studio next to mine. Bryan had a studio on the courtyard, you know, with a legitimate window—real luxury. He was next to Bob Durham who probably had the best studio at some point. That place was filthy. You could crawl through holes in the floor and get underneath the foundation. And because the drainage was so bad, the mosquitoes inside of The Fugitive, they were so bad year round. I've been in swamps on the equator and it was not unlike that—the density of the swarm.

JEFF DANLEY: I was always the artist in the class. I went to college to be an art major. And then when I left school, I thought "I'm going to play drums," because I started doing that in middle school and just decided I really wanted to do that instead of art. A buddy of mine was a bass player I met in Georgia and he moved to Nashville. I was living in Georgia and he contacted me, and he's like, "You should move to Nashville." I had been introduced to Bob Durham, and we stayed in touch when he went to grad school in Georgia, and that's where he met Greg and all of those guys. And at that time at The Fugitive, it was Bob, and Gadsby Creson was in there, and maybe one other person. And they were in a big room at The Fugitive and they didn't have any walls or partitions between them. And then Greg Pond had that weird space.

BOB DURHAM: Greg's studio was misery. I mean, I was in there probably a month or two and one day Greg comes in, and you know how Greg'll just start talking like you know exactly what he's thinking about? He's like somewhere else in the universe, and he would be talking about his office space right there in the building, and it sounded like it was some other planet. And then I went back there with him—or tried to go back there—and it was impossible to even get to. It was so fucked up. It was the worst place.

JACK RYAN: Greg had a permanent space, but no one wanted to go in because it was terrifying. It had no windows. It was at the front of the building next to mine, but at the corner. There was no lights in there. It was just a series of clamp lights. Only he knew where they were at, but to even get those to work you had to plug in like a series of extension cords in the dark. And it smelled terrible. It was completely dark and it was next to the gallery and on the other side, so it was really out of the way. And Greg was extremely prolific and he also made big work. And so there was like all kinds of objects, and it became kind of a storage facility for him. There was old boxes that were covered with dust. There was nothing archival. So it was just a disaster and it was piled up everywhere. Stuff was literally wet. The ceiling was falling in on most of it. My studio was really small, but it was clean, right?

BARBARA YONTZ: When I first moved into that studio it was so gross. I never saw so much dust and dirt. It was disgusting. I literally like spent a week cleaning. But it was such an amazing space. It was a really fun place to be and it was a little bit scary.

JEFF DANLEY: So I had some space in the back of my room where they'd built a riser because there was no floor under it—the floor had collapsed. I remember that the floors in other parts of my studio would almost have made a great skateboard half pipe. You had to pick a level spot to put your easel and stand there all day. My studio was frequented by possums and raccoons—some kind of wild animals, as well as rats. It all lent itself to the romanticism of having a New York-style warehouse space, and the rats weren't as big and mean as the New York rats. They were a lot more Southern in their style. They were much more polite, but still rats. I had to leave my dog there because I was living in this tiny little apartment and I couldn't have a dog there. So my dog Jack stayed there at The Fugitive, and Terry Glispin loved Jack and would let him out at night. Jack and I would play in that long hallway. I would throw the ball down the hallway and he'd run down to the other end and get it and bring it back to me. That was kind of his indoor exercise trail. I didn't have the visits from the critters as much when I started to leave Jack there overnight. So he was kind of my guard dog.

TERRY THACKER: It was a big open space, probably nine hundred square feet. There was no electric—there's one or two outlets in there. And my brother and I ran electrical and probably not coded. And there was only one sink and one toilet. And there was one heater and there was just enough heat to keep the pipes from freezing. And of course there's no air and it's humid as hell in there. You got sweat rolling off of you. And Patrick [DeGuira] caught me one time while I was painting in my underwear and he knocks on the door and I stuck my head out sweating like a pig.

JEFF DANLEY: I remember in the summer it being miserably hot and we would sit around pretty much sweating to death with no shirts. And then in the winter, freezing to death with a scarf wrapped around my face and a toboggan on and gloves and layers of clothes on, painting. There was absolutely no climate control. And if you turned on one light bulb too many you blew fuses. God forbid you plug in a heater. The whole building would have gone up in ash. So we barely had space heaters in there. But it was a beautiful space in its way.

HANS SCHMITT-MATZEN: My truck got broken into so many times out there. It was that kind of a place where you just didn't leave anything in your vehicle. There was a lot of water problems too that were crazy. The loading dock would just flood. And it would just be like, two feet of water, like almost up to the top of where you would back up your truck.

BETH GILMORE: It was a rickety old building. The floor would kind of bounce. Like when we would have parties after the openings we would jump on the weak spot in the floor. There was a boxing speed bag mounted on one of the walls and there was a lot of dangerous wood-working equipment and like a bunch of magazines that we could cut things out of to collage. It was great.

HANS SCHMITT-MATZEN: For somebody like Greg who was a sculptor who had heavy stuff he needed to get in and out of the back of his truck, the loading dock was kind of perfect. We set up a communal wood shop—that was really important. I bought some tools—just basic table saws and chop saws. Terry Thacker moved in for awhile there. We were right beside each other, and it was cool to be working with my old college painting professor. Terry brought some chop saws for everybody to use.

DAVID MADDOX: I remember talking to people on the West Coast about the Ghost Ship warehouse fire and that reminded me of The Fugitive. There was really good work being done there, a lot of interaction going on. And the place itself wasn't orderly. You might turn the corner and it's like, "Oh! Wait a second. Somebody has carved out some space here." And so it felt kind of like a labyrinth. It felt like you might find anything.

TERRY THACKER: It was a really fun space because adjacent to it is an old hosiery factory and there's several artists in there. And then there's a big loading dock next to it. So you can go outside and work, whatever you need to do outside. And then the people that came to us, sometimes they wanted to be really private and they would never talk. And other times they're very chatty and invite you into their studio. I think K. J. Schumacher was there for a couple of years and he was always asking me to come over and look at the work, and he was really energetic.

MARK HOSFORD: After I got my MFA I applied to a bunch of programs and Vanderbilt offered me a job. I came from Knoxville right out of the program as a graduate student and one of the first people I met was Terri Smith. Someone hooked me up with her as a person I could show my art to. She was curating all those things with Temporary Contemporary at Cheekwood. And so from her I met Terry Glispin at Watkins and all those people that became the center of the artists that I knew. I got to know Terry and Greg Pond and see what they were doing at The Fugitive. It was all artist-led. They had that combination of studio space and art space that had no desire or no need of worrying about money. The board kept it afloat and invited interesting artists they were friends with to have shows. And so without sales involved, with just wanting to have interesting art come to Nashville, it was just a beautiful mission of bringing cool stuff just so everyone can appreciate what's happening.

JONATHAN MARX: The thing that tainted the music scene was the presence of the music business. There's always so many people moving here trying to make it. Whereas, in the art scene, there was nothing to make. There was no way to make it in the art scene here. And I think the magical part about The Fugitive was that it was very much this kind of communal enterprise where it was like, "Let's bring new and exciting things in." And even though the art that was on the walls in the space was important, the community being created around that was actually even more important. It had a huge impact on my life because it's how I met my wife.

LESLEY PATTERSON-MARX: I actually met Jonathan at The Fugitive. I made cupcakes—we would bring snacks and stuff. And I was wearing this Florida, 1960s, boldly colored, Loretta Lynn kind of dress, carrying a tray of cupcakes. And he looked at me funny. I'm sure he was just like, "Who is this freaky person with the cupcakes?" I remember that's the first time I ever saw him.

GREG POND: The casual conversations that happened around just all of us working together were incredibly important in terms of pushing all of us forward. Between The Fugitive board members and all the people who were there, we didn't resemble each other in terms of what we made. We were all very different artists, but I think that was important because that's how we learned from each other.

LESLEY PATTERSON-MARX: I remember it was one morning after my 2D class over on Powell Avenue at Watkins. Terry walked in and said, "Hey, would you be interested in being on the board at The Fugitive." And I said, "What's The Fugitive?," not really knowing what I was getting myself into. It was never any kind of huge job for me, but I just remember a lot of like Sunday morning meetings or Sunday afternoon meetings. Everybody would sort of sit on some old rotten couch in the back and either talk about organizational stuff or go through slides.

RICHARD MITCHELL: I think I was on the board of The Fugitive. It was all so loosely organized. We'd have these meetings and we'd drink beers and people would propose shows. Or, sometimes, we'd just hang out and look through tons of slides and see what the artists were sending us.

MARK HOSFORD: The Fugitive board was pretty loose. Basically, there was a small group that all went to UGA. So they had that tight friendship and connection. They were operating for quite a good amount of time doing great stuff. But, then there was a moment where I think they saw that it would be interesting to expand the network. I think part of it was kind of increasing those voices from outside of just the founders. They brought in myself, Lesley Patterson-Marx, Julie Roberts, Iwonka Waskowski.

RICHARD MITCHELL: We did a bunch of really good shows there. I did one where I had four nudes: two men, two women—I had taken photos of them. And then I was projecting the nude photos on them and they were wearing these white bathrobes. They were in the dark and surrounded by this perimeter of gauze. If you wanted to look at them, you had to bend down and look through these little windows in the gauze. You couldn't tell if they were naked or not. Your perception would be switching back and forth whether they were really naked or if they were being projected as naked. I was trying to disrupt that whole notion of voyeurism.

BARBARA YONTZ: Here's the first time somebody puts together an exhibition space for the purpose of bringing in interesting things from the outside and not for their own purposes. This was an extremely non-competitive group of people. It was like, "Oh sure, you want to do this? Yeah, I'll help you. Oh, you want me to do this? Okay, I'll help you." There was no sense of competition among anyone and I think it's super rare. And you know, I've hardly ever had an experience like that.

LAIN YORK: We saw so many people that were going through sculpture programs, that were abandoning sculpture and going to video. And then eventually a lot of those artists dropping the image altogether from video going straight to sound only. We were seeing these big transitions in these different media and Fugitive and Ruby Green were the only places in Nashville where you could see this stuff.

MARK HOSFORD: You'd go through the door into a hallway. The big room was on the left as you came in that space. One thing that was different about Fugitive, that I found so magical, was the scale. I mean that space was massive in there. Artists were allowed to just do a lot more because it wasn't confined to this ten foot by ten foot cube. Artists could just do their wildest dreams because there was just so much space—wall space, floor space, ceiling space. People brought in a bigger arsenal to play with that I haven't seen within an artist-run space since. So you'd get to the studios through there and of course the one bathroom in the place was way at the end. I think people just realized like, "Why should a hallway just be a hallway?" We decided it might as well be an exhibition space. Then we could have a bigger space and smaller space. The out-of-towner could get a big space and someone local could have a small space just to make those connections in that hallway. We wanted those two spaces to have a dialogue together, where the artists that we're bringing-in get the benefit of really learning about someone else's art by how we're pairing them together.

PATRICK DEGUIRA: I joined the board in the middle of the run. I tried to help them organize responsibilities: Who's doing press? Who's doing installation? Shipping is always a huge issue. Who's finding artists who are willing to send work or even deliver work for free? Carol Mode came on the board basically as a patron. She wasn't rich, but she knew we needed help financially. And so if we got into pickle with shipping or when we ran out of paint for the gallery walls she could help. The $15 a month that we put in every month helped too. But the money that was generated from studios helped a lot and made sure that artists had spaces to work in. Those fees even let us give free studio spaces to our interns: Shaun Slifer's first studio was there. Chris Doubler's first studio was there. The interns would gallery-sit on the weekends when nobody else wanted to be there. We started running the place democratically. Greg and Bryan were really the go-to people when it came to like the history and the pedagogy and philosophy of the space. When Mark Hosford joined the board I was like, "You're gonna do our posters and you're gonna do a lot graphics." And that's how he started making those beautiful Fugitive posters. We really started treating the exhibitions like band shows. We'd put our posters up in all the coffee shops or whatever.

RICHARD MITCHELL: We weren't exactly Marxist or anything like that, but we were outside of the whole system. We had a show at Fugitive and somebody complained that we were serving drinks. We'd usually have like Cokes for a dollar and maybe $2 glass of wine. But that was just to cover our costs. We weren't making money on it, but somebody down the street from The Fugitive complained that we didn't have a business license and we were selling alcohol illegally. And the people from the city government came and started talking to us. So I finally said to one woman, "Just come with me to The Fugitive and I'll show you what it's about." And she did. She came and we were walking around and I was telling her what goes on here, and what goes on there. I told her about the very minimal rent. I described the shows to her—there might have been a show up then. So this is what it is. And when we were done with the tour she's like, "You mean, you're not doing this for money?" We're weren't interested in anything to do with money. We were doing it for love, basically. She was very confused, but she thought it was really cool. I could tell she'd never seen anything like that. Everything that she deals with is people trying to make money.

MARK HOSFORD: I can't think about The Fugitive and not remember the importance of Terri Smith and the horse stall video exhibitions she was doing at Cheekwood. I felt like she had the same sensibility as The Fugitive, but was able to sneak it into an established museum. And the works that she was showing would be like Tony Oursler— really important video artists that no one else was showing, but in these weird horse stalls at an old mansion. She took it as a mission to find an unused weird space and fill it with important things.

JACK RYAN: Terry Glispin was the expert at casting. And so, I wanted to do a death mask, you know, of my head, and I wanted to do it three dimensional. And so he helped me get all the materials I needed, and, first of all, I shaved my head. We put the Vaseline everywhere. And then he got the kind of low temperature wax that you could put on your face. So we did this thin layer that was low temperature and it still hurt my ears. And I had straws going up into my nose and my mouth, and I was encased. And then on top of that, they put what's called a mother mold. So Terry was the technician and we brought in Patrick, too. His job was just to stay in touch with me. Make sure that I wasn't suffocating. And Barbara Yontz showed up—she was renting a studio in the back. And so she came and she saw this like, experience of Terry Glispin doing my mask. I didn't even know she was there. Patrick and I, we had a series of codes. Like, "Can you breathe?" Or "Are you okay?" He's tapping me on the shoulder, "How are you?" And Barbara began to cry because she was so touched by the sort of like masculine tenderness that is going on.

SHAUN SLIFER: I had a studio at The Fugitive and I was also a gallery attendant. Growing up in Omaha I went to the Bemis Center, which is now a huge thing. But at the time it was a warehouse full of weirdos making things. And as a kid, I went to some classes there. And I just think I normalized the idea that people might huddle up in these poorly environmentally managed buildings, without heat or something, in order to make things in the rooms that were maybe not totally safe. But it's okay, because we're artists. And The Fugitive was an amazing experience for me.

TERRY THACKER: I really wasn't a part of the initial group like Greg and Lain and Terry, and those people that sort of started that place up. They built out a new studio space and I rented it. And that worked out so well that they said, "Well, we got room for more spaces. Let's bring more artists in." And that's when Hans Schmitt-Matsen and everybody else came in. Hans was right next to me. And then Patrick and Lain were on the other side of the doorway.

PATRICK DEGUIRA: I was across from Lain and then John Donovan was next to me.

HANS SCHMITT-MATZEN: The first time I ever went to The Fugitive I was in college at MTSU. My professor John O'Connell had a studio space there. And so I met Lain for the first time then, and I met Bob Durham. I thought it was just so cool. It almost felt like everything we were learning about, about the happenings in the 1960s in our contemporary art history classes. MTSU provided us with studios up until our senior year. They let me keep it through the summer, but I had to move all my stuff out by the time the fall semester started. I got in touch with Greg and Lain and Bryan Hunter and lined up a studio there. It's crazy, man, at that point in time it was like fifty cents a square foot or something like that. It was the biggest studio I'd ever had—it was like three hundred square feet and it was like 175 bucks.

BETH GILMORE: This was around 2004. Terry Glispin was there and Jack Ryan and Margaret [Pesek]. Lesley [Patterson-Marx] was there. Mike [Bielaczyc] was there. I think Terry Thacker was there, but I didn't see him much. Hans [Schmitt-Matzen] was across the hall from me. Lain [York] was there, but he was on the other side of the building through these big metal doors. I was always working when no one else was there. I was pouring paint onto big canvases on the floor and then painting on top of those. I would pour a bunch and make it look marbleized, like make my canvas all ready. And once that was dry, I would paint on top of that with oil paints and do Victorian-looking stuff, this sort of Technicolor, whimsical, psychedelic Victorian.

MARK HOSFORD: The Fugitive was right by the baseball stadium. When we had openings on a Saturday, they did fireworks at the stadium. So we always got a free firework display as part of the openings.

JACK RYAN: Lesley Patterson and I were DJs for one or maybe two of the after parties. We would wait until after the exhibition until we started the music, and it was such a blast. If we started the music too early, you know, we didn't want to step on the toes of the exhibitors, but Lesley and I worked the music for at least one or two shows, we called ourselves DJ Tape Cassette, everything was on tape cassettes, and one of us was on a machine rewinding to the song we wanted to go next and the other one was playing it. And they were mostly from Jonathan [Marx]. Jonathan gave them to us. It's like boxes of tape cassettes that we had to forage through.

LESLEY PATTERSON-MARX: Oh goodness. I don't even remember how we came up with that idea, but I lived like one street over from Jack and Terry. And so it was a regular occurrence for us to porch sit, you know, a couple times a week, at least or even if one of us was walking by and we'd see somebody outside. We'd just sit on the porch, and it was back when a lot of people smoked. So it was just like a good excuse to just sit and have a cigarette on the porch and it probably occurred to us one of those little times when we were just sort of blurting out ideas. We both just have had so many cassettes. I mean everybody did, everybody was transitioning to CDs. I mean, I think we just wanted to like go through that arduous exercise of like cueing-up and rewinding. And it was an ordeal that was like part of it. Can we do this? Can we meet this challenge?

BETH GILMORE: The toilet was very like, it felt outdoorsy, but it was technically indoors. It was like, they built it up on a platform in a closet and it had a stone wall around it.

TERRI SMITH: The Fugitive bathroom was a little intimidating. It was just tiny and up some weird stairs. And there was like an unfinished wall that had like two by four studs in this corner and that was the spot where I hid my wine, every single opening because I didn't want to drink the keg beer. I remember Terry Glispin's weird sculptures being around all over the place. There was like a My Little Pony and a dolphin

I think. There was some big cat with giant balls, like testicles. I think there was a big sexualized raccoon. There were these large animals with prominent genitalia basically that you'd find just lurking in these weird little transitional spaces in that building.

SHAUN SLIFER: I remember standing in line for the bathroom which had been plywood-ed out in the very back, there was like a toilet up on a step—who knows how that happened? I was standing in line with Bob Durham behind me. And I'm sure we'd been drinking beers and we're just, you know, shooting the shit. A ton of people were there for the opening. And the bathroom door opens up and like two or three people come out and just walked passed us. And Bob watched them walk past and he goes, "Man, you know, if people are doing coke in the bathroom this place is becoming awesome!" Like that was the sign—if people showed up to do a couple lines in the bathroom. We fucking made it. Definitely.

JOE NOLAN: The Fugitive, for all of its rough edges, really did bring in a lot of very talented people, and they treated those people with as much respect as you could muster in this shitty old building. Like there was never really a big party happening when the exhibition was happening. But, when it was about 11 p.m. you knew it was going to turn into a disco.

BETH GILMORE: It was like, "It's gonna get sweaty in here." Gosh just dancing and dancing. Mark Hosford would DJ. He would bring records. I remember things like the box fan blowing so that people didn't get totally overheated on the dance floor.

MARK HOSFORD: It wasn't just even the art. On opening nights people would stay around and I would DJ occasionally, and we'd have dance parties. It was a way to get to know each other. It was a way to see art. It was a way to just bond and have a good time. It was kind of a hub for so many things. It was great.

JEFF DANLEY: It seems like I was in there for a lot longer than I was—there was just so much that went on there at that time. It wasn't a major scene, but it was expanding and it was revving up and changing and getting faster and better and bigger. I know I was there on September 11, 2001. I remember that Richard Hall had a tiny little black-and-white TV set in his side of the building. I found that little black-and-white TV set and turned it on and I watched the towers fall while I was sitting in The Fugitive.

HANS SCHMITT-MATZEN: I think that what was happening was we were creating this like kind of support group where everybody kind of understood, I just have this innate creative urge to make things. And it's good for me to be around other people that have that too. I want to be with the people doing the philosophy and having the ability to talk about it. You figure out what it is you're interested in because you're having conversations with somebody in the studio.

BOB DURHAM: It was really nice in terms of having that space because I came in there and I painted and I got a lot done. That was the most productive time of my life. You had people around you who were interesting and they would always be willing to talk about stuff, even if you didn't see eye to eye, it didn't matter. It was a really interesting time. I'm sort of nostalgic about it, you know? Damn, it was so nice to be that young and sort of frivolous and think everything was possible. It sure seemed like it was.

SHAUN SLIFER: There was a lot that went on there that was beautiful and strange. I learned a lot about how to operate in a space that involved other people. Those people took me in as another artist, but I was this twenty-one-, twenty-two-year-old kid. They treated me like another artist in the scene, which was exactly the thing that turned me into who I am now, and gave me a lot of confidence.

HANS SCHMITT-MATZEN: After I started making work at The Fugitive, I became more interested in curating as a creative outlet. But that was right around the time that David Maddox wrote that piece in the *Nashville Scene* where we were on the cover—it was really awesome. It was like "We made it!" At almost exactly the same time, everybody voted for me to be part of the board. And that's exactly the same time that the article got the Fire Marshal's attention, and they realized we had hundreds of people showing up to art openings at this warehouse. After that we weren't allowed to continue to have the gallery open to the public. That was around 2004.

PATRICK DEGUIRA: It was really funny. I mean, we had been in *Art in America*, *Art Papers*—there was good coverage. I think *ArtForum* had us listed as a legitimate cooperative space. And then Dave did that story on the front cover of the *Nashville Scene* and the gallery went completely belly-up.

HANS SCHMITT-MATZEN: We talked about becoming a nonprofit at The Fugitive, but somebody was going to have to have a part-time job to keep-up with all the paperwork to be a 501(c)(3). There's all these accounting requirements that have to go to the IRS and stuff like that. It didn't seem like there were enough benefits for us to try to go through that.

PATRICK DEGUIRA: Our curating in Nashville got shut down so we did the video project festival for two years and there was probably more attention in a way for that internationally than anything else.

GREG POND: These video projects that took us to Cairo, we took it to Basel, took us to various spaces. That was how we continued to kind of curate. It wasn't so much curating, it was more about—again—creating a space for artists to make things and engage in it. And so when we lost the physical space we went to the closest thing that we had to virtual. The spirit of the entire endeavor was to be this sort of itinerant space that shouldn't have existed. We were a little punk rock, I guess. We told ourselves we'd last for two years, but we ended up with ten.

RICHARD MITCHELL: It's been totally renovated. It doesn't have any of the charm it had before, but at least the floors are safe. You don't fall through them. I met up with Lain and Greg and Terry in 2019. We were at one of the bars that's there now. We were sitting up in the corner and Greg's like, "Oh my God. This is where I used to sleep." Once the artists start moving in the yuppies aren't far behind. They totally just took over and then pushed the artists out without even so much as a thank you. "Thank you for making it possible for me to make millions of dollars on this building."

LAIN YORK: The Fugitive sign was above what's now the bar at Earnest's. You can sit there and have an eight dollar whiskey, and if you look at the support pier it still says "Greg is a big fat . . ." you can't read the rest. Bob Durham wrote it all those years ago. That's all the validation we need.

JACK RYAN: I was back there maybe eight years ago. I went to the old Fugitive and there was a model draped across a Harley-Davidson with a photographer going, "You look stunning! Make love to the camera, darling!"

Chestnut Building

1990–2016

THE HISTORY OF NASHVILLE'S MAY HOSIERY MILLS touches on both the Holocaust and the space race. But the big brick building on Chestnut Street functioned as a studio community, a gallery incubator, and even an artists' squat to a generation of do-it-yourself creatives beginning in the 1990s. Alongside the Fugitive Art Center, the "Chestnut building" helped to define Nashville's Wedgewood-Houston neighborhood as an arts district. And its long, dark hallways, terrifying elevator, uncontrolled climate, and occasional animal visitors made the place a rite of passage at the beginning of the city's contemporary art renaissance.

JAMES THREALKILL: I had gone to visit an artist friend of mine—Joe Sorci, the sculptor. And he said to just come by his studio. And that's the first time that I had gone down there to see that artists were using some of those spaces as studio space. Because, when I was growing up in JC Napier Homes, our mom would take us to the old May Hosiery Mill that had the outlet store next to the factory. You could go in there and get a bag load of tube socks for like $2. Man, you go to school the next day with them tube socks all the way up to your knee with the two stripes on them and couldn't nobody tell you nothing. You thought you were the coolest walking dude in the school. So, you know, we got really excited when mom was taking us to the outlet store. When May Hosiery Mill closed the factory, I realized that artists started looking at those spaces for workspace. I called Michael and said, "Hey man, there's some available space over here at May Hosiery Mill." We went and applied for one of the spaces, and turned it into our studio space.

MICHAEL MCBRIDE: I'm from a rural community right over by Memphis. I was in school in St. Louis for two years at a community college playing basketball. And I transferred to Nashville, to Tennessee State to play, but I hurt my knee. I just kind of gave up on that. I just concentrated on my art.

JAMES THREALKILL: I actually am a native Nashvillian who grew up in South Nashville in the JC Napier public housing community. It was my first-grade teacher at Napier School who told my mother that I was drawing in class all day. She said, "There's a good chance this young man's going to be an artist because that's all he's doing." So my mother said, "It is OK to draw, but you have to do your schoolwork as well." She made sure that I had art materials and she enrolled me in art classes in the Children's Museum over by Howard School. I was the oldest of six kids, and when I turned thirteen my mother bought me an oil painting set from the old Acme school supply store down in Hillsboro Village. So that just demonstrated to me that she had the utmost confidence in my abilities as an artist. I was just trying to draw and paint everything I could get my hands on.

MICHAEL MCBRIDE: We went over there and found this guy on the first floor—he had that space where he sold furniture across the country. He had a big space, and we talked to him, and he let James and I have part of it. It was big. It was hot. We had to try to put some air conditioners in there. I mean, it was treacherous. So we were there for about maybe six months, and then Joe said there was a space opening up near his on the fourth floor. We ran up there. We called the owner of the building and told him we wanted to move up to that space. And that's how we got up to the fourth floor.

JAMES THREALKILL: The view was absolutely incredible because you had those high windows and then, we used to even go up on the roof and look at the fireworks at night, and just sit with lawn chairs up there. We had great privacy up there until we opened it up for a reception and stuff. And so photographers started asking us if they could use the space to do photo shoots and different videos and that kind of thing. So it was a pretty cool spot up there on the fourth floor. The building address was 427 Chestnut and we called our studio Atelier 427.

JOE NOLAN: There was vintage signage and industrial carts and things all over that building. You were aware you were in an industrial space—ramshackle, but mostly clean. We all knew it was a former hosiery factory, but everybody just called it the "Chestnut building." Even nowadays you can date people in the art scene when they say "Chestnut building" and just assume you know which building on Chestnut they're talking about.

JAMES THREALKILL: I knew that if I ever had an opportunity to go to college, that art was what I would want to study. But, being the oldest of six and growing up in public housing, I didn't have a very confident idea that I would be able to afford college. So by the time we moved to East Nashville I was entering the ninth grade and attending East Nashville High School. After the tenth grade, I had this tremendous growth and coordination spurt and ended up being a three-sport All-American, All-State, All-City athlete in football, track, and basketball. So I had my pick in terms of where to go to school, and it wasn't no question about what I was going to study. After being recruited by Lee Corso at Indiana University, and Arizona State, and Notre Dame, Tennessee State with coach John Merritt, I was also recruited by Bill Parcells, who was the defensive coordinator at Vanderbilt in 1974. And so I signed a scholarship to play football at Vanderbilt, and that's where I studied art. I got my fine arts degree from Peabody College after finishing my playing career.

MICHAEL MCBRIDE: So when I came here in 1977, it was very limited in terms of what was happening art-wise. My first art studio was in 1982 and it was in the heart of Green Hills. My studio was where Macy's is now. It's crazy, man. There was a Castner Knott, Cain-Sloan, and a place called The Game Store, and my studio was up above The Game Store.

JAMES THREALKILL: In terms of trying to have an art career, Nashville was the last place to try to do that. It was slow and people considered us a one cart, horse-and-buggy town—that kind of thing. I just felt like in order to be an artist, I needed to leave Nashville. So I had an uncle who lived in Chicago on Lake Michigan. He told me I could come up there and stay with him and look for a job. And after the first snow I tried to walk to the store and I was knee deep in snow at six feet six inches. And I said, "The snow is this tall? I'm going back to Nashville."

MICHAEL MCBRIDE: Somers Randolph was probably the first artist in May Hosiery Mill doing stuff, because that's how Joe Sorci got there. Somers was doing these huge sculptures and stuff, and so he needed the big space. I think he was the first one in there making a space for art and artists.

JAMES THREALKILL: My grandfather's sister lived in Sacramento, California. So I said, "I'm going to try my hand at California." So I moved out to Sacramento and just got frustrated that the job didn't come around as fast as I wanted it to. And Sacramento seemed too much like Nashville. I called my mom, told her I wanted to come back home. She sent me a bus ticket, and as I was leaving on a two-and-a-half-day bus trip, the bus went through Southern California. And I realized, "This is the California I was looking for!" I wanted to jump off the bus at that time, but I came back to Nashville. And it was at that point that I started to see a change in what was taking place in the city.

MICHAEL MCBRIDE: The thing about May Hosiery, what James and I did was a whole vibe. Our idea was to make it not just a place to make art, but a place to hang, a place to entertain, a place to do all of it. That's what art galleries and people are trying to do now, but we started that whole vibe. We had these sessions called "Soirées" where we invited people in and we talked about art. We painted live, we had music. We were doing all that in that space.

JAMES THREALKILL: Me and Michael were working with a friend of ours, Derell Stinson. We would invite people to come to our studio, and our space was big. I mean, we had sofas and work tables and a bathroom and a refrigerator. I mean, it was the full gamut in that space. And so we could invite say thirty to forty people inside the space. And we would do this thing where we would give them a topic and then they would have thirty minutes to discuss this topic at their tables. And Michael and I would walk around and just listen to the different conversations that were taking place. Michael and I would then go to our studio spots and create a painting based on the conversations that we heard. And then at the end we would auction them off to the group and discuss what our interpretations of their conversations were. Man, those things were such cool parties. We had people that just couldn't wait for the next one. It was a really exciting event, and people were willing to pay money to come and participate. And those went really well.

MICHAEL MCBRIDE: Nothing is new. People are thinking that these things are new, but we were just so far ahead at that time, Nashville had to catch up with us.

JAMES THREALKILL: And then, it was great in terms of just inviting groups of artists to come and talk about strategies for promotion and continuing to grow the art scene. Whenever clients wanted to meet with us and they came up into that space, they were blown away. The building looks one way on the outside, but when you come inside you got all of these amazing creative art spaces. We started doing tours of all the artist studios that were in that building, and so word got around that it was a hotspot for this vibrant community of artists.

DANE CARDER: So that time in my memory is pretty fuzzy. I got sober in May of 2000. I moved into the building in the fall. So I was on the ropes. Adrienne Outlaw was there. I think Somers Randolph was there, but I never met him. There were like some wood hoarders there. They had like 3000 square feet and it was just lumber. I shared a space with Paul McClain next door to Adrienne.

ADRIENNE OUTLAW: I moved to Nashville in 1996 from Chicago. I grew up in Nashville, but I left as soon as I could get out of high school. At that time I knew I needed to go to another area to pursue my art. So I went to the School of the Art Institute of Chicago, and then I came back kicking and screaming. I felt like going back to Nashville was going backward. But, in Chicago—or probably any bigger city—I would have been kind of another cog in the wheel that had probably already been developed. But, as long as you were doing your homework, jumping in and doing, I quickly realized that Nashville was a city that we could really make into whatever we wanted.

DANE CARDER: So I never graduated college. The last time I left college, I helped my brother build a house and painted the house and started painting interiors for a living, and rented the studio at that time. Moving in with Paul McLean, who was almost ten years older than I am, and had shown extensively, and had a lot of willingness and desire to espouse his wisdom, I kind of fell into like a mentorship with him. When I moved on to my second space on the other side of Adrienne's studio, I was running through trial and error, learning techniques with acrylic paint after I had kind of abandoned oil painting. There was no cohesive body of work. I wasn't exhibiting. My studio practice was just practice, practice, practice, practice, making average paintings.

JOE NOLAN: Real artists are compelled to build their lives around their creativity. They don't replace it with adult responsibilities, they make it an adult responsibility. The first artists-in-residence at the Downtown Presbyterian Church referred to themselves as "art monks," and Dane's studio was a little monastery, too. He was devoted, and he broke through.

DANE CARDER: I had given a couple of siblings some paintings of old, black-and-white family photos that I had done. And being Southern born, I had a Civil War book of photographs. And I just pulled it down and was flipping through it. There was some emotive quality to the imagery that struck a deep chord with me. And because I had just done a couple of black-and-white paintings, I thought, "Paint one of these and see what happens." Then, suddenly I was probably three or four paintings into it. They were all pretty small format. Just kind of trying to see what happened with it. It occurred to me that like the storyline of the Civil War, my storyline was of having lost my dad when I was sixteen, and kind of spent ten to twelve years in this sort of state of depression and grief and loss and eventual recovery from that. So I'd dialed in on the soldier's journey. And this symbolic approach to life and how to be a human in a world that's ultimately going to kill you. It was sort of steeped in death, my investigation into death and what it means to be human. It evolved into contemporary dialogues around politics and Southern heritage and race, and then the spiritual duality of this side versus that, wrong versus right. I started making the Civil War related work in 2007. And from then on that was most of what I did at that time in the studio.

JOE NOLAN: The Chestnut building was a fascinating place if you were into art and you knew those artists. If you weren't immediately connected with the art scene you'd have never known what was happening in that building. A new experimental gallery/curating culture started to sprout there. Artists wanted to the show the work they were making, and some of the bigger studios had more than enough room to accommodate a small group show or a nice selection of one artist's works. And it was all artist-led so you saw every type of makeshift display starting to go up. Seed Space was basically just a tiny portion of Adrienne Outlaw's studio. Dane Carder started Threesquared because he had this one giant wall that was really just dying for work to hang on it.

DANE CARDER: I had this thirty-foot, straight, white wall. And most of my painting was done on the other side of the studio. I kept looking at it thinking, "How lucky am I to have this space and this wall? I should share this." Kaaren Engel was the first person I invited to show, and then I kind of kept it going and had several shows. Maybe like a year or so later is when Adrienne opened up Seed Space.

ADRIENNE OUTLAW: I think I was in a really unique position. I had this dual role of being an artist and a reporter. And when I stopped being a full-time reporter in my twenties I realized what incredible power you wield as a reporter—everybody answers your phone call. Everybody's ready to talk to you at any time you want to talk to them. I'd always kind of known that, but I took some of it for granted because I came into it so early. So when I left that field, I realized with much more clarity how powerless many artists are in the hierarchy of positions. I also did a fair amount of traveling nationally and internationally. And I came to the conclusion that all cities had the same level of artists in terms of the quality of their work. And I came back thinking that Nashville had just as high a quality of work as you see in London or Paris, but our city is so much smaller. And the last time I went to New York I was pregnant with my first daughter, Casey. This was in 2006 and I was so motion sick. I realized I just couldn't pull it all off, all this travel networking anymore. I realized I needed to stay put for a while if I was going to be having babies. And I didn't have these connections as a reporter anymore. I decided that I really wanted to start bringing people to Nashville to show them that—in fact—we do wear shoes, and we're really able to extend the kind of hospitality that you can't find in big cities. That became something that we really sort of prided ourselves on with Seed Space. We specifically tried to bring people in when we had really good weather, so they could experience the weather. We really tried to pair really well known curators up with emerging artists, and really well known artists with emerging curators. I was always very much trying to break down that hierarchy. I really wanted to open the city up, open up dialogue, extend networks, reduce the hierarchy.

DANE CARDER: Seed Space was like a totally different model than mine was. They were a good play off each other because Adrienne's was cerebral and academic and project-based. And mine was like kind of rough shod—"Hey, bring some paintings. We're going to hang them on this wall!" That's when we started calling it Threesquared and I brought Sara Estes in as somebody who could do it better than me. I offered the space and I assisted with anything and everything, but I wanted somebody else to sort of take it and make it their project. I wrote to Lain York and just said, "Hey, do you know anybody that would be interested in curating shows?" She was the first person he said. She was perfect—new and young and excited and perfect.

SARA ESTES: So while I was working at the galleries at Fisk, I had a lot of downtime—gallery work is a lot of downtime just waiting for people to come in for a tour or whatever. So I was studying Georgia O'Keeffe and Alfred Stieglitz' little galleries that they had in New York. And I was bowled over because they were so small, you know? These were not big operations. These were tiny little one-room things. And so for me, I was just like, "There's so much potential." You don't have to have a bunch of money. You don't have to have a big space, you just need anywhere. You just hang that art on the wall and you can make shit happen. So I got really inspired by Stieglitz's legacy. I decided I wanted to start my own gallery. I'd gotten to know a few people just from being in the art world. I think I told someone that I was looking for studio space. Someone put me and Dane in touch and he had that massive space in the May Hosiery Mill. He had curated a couple shows there and he was looking for someone to take over. He liked the idea of stuff going on in that studio and not being so like, lonely and quiet. So we got together and like we were on the same page immediately.

DANE CARDER: Jodi Hays had a real early show. Paul Collins had his first show in Nashville at Threesquared. Lisa Bachman Jones had an early show there. Mike Calway-Fagen showed collages there.

SARA ESTES: At the time it was only Dane and Adrienne Outlaw. There were other people in the building that had studios, but in terms of people who were trying to be public facing, they were the only two in that building. Dane was super cool. He just let me run with it. I was dating this like web developer guy at the time, so he made me this awesome website. I wanted professional stuff happening in the art world. I felt like a lot of stuff looked bad. The emails going out didn't look good and the websites that people had didn't look good. So, my mission at that time was to make real sleek stuff. I wanted to be sending out sleek emails. I wanted the show pages to look really good. With that website we made sure to document everybody's show and have all the photos. I was making and sending out press releases and doing whatever I could at that time. I had downtime to do it while I was working, so it was awesome. We ran that gallery for three years doing monthly shows and we started the Art Crawl in Wedgewood-Houston. We got with Adrienne and we were like, "Why don't we just do our openings at the same time because more people will come?" We started doing that every month, me and Adrienne doing those openings. People kept showing up. And we would do other little events. We had a screening of one of Matt Christy's films and we did artist talks and stuff like that. It just kind of grew. And then when Fort Houston moved in downstairs, that was, "Oh shit! This is really happening!" Because they made the party even bigger. So that was a really, really, really fun time. We started in 2011 and went through 2013.

DANE CARDER: So when it was just me and Adrienne, we very intentionally wanted to get people to the shows without drawing a crowd. The building was not up to code and they would shut it down just like The Fugitive. You kind of wanted to fly under the radar, but you wanted to be on the radar. And so then Ground Floor Gallery had opened. Julia Martin moved in, and Channel to Channel was upstairs. And SooPlex Gallery was across the hall. I mean, at some point, Ovvio Arte moved across the railroad tracks basically in a garage. It tipped the scale from something I enjoyed to something that I just didn't. There was a point where it was just too much of a party thing. Sara and I had kind of gotten to where we weren't showing consistently with the Art Crawl so we just kind of pulled back on it all.

ADRIENNE OUTLAW: Seed Space was really supposed to be by the artists for the artists. It was not supposed to be a drinking stop. I always wanted to be much more serious. I've never enjoyed this duality of we're all drinking and talking and no one's paying any attention to the art. That just always made me crazy because I feel that our society here in America has always used art as this gathering tool. And the artist does not gain anything from that at all, ever. I especially see it when cities try to use these art districts and it becomes this drinking tour and the galleries are just losing money from like trying to give everybody like two ounces of wine. So for me it was that, but it was also that we had real concerns with the building: Would people get lost in the building? Would they get hurt in the building? Would the building shut us down? What about the fire marshal? We knew if we reached a particular capacity, the fire marshal would come and we would not survive.

SARA ESTES: The Wedgewood Houston Art Crawl sort of started to be a whole thing. And then of course it grew into whatever it is now, you know, which is insane.

JOE NOLAN: Sara Estes was running Threesquared with support from Dane, but Adrienne turned Seed Space into an incubator via all these artist internships. She had whole groups of young artists—mostly young women—learning about creating exhibitions, scheduling, doing press, actually installing shows, networking with curators and galleries and institutions all over the city, but also all over the country. There's a remarkable number of success stories in Nashville today that got their start programming that tiny gallery space in Adrienne's studio at the Chestnut building.

ADRIENNE OUTLAW: I wanted them to see the joys and the challenges of being an artist, and to understand the reality. A lot of them, probably, went on to not become artists—which is also great. I sometimes felt like I was influencing more people for art de-appreciation than anything else, because they would see the challenges we went through in the studio: you still have to sweep the floor; you still have to pay your bills. I let anybody in the studio. I had a lot of high-school interns. I had a lot of PhD scientists who just wanted to do something wacky, and I always needed just drudge help. I think the person that has had the most success coming out of the studio would be Lisa Bachman Jones. Lisa came in as a more realistic figurative painter. Then she loved being a much more abstract painter. And you know, now she's gone through grad school and has had another evolution of her work. It was also interesting having people there for short periods of time or long periods of time. I think Alicia Beach was there for two years. We were working to get her ready for grad school. And just having these really long term relationships with people was cool. I felt that I was like the spiritual counselor for all the young ladies in town. I didn't understand why all these young women kept coming to me for like relationship and spiritual advice. I know for me it was really wonderful. But it was also indicative of my total inability to do time management. Like we would just sit around and like shoot the shit in the studio all day some days.

JOE NOLAN: The Tri-Star Arts organization just held the inaugural Tennessee Triennial in 2023. That's a statewide arts booster that grew out of a merger between an organization based in Knoxville called Locate Arts and Seed Space. It's not crazy to say "No Seed Space, no Tennessee Triennial." Janet Decker-Yanez ran a space called Ground Floor Gallery + Studios on Fourth Avenue South for years. It rented studio spaces to artists and programmed a small gallery. Tons of artists started their careers there. But Ground Floor first opened in the Chestnut building, and Janet was one of Adrienne's interns once upon a time.

ADRIENNE OUTLAW: The thing that Janet brought to the table was just amazing. And I saw this happen a lot in the studio with interns. The fantasy is that artists completely make things up within our own mind. And like this solo person makes everything happen. But, really, to make anything successful, it requires a team. I would often sort of think about visual arts and music: In music you've got a songwriter, but then you need to have someone sing. You need to have someone play the instruments and you need to have a producer to put it all together. You need that in the visual arts too, but nobody ever talks about that. Seed Space was so awesome because people would just come out of the woodwork to help us. Janet came out of more of a business background and kind of transferred into art.

JANET DECKER YANEZ: I had two kids and sort of just relished in motherhood for a few years, and we actually moved back and forth from Nashville. When I got back here in 2010 I met Adrienne Outlaw and I did a couple of projects with her. She had Seed Space and she was doing the CSArt project: she took local artists, packed their work in a food crate and we sold art shares basically just like local farmers. I told her I'd always wanted to have this studio/gallery collective type of thing. And she's like, "Janet. Just do it." She said that Bookman was leaving the May Hosiery building—he's the guy that was at the end of the hall. He had a ground floor space that was just filled with all these old books.

ADRIENNE OUTLAW: One thing that I was very, very adamant about all throughout Seed Space is, probably every three months, I made us all sit down and look at ourselves with as critical an objective eye as we could. And I started doubting the relevancy of it at the end of my time in Nashville after The Packing Plant grew and Zeitgeist moved from Hillsboro Village to Wedgewood-Houston. I wasn't sure Nashville still needed Seed Space. Nashville had gotten recognition. We had gotten a Warhol grant, like things were really starting to move and groove by the time I left and it was time to transform.

SARA ESTES: It just felt like a lot of possibility was there, you know? And I think everyone who walked in the Chestnut building had the same reaction. Like, "This is so fucking cool!" It just had a magic to it that, for artists and musicians and anyone who had any kind of creative mind, it just pulled you in and you just wanted to spend time there. We always got to tell the story of like, "This is the place where they made socks for the Apollo astronauts," or whatever—I can't remember the story anymore. It felt like at any time when you're walking in the hallways, you would cross paths with somebody cool who just happened to be visiting a studio there or whatever. And then when Jimmy Abegg and other people got studios down there, there was a lot of people in and out. It felt like something very magical to me, which is why I just loved being in there.

JOE NOLAN: Three hundred Jews fleeing Nazi Germany stayed and worked at the hosiery mill—it was retooled to make weapons during

World War II. During the 1960s and '70s all the Apollo astronauts wore socks manufactured at the mill on their missions to the moon.

MICHAEL MCBRIDE: Oh man, that building was so old and sexy, man. It's the closest thing to being in New York. You know, with the high loft ceilings and everything. We had the big tall windows and we were up on the penthouse. We had that big old elevator that closed up like you see in the movies. People loved it, man. That place was buzzing because we had more photographers and models doing photo shoots in the elevator and in the hallways. It was that kind of a building. That's really what it was, man. The building had its quirks and its issues and stuff, but that was part of the sexiness of it—it was authentic. At one point we had about twenty-five artists in there, man.

JANET DECKER YANEZ: One of the early days when I was moving into the space, cleaning it up, getting it set up, we were hauling things in and out of that freight elevator. There was this cord that you would pull on to get the top to close down, and I nearly lost my hand or at least my finger in the freight elevator. This cord that you pulled would get closed inside the elevator and I thought, "That shouldn't be inside. It needs to be outside." At first the elevator door closed really slow, but it speeded up as it closed. It looks like there's all the time in the world to just stick your hand in and just push that cord through real quick. It slammed my left hand and I had a crush injury. My first finger was in the gap and I felt my first finger hook around the latch and I like ripped my hand out and I really thought I lost my finger. But I looked down and my fingers are still there, but I thought that my knuckle was like pushed into the middle of my hand. I thought, "Holy crap, I've just messed up my hand really, really bad." Will ClenDening was working there with me, and he comes running because I'm screaming and crying, and he thought maybe he did it because he called for the elevator on the other floor, but it was all me. I was going to drive myself to the ER and he's like, "No, I'm gonna drive you." And I'm like, "I got this." And so I'm getting my stuff and I wrap my hand with like some cloth because it was bleeding all over. I'm walking out the front door and Will had already made it to his truck and like pulled right up. He was like, "Come on. Get in. I'm going to drive you." And thank god he did because just from the Chestnut to like the van to the ER, like I was starting to get like woozy, and really lightheaded. So the ER doctors were totally taken aback. They're thinking I'm going to have to have surgery. They're telling me they're going to have to put metal pins in my hand. So then they x-ray and there's not even a break. My knuckle hadn't actually moved at all—that was just the intense swelling that had taken place, and it looked extra bad with the bleeding. The thing that saved me was my 18-karat gold, thick wedding band. It didn't even dent, which was pretty cool.

ADRIENNE OUTLAW: Being at the May Hosiery factory was kind of like being in the Wild West. I mean, you had to really be careful about being there at night—you had to be careful about being there in the day! I had a raccoon fall through the ceiling once—a big thirty pounder. We caught some birds, some squirrels. I always felt that the building really had good juju, but a lot of people who had come in were kind of freaked out. I loved walking around that building into the parts where I really felt like it would be helpful to have a construction helmet—I was just waiting for something to fall at any moment.

SARA ESTES: It had a good vibe. There was a lot of natural light too. It had these big industrial windows. It was just unlike any other space in Nashville where you could go see art and make art and hang out. The ceilings were really high and the hallways were cool and there was all this like old furniture and old signage. Everything about the feeling of it was just homey and it was cozy despite it being just absolutely rundown.

JANET DECKER YANEZ: Our gallery still had the yellow stripes down the center of the floor that were the lines that these big bins on wheels would roll down. It was so gritty and dirty, and it was just the exact space that I wanted. We had open air to the outside because some of the windows didn't have glass or wouldn't shut all the way. You really couldn't work in there more than like nine months out of the year. It was either too cold or too hot. When it drops below 50 degrees your fingers just don't work so well and your paint doesn't flow. And then in the summer in Nashville it was just way too hot.

ADRIENNE OUTLAW: I think the thing that May Hosiery Mill gave me was a real sense of place and a real sense of community. I loved having that unbelievably gorgeous studio—as dilapidated as it was. I loved that place. I loved the floors. I loved the holey ceiling. John Reed had built this really sweet deck off the back that eventually they closed my access to. And then, eventually, it just fell off the building. The thing that was really great about that place—you definitely had to have your bearings about you, particularly if you were there at night as a woman—but I never really felt unsafe. I never felt that there was any super weirdo in the building. It was just normal weirdness.

JANET DECKER YANEZ: So then, a friend and her daughter came to one of the openings. And a few days later she tells me "You're not gonna believe this." She knew about the accident with my hand. So when her and her daughter were leaving the reception they were passing the freight elevator and my friend said to her daughter, "That's the thing that almost took Janet's hand." And just as she says that, the doors open and a guy is standing there holding his bloody hand, because the same thing had just happened to him as well. And he was like, "Were you just talking about this elevator?" I literally never used that elevator again. I think it was possessed.

JOE NOLAN: That elevator was spooky and I only remember taking the stairs in that building. It had a reputation for biting people. It reminded me of the Stephen King short story "The Mangler," where this industrial laundry press becomes possessed and acquires a taste for human blood.

JANET DECKER YANEZ: So if you're walking in off Chestnut, those main front doors, you just walk straight back. And so I went in there, I looked around and I talked to the slum lord and arranged a lease and he rented the space to me, super cheap. I was able to carve out four studios with the help of Will Tucker and his students from Watkins. They came and built walls so that there was a central gallery and then four studios. My whole plan was that I would have one studio and I'd rent the other three. And I was going to do quarterly juried shows. The first show in 2012 was called *From the Ground Up*. It was a lot of work, but it was really, really cool.

JOE NOLAN: Ground Floor Gallery + Studios added a new attraction to the gallery-going at the Chestnut building, but it was also kind of a throwback to a smaller Fugitive model in the way it was more deliberately set up with simple, but purpose-built studio and gallery spaces. Janet had worked with Untitled and knew exactly what she needed. You could say "No Untitled, no Ground Floor" because Untitled taught people a lot, but it also frustrated people and spurred some artists on to make the kind of spaces, and build the kinds of organizations, and curate the kind of shows that they wanted to see and be a part of.

JANET DECKER YANEZ: I originally landed here in 2003. As an artist I really always wanted to kind of dig in and find community where I was at. That was kind of harder as an adult, you know, it's kind of a little easier when you're a kid. I had graduated from the University of Houston many years before I got to Nashville, but I always took away something a painting professor told me: "Just don't put down your brushes." The Untitled concept was to let everybody who wants to show in, but then lots of people just drop off work and don't put anything into the show, but then they're back for the opening. That started rubbing me the wrong way. After doing a few shows I wanted to have a little bit more of a selection process. That's part of why I opened Ground Floor. I wanted to show quality artwork, and at that point I decided that I wanted to help other people show too. I think this just goes back to wanting to be a part of the community. Dane Carder's Threesquared gallery was there, Adrienne had Seed Space, Dustin Hedrick's Channel to Channel was upstairs. Jimmy Abegg and Kit Reuther were sharing a studio. They'd open up and invite people in.

KIT REUTHER: I was born here. I studied commercial design, but I loved art history. I found my way into the art world slowly. I was self-taught and did a lot of peripheral jobs. I kind of fell into the art world when people started buying my work. I'm sixty-five, and I've been full time as an artist about thirty years. One day I started making a living. I eased into it.

DUSTIN HEDRICK: I'm originally from Mississippi. I moved to Nashville from Los Angeles, after being in a band. They kind of fell apart in LA. This was back in 2010. The gallery started off as my studio. When I moved to Nashville it was super sleepy. I would drive around and it was kind of uninspiring because it was like going from LA to a small town. I had to really seek out inspiration, and I thought that I would move to Nashville and still play music, actually. I have a degree in art and I was still creating paintings here and there when we weren't on the road, trying to supplement my meager musician per diem with selling paintings. So, when I moved to Nashville, I started working at [restaurant and live music venue] 3rd and Lindsley. I was already kind of jaded from being on the road. Eighty percent of the time I didn't like the music that was being played. So that made me 100 percent full-on jaded with being a musician. So that made me want to get into the art studio more. I actually went to Marathon Music Works [formerly Marathon Motor Works] first. While I was still living in LA, I was researching studio space in Nashville. I went over there and a guy named Barry—I think he's still owns it or something—he told me to go to this building on Chestnut. Nobody was calling it the May Hosiery Mill at that time.

KIT REUTHER: So my first studio at the Chestnut building was around 2007, 2008. I wasn't painting over there. I was doing sculpture because

I had inherited my dad's tools—he was a pilot and he rebuilt vintage aircraft. And when he passed away my sisters and I inherited all this stuff of his and I didn't want to get rid of it. So I brought all the tools and stuff over and I needed a space to put it in. So I got a space at May Hosiery, I was in with Julia Martin and John Reed. It was a great energy. Julia was fun! And then I decided to take a bigger space across the hall, but I couldn't really swing it financially myself. So my friend Jimmy Abegg, he needed a space, too, and we took a bigger space across the hall. Dane Carder and Adrienne Outlaw were all in that main hallway. Jimmy and I were in the last space on the left.

JULIA MARTIN: I was born and raised in Nashville. I did a pre-college program at the School of Visual Arts in Manhattan, and then found out they were opening their only satellite branch in Savannah, the School of Visual Arts. And so there were only two classes that went through and I don't think any of them made it all the way through because Savannah College of Art and Design—during my first year—sued School of Visual Arts and like ran them out of town. So I don't have a degree. I got really jaded by that experience, but I had an incredible foundational education because of those professors. I got a really solid foundational understanding of color and composition and the minutiae of oil paint, which is still my greatest love.

DUSTEN HEDRICK: I remember walking in there and just going down that long hallway and like, nobody was there. Nobody was even in the neighborhood. I get down the way a little bit and finally I find these people running this drapery shop—they'd been in the building for years. They gave me Tom's—the property manager's—phone number. I called him up and he was cool. He showed me the upstairs, there was a few places that were super run-down. There was paint flaking everywhere, and moisture issues. They weren't even renting the spaces on one side of the building because they were in such bad condition. Victor Schmidt had been doing his sculptures there for a long time, and then other artists like Daniel Holland started coming in. Emily Clayton was upstairs above me and then Amanda Joy Brown was there for a little while. Carlton Wilkinson, James Threalkill, and Michael McBride were all on the fourth floor.

KIT REUTHER: Joe Sorci was upstairs. He did sculptures and was kind of all over the place. He had a lot of the upstairs. He was really spread out up there. And then there was kind of an alcoholic that lived up there. He wasn't supposed to. It was sort of hush-hush, but he was buddies with the maintenance guy. He had a spot up there that was all tricked-out.

JULIA MARTIN: I remember getting my foot in the door at the Chestnut building with Dane Carder. He let me kind of pitch in on rent and have a space in the back there. Then that huge space directly across from Dane came open. I mean, fucking enormous. Even a quarter of that was too much space for me. So I ended up with David Guidera and John Reed and Kit Reuther. The four of us just sort of split it up into quadrants and went to town. And that was when Kit just starting experimenting with the sculpture stuff. That became problematic because Emily Leonard had just turned me onto this MSA varnish—it's so beautiful. And I'd just done this pristine—for me—like super minimalist triptych of faces. I'd just done the MSA varnish and Kit had to do a lot with the torch on wood. And it creates all these little like black floaters. I came back the next morning and all three pieces were ruined. They're just little flecks, like fucking torch rain. But I did a lot of fun work there.

KIT REUTHER: Jimmy Abegg was great fun because we would just go all over that building. We would scavenge the old wood shops downstairs. Fort Houston ended up down there. There had been a big wood shop there. We would just take a cart and go down and come back with a haul of wood, which really started me working in wood was just from those scraps I would find in the building. There were ceilings falling through. And the squirrels kind of ran freely through the ceilings. We were thriving in that environment. Jimmy was all over the place. He was doing his painting. And he would have people in and play guitar. He had this giant, long table—like twelve-foot-long table—down the middle of the room. And he would just hold court and play guitar. And his buddies would come and they would draw and write. It was just a really fun time and a good place for him as he began to lose his eyesight. It was a familiar place that he could still function in and he really made the most of it. I was in that space quite a long time with Jimmy—seven or eight years. But then a space became available across the hall, and I needed my own space because my work was getting a little messy.

DUSTEN HEDRICK: I was living in a six-hundred-square-foot apartment when I first moved to town. I wanted a place where I could work but I also wanted to network and meet people and other artists. That first space I had helped, but it was really tiny. Then one person who was renting a bigger space there—I think she was a retired attorney—she had put linoleum tile down, did like asbestos and lead paint testing. She painted the whole thing. But, she wasn't in there much. So she asked me if I wanted it, but with my rent for where I was living plus her space that was kind of a stretch. But I really wanted this place. I was reading *Walden* at the time, and really getting into like a minimalist mindset and wondering what I really needed in my life. So I moved in there and I had these partitions that I built. Half of it was my studio and half of it was like my living quarters. And it was nice enough. The biggest thing was the train rolling by like three times a night. I would like crank up my sound machine and put in my earplugs cause I'm a light sleeper anyway. I hardly got any sleep when I was there. I was trying to be like really sneaky. I would shower at the Y. I would get up really early before Tom, the property manager came in so he wouldn't see my car there. I'd workout and shower and then come back around 6:00 AM or something like that. Sometimes he still wasn't even there. And then it transitioned from my studio into a gallery. I only lived there for half a year because that winter was super cold. There's no heat in the building so I bought this window unit from Home Depot and when that went out I didn't want to buy another unit. I had a friend whose basement was available. That's when it transitioned into just a gallery and a studio. That was in 2014. In December of 2014, I showed a small exhibition of Robert Scobey's work. It was the first show that wasn't just my stuff. It sounds like the quintessential poor, starving artist story, but it didn't feel like that at the time. I was just doing whatever I needed to do.

JOE NOLAN: Dusten Hedrick called his space Channel to Channel and it became must-see viewing very quickly. It was just a small room with his studio gear tucked in the corner and a handful of works up on the walls, but that was all you really needed in a space like that if the art was good. He had this connection to the Knoxville art scene and he was constantly introducing Nashville to this great contemporary abstract painting that was happening in East Tennessee.

DUSTEN HEDRICK: I didn't really know what I wanted at the very beginning, so I just put artwork up. It was me and my friend, Tim Cook, who's a graphic designer. I went to Mississippi State and majored in fine art. He majored in graphic design, and our first show at the May Hosiery Mill was May of 2014. Our work didn't go together well at all. It was my big, bulky, abstract painting. I was working really textural, like thick. I was using molding paste to build-up texture, and doing completely abstract, minimalist, zombie formalist type stuff. And he was doing these *Star Wars* prints, because that's what he was into. And so we put that work up together and like, it just didn't work. I knew that I didn't like that. So then I switched to doing solo shows. Solo shows were a lot easier to curate than group shows, because then I was curating from one artist's work.

JANET DECKER YANEZ: A really important part of my juried shows was that I always tried to crank it up every time, you know? I'd get submissions from artists that were a little bit more experienced, a little bit more well-known. Later on [Brooklyn-based painter and curator] Catherine Haggarty was a juror, and Austin Thomas, who did Pocket Utopia in Manhattan, he juried a show for us. It was a way to show people outside of the city and outside of the region what Nashville can do.

DUSTEN HEDRICK: I kind of felt like if we were to sell one piece from a show that was pretty successful. And the price point was always pretty good because we weren't doing a 50/50 split at the very beginning. I was just taking like a hundred bucks for like each piece sold. And then the more that I did, the more I felt like I was earning a certain percentage.

JOE NOLAN: The first time I met Daniel Holland he had his work hanging at that tiny gallery area where Fort Houston was sharing their maker space with a motorcycle repair shop. On First Saturday crawls we'd head straight upstairs to Dusten's and then work our way down to Seed Space and Threesquared and then to the basement. Fort Houston wasn't showing a lot of art then but they always had a little display up and they'd play music and open the loading dock doors. There was always a keg. Fort Houston was kind of the permanent after party at the Chestnut building.

DANIEL HOLLAND: I grew up in Greenville, South Carolina, and there's a college there called Furman. And, at least at the time, there was a big crossover of people coming from Nashville and going to school down there. And so I wound-up meeting a couple of these guys. We became good friends and then they were going to move back to Nashville. I really wanted to get out of my hometown, you know, like everyone. And so me and Lauren decided, "Well, let's go try Nashville." That was twelve years ago, I was twenty-five.

JOE NOLAN: Mike Calway-Fagen and Julian Rogers worked out of the SooPlex space, which was across the hall from Dane Carder's and Adrienne Outlaw's studios. That space was emblematic of the studio-as-gallery model at the Chestnut building. Mike and Julian organized shows and also asked friends to curate exhibitions.

VERONICA KAVASS: I was living in London and just visiting family in Nashville. Mike was running that space and he was like, "Do you want to do a show here?" Mike brings a certain energy to his projects—there's an urgency. Whatever he's working on, he basically acts like it's the most radical thing in the world, and sometimes it is.

DANIEL HOLLAND: Our first house was around Twelfth in East Nashville over by The 5 Spot. It's really fancy now. We rented an entire house for seven hundred bucks in 2010. I was working out of my house and still really developing artistically when we first moved to Nashville. I got enough of a portfolio together to get into Watkins. That wasn't even the plan. I actually just met David Hellams, who worked at Watkins at the time. And he encouraged me to get some stuff together and bring it to Watkins. They were like, "Oh, this is cool. Here's some money." That was totally foreign to me, and it was really exciting. It's like when you get in the right stream, you know, everything starts flowing. I mostly started out working in my basement in that first house. And then once that kind of snowballed, I met Katie Howard. It was Katie Howard that found the space.

VERONICA KAVASS: Since I had limited space to work with in terms of what I could bring over, I decided to make it a sound-based show that was like a response to Nashville as a country music scene, a music city. So that was the artists' prompt, and I selected artists who I knew made that kind of work. So I remember I brought their work over in a suitcase and it was mostly sound and video. I made some fliers for it and put them all over town and it had a really good turnout. But a lot of people were pissed about what it was. Like, there was some people that showed up from Belle Meade—older women who I guess thought they were gonna buy some like English artwork for their homes. They walked in and there was really nothing to look at. I mean, just a few things. They, they were like, "What is this? We came all this way to this place." They were really pissed, which I thought was hilarious.

DANIEL HOLLAND: I think we were on like the third floor. It was quite big. Maybe it was like twenty by forty feet or something. It was a big space and it was me, Aaron Martin, Kuntal Patel, and a kid named Jesse Matheson who's a writer. He didn't take up any space, he just kind of had his typewriter. I think he kind of secretly lived there. There was a girl in the beginning, but she never showed up. She brought some plants in on day one and like a desk, but never, ever came back and didn't pay. So we just kind of took her stuff out and brought somebody else in. The building was not well maintained, but it was perfect for art. We got paint on the floors. We wrote on the walls. We didn't pay much for it at all—nobody did. I think we paid like three hundred bucks or something split between all of us, but we could still barely pay it. We would have huge parties there. Aaron knows everybody, so he would get kegs brought in and it would just like turn into these like wild parties. We would call them like studio-wide art shows, but I feel like we were the youngest wildest ones. So I feel like the other studios kind of like didn't want us to bring all our hammered friends into their studios. But we had a blast, you know. It was fine.

JOE NOLAN: David Lynch talks about how important it is for artists to have a "set up" so they can be ready to jump into action when the ideas come. Those cheap studios made those set ups accessible, but the Chestnut building was like a whole warren populated by all these creative folks, involved in all these varied practices. That meant there was conversation and networking and learning and inspiring happening too. It was a fun place to look at art on a Saturday night, but it was a lot more than that. It empowered the entire art community at multiple points of contact.

DANIEL HOLLAND: Getting into the studio was just such a breath of fresh air. I was able to just focus completely on art and talk to people who only wanted to talk about art and creative things where nothing is weird. Everybody was on the same page. Everybody was encouraging. The more abstract the idea, the more excited people got about it, the more rewarding it was to have those kind of conversations. Once you get a good rapport with your artist friends, and you trust them, it helps you produce work faster. They can kind of just stop you from going down dead ends and wasting time. Just having support and being able to have ideas come to me, and being able to speak them to other artists was so important. And you can do whatever you want to do, you know? You just roll cigarettes and read Michel Foucault or like, whatever. You just pee in a jar and paint because you don't want to walk down a couple flights to use the bathroom. That's when I started working big as well. Just the idea of having like a twenty-by-twenty-foot section of the studio where I can see six of my paintings at one time. I think that's when you start thinking macro. That was really great. I was able to start formulating long ideas, and once you develop that muscle that's a big change. Once I zoomed-out, then I was like, "Oh, this is how I think now?" It's like the monolith in 2001 or something and you just keep going back, back, back.

JOE NOLAN: The studio/gallery spaces in the Chestnut building weren't traditional retail/commercial spaces and they didn't run that way. You really needed to go to the opening receptions to see the shows. There weren't usually regular hours at those spaces, and if you didn't have the artists' number or email there was no way to contact them. On the other hand if you popped into the place on a Thursday afternoon you might find an open gallery and a working artist at the same time. That Chestnut scene was very accessible in that way. Just the nature of the environment in that building helped to educate the city about what contemporary art is, who makes it, and how it's done. If you were gallery-going there, you were also doing studio visits simultaneously. There wasn't room for artificial walls between the artists and the audience and the artwork.

VERONICA KAVASS: There's that long hallway with all these little rooms coming off of it. And there's this industrial classroom look to it all. So the SooPlex space wasn't huge, but it was just one of those rooms—and then it had those giant windows. The space had the feel of the building. It wasn't like they paved it over and tried to make it look like something else. It was kind of hard to get to for people that hadn't been there. They're going in this creepy building that is like unlocked all the time and you know, who knows what's going on in there. I would send people to go see the show and they wouldn't always find it or they didn't trust it because it was like such a quiet, weird building to enter into. Mike was in there a lot and so was Julian. And they did a lot of appointment-only type stuff. They would meet people there and I think they were just trying to make it a part of the larger contemporary art scene. They just wanted to show work that was way more experimental. The gallery lasted, I want to say a year or a year and a half.

JANET DECKER YANEZ: People kept coming to me asking if I had space, but I was full. So I was walking around the building one day and wondering if there was a space where I could expand. And I was looking upstairs they had like this huge open room with all these little tiny rooms around it—it was perfect for a gallery and studios. I started talking to the maintenance guy and he said there had already been developers sniffing around. I was like, "Oh, shit!" And so I then just started scouring the neighborhood because I knew the end was coming and I didn't want to get caught.

KIT REUTHER: I moved into that last space around 2015. We didn't sign any leases. We were month-to-month so we knew we were on borrowed time. I was able to stay in that last studio for a couple of years.

It was good. That was a real productive time for me. Then we all got the boot.

MICHAEL MCBRIDE: We were there from 2000 until they kicked us out. They sold the building and kicked all of us out. We had a good run, man. James and I had been doing art together at least fifteen years prior, and then we were in that building for I guess almost seventeen years, something like that.

JAMES THREALKILL: We spent a good twenty years in that space. And it was just amazing what happened in terms of the collection of artists who were there. The receptions that we would host and have an incredible turnout of people coming to visit our studios. We started working with University School of Nashville who started doing some programming. They would invite the parents and the kids to come down to the studio. And so it was a vibrant space to be in. I created some of my best work in those spaces. And so Michael and I were rolling along with having space to work, having space to hang our work and store our work. And eventually development started to come through and that's when we were informed that we would have to vacate the building. But we had a good twenty-year run at May Hosiery Mill.

JANET DECKER YANEZ: I've got this group of friends, they're mainly educators, but one of them is the granddaughter of the founder of May Hosiery—she's a May. So I was telling her about my space and talking about the Chestnut building and she's like "Oh yeah, that's my grandfather's place, the hosiery factory." She said her fondest memories are going to visit him when the circus was coming into town because they would stop the train right there at the tracks, where they cross Chestnut just down from the May building. They'd stop the train and let the elephants out to walk. And when she was a little girl she got to ride an elephant from the Ringling Brothers Circus down Chestnut Street.

Ruby Baby

1998-2009

RUBY GREEN WAS ONE OF THE FIRST, permanent artist-run venues to emerge from Nashville's 1990s contemporary art scene. That era was defined by pop-up exhibitions and the itinerant projects of the Untitled Artists group. Ruby Green founder Chris Campbell brought a passionate curatorial vision to her space, and the gallery's nonprofit model further distinguished Ruby Green and Campbell's programming from the city's growing commercial gallery marketplace. Ruby Green managed to be as challenging and sophisticated as Untitled was disruptive and irreverent. And—along with the Fugitive Art Center—Campbell and her gallery showed the city that the kids doing the heavy lifting in Nashville's contemporary art scene were more than alright.

CHRIS CAMPBELL: I'm from here. I went to Hillsboro High School and graduated in the mid-eighties. I dated Jeff Johnson of Jason and the Scorchers my junior and senior year in high school. And through him I was able to meet lots of people and go see lots of bands. It kind of opened my eyes to things I wanted do in the future. I wasn't very musical at all though, so that's when I decided to go to art school. And so I left Nashville and went to the Art Institute of Chicago. I had actually never been there except to see The Smiths. I stayed in Chicago for a few years and then left, and decided I didn't really see the future in paying for the high-dollar art degree. I went to live in Arizona. I got to travel out West and see things. I had a lot of friends that lived in Olympia

59

and San Francisco or Portland, things like that. So I'd go and visit them. And then that's where I first experienced a nonprofit run by artists. And then I eventually did go back and finish my degree. I got my BFA in Chicago. I came back to live in Nashville and joined up with Untitled.

JOE NOLAN: Untitled was really the breaking point where the contemporary art scene became a DIY movement to work-around all the gate-keepers in Nashville. The Untitled pop-ups were groundbreaking, but the next logical step was artists attempting to establish more permanent spaces.

CHRIS CAMPBELL: Untitled had been going on for a few years by the time I joined, I think. The best part is I felt like I'd found my people, you know? There was all these other artists and we would get together and talk about having shows, because we didn't really feel like we had access to the gallery system here in Nashville. They didn't really care about us, especially if we didn't have a masters degree. That was a stopping point for entrance or just the kind of art we were interested in wasn't necessarily Nashville's interest. And we knew that. We were very inclusive or we tried to be. If you said you were an artist or if you said you made art that was good enough, you know?

JOE NOLAN: Untitled was defined by being open to all artists. But that also meant no curating. After a while, artists wanted to be shown in more focused displays, and many also wanted to curate shows in addition to making work.

CHRIS CAMPBELL: I had a studio space at 514 Fifth Avenue, and that was the name of the studio. It was "514" and it was founded by John Reed and David Glick maybe four or five years before I ever came along. It was a very long, narrow space, and the studio spaces were divided with horizontal stripes. And you weren't allowed to put up any kind of barriers or walls between each other. You could only work on the end walls. I kind of did painting and I had started sculpture. I really like textile sculpture. And that's always been something that I could afford. I never could—even at art school—afford paint and the materials needed. And then also, I was at art school at a time when found objects were the big thing. Where you remade things that you found and re-presented it. I wasn't actually that into buying brushes and paint and all that kind. The studio space was all men until I got there. They were all serious painters.

LAIN YORK: So in 1997 or 1998, I remember hanging an Untitled Glow Show at The Cannery with Chris Campbell. Nobody showed up to help, and you've got to hang the pieces and then you've got to get a black light properly illuminating each piece. And Chris just lost it. Chris already had a studio space and she was like, "This, is it. I want to break off. I want do my own thing. I want to do curated shows. I'm done." And that was it. She finished hanging the show with me and then she started Ruby Green. And Ruby Green was the first of that wave of artist-led spaces.

CHRIS CAMPBELL: I think a lot of us were serious artists even though maybe our art wasn't serious. But it was as far as the idea of art making and why you did it, how you did it, that kind of thing. There wasn't that many of us in Untitled. There were a lot of musicians who made some art, wanted to be part of the group. When you brought in your work for the show, you could price it at whatever you wanted. A turning point for me was somebody like literally kisses a piece of paper with lipstick on, puts that on for $1,500 and makes us all look bad. A lot of artists just started thinking about other things that we could be doing. And then the original 514 members kind of left, more people came in, more divided space. And then it just kind of got out of hand. There were like twenty people there, some people sleeping there that weren't artists at all—just kind of a hangout place. I'd heard from one of these people that the owner, Fred, was really unhappy with the way things were going. So I just went straight to Fred and asked him if he would rent it to me. I thought I'd have it as a gallery and studio space for myself so that I could still work on my stuff. At that time it was about $500 for the whole space.

JOE NOLAN: Ruby Green operated out of the space where Bar Sovereign is today. There weren't bars or restaurants or anything like that down there—there weren't even enough street lights. The gallery was well off Broadway, but you always had foot traffic. Homeless folks. Some prostitutes. People up to who knows what. That's why the rent was so cheap.

CHRIS CAMPBELL: The Ruby Green name was just colors. A lot of people thought it was a person. Richard Reesman [artist] looked it up on the internet and the only thing he could find at that time was a painting of a little Black child singing in church. "Ruby Green Singing," I think is the title of the painting. But that was it. It was just colors. I'm actually against vanity gallery names, you know? They've always just kind of turned me off. That's that concept of naming it for yourself or a person. So that was kind of my take on that.

JOE NOLAN: Ruby Green was a nonprofit space and that was part of what made the scene there so different and unique. It was a nice, finished space, but it didn't have the retail vibes of a commercial gallery.

CHRIS CAMPBELL: I talked two of my Untitled friends into starting it with me, but that only lasted maybe a couple months. But I was just kind of steadfast on my vision. I really wanted to give the space and the art the respect of clean walls and a clean floor. I had this vision, I was just naive to how much money it was going to take to pull it off. I had come into a little bit of money because my great aunt had died. I had taken care of her. She'd had Alzheimer's and she didn't have any family, and she left me what she had. And I had no idea I was gonna give it to Nashville like what ended up happening. The space didn't have any electricity. It didn't have any lights. It was a concrete floor. The roof leaked, all kinds of stuff. I thought, "Oh, just run some wires." The electricity alone was like $15,000 or something, you know? My friend, Chris Dugger, thank god he had construction experience and knew some other people—friends of his that basically worked for next to nothing. They put up the drywall. They opened it up because there was like a house door size—you know, like eighty inches tall, thirty inches wide—opening in between the front room and the second room. They were able to open it up to make it more of an entrance into the space. And then they built a wall, I call a floating wall, in the middle that could kind of be pushed to divide the space or not. It just sunk a lot of money and the landlord made me buy a new roof, stuff like that over the time. It really took a toll on me because I didn't have any money and I didn't have a job. I didn't have anything. I just had a dream of doing this.

JOE NOLAN: Ruby Green was my favorite space in the city for looking at paintings. Part of it was the programming, but part of it was just that room itself. That place had big vibes no matter what was on the walls.

LANDRY BUTLER: It was the people and it was the work. Ruby Green had energy. I got stuck in that building one night overnight. I was helping Chris set up for a show and I didn't have a key to lock up. So I could only lock the door from the inside. So I ended up spending the night there and I had interesting dreams. There was a lot of good energy in that place.

CHRIS CAMPBELL: Because of the nonprofit stuff I had seen out West, I thought "I'll do nonprofit." I didn't know what that was either. "I'll just wing it," you know? Which I did. And the first and fatal mistake was I wrote that we were going to sell art when we were filing the papers to get approved by the IRS for the 501(c)(3). I wrote on there that we were going to sell art and we were going to get donations and write grants. Seems reasonable, right? Well, first thing I found out is you can't sell art. I never recovered from learning that as a nonprofit the only thing you can sell is something completely unrelated to your mission. Which would be like if we sold jam or cookies or something. I was sent warnings by the IRS. I had to say that I would not sell any art. It got serious and I never got over it. Once I say I am not going to break a rule, and you've asked me not to break a rule, I'm not going to break the rule. We couldn't put the prices on the walls. We would have to like have it on a separate paper and let people know it was for sale by the artist, and then it was an honor system with the artists: We asked the artists to donate 30 percent to us. Well that worked maybe 60 percent of the time. Sometimes they just made their sale after the show came down.

JOE NOLAN: I'm not a fan of the nonprofit model in the arts. I want to see contemporary art in a valued place in the marketplace both culturally and economically. I've been able to make nonprofit and public funding work for my practice here and there, but if you go the nonprofit route you can lose all your personal sovereignty in the project you created.

CHRIS CAMPBELL: It was a foundational mistake to have set it up that way and not have a plan. I really didn't have any guidance about it. So I ended up not working on my art because it was just too much. There was so much paperwork, so much administration. I had to learn how to write grants, and then besides just writing the grants, you have grant management. And then I would get audited by the arts commission and things to make sure that I fulfilled the way I said it was. When you write a grant and they give you the grant, you have to prepay it. It's like a reimbursement situation. On all the state art commission grants, you had to put up all that money first. Prove you did it. Then they give you the money by like the end of the next year. I sure hope the Tennessee Arts Commission is now a better organization than what I had to deal with.

JOE NOLAN: Ruby Green won a Warhol Initiative grant in 2005.

CHRIS CAMPBELL: What started the whole getting attention from the Warhol thing? I don't really know. We had been getting best programming notices and being recognized for the artists and the things we were doing. But I think what set off alarms and stuff is when I had these Memphis artists—Jan Hankins and Christine Conley—show. Jan did political paintings and it was right after the Iraq war started in 2003.

CHRIS CAMPBELL: The Tennessee Arts Commission was run by Rich Boyd. He came with a theater background from I think Jackson, Tennessee, and he really had no idea about visual art or defending it. He didn't really understand or know what Ruby Green was or what the kind of art we showed was. And the kind of art he promoted was craft and nice, acceptable, traditional kind of art. He was protective of how the state senators and everybody like that viewed the Tennessee Arts Commission because a percentage of the specialized license plates went to the commission. And part of my grant from Tennessee Arts Commission was promotion of the shows. Part of the contract that you signed with them is that you're going to use their logo. You're going to mail this stuff out to all these representatives and state legislators. So I had all of them on my list, and they all got that card with this woman driving a Hummer with Rumsfeld and somebody in it, running over the planet. The artist said it was Lady Liberty. That's why she was kind of like naked or something. I don't know. But, the Tennessee legislators got so upset. They said that I had sent them pornography and it should have been in a brown bag. The dude wanted me to write a mea culpa and send it out to everybody about how sorry I was that they got this, and I said, "No, I don't have anything to apologize for." And then that was kind of the end of the support. A Metro Nashville Arts Commission employee said I had "shot myself in the foot" and they were right. But I felt like I needed to stick up for it. He was speaking through art, you know? I lost all my support from the government agencies. It really offended a lot of people.

JOE NOLAN: It's no coincidence that Chris did her time in the trenches of Untitled. Ruby Green rubbed some people the wrong way just like Untitled did. A lot of the Untitled shows were objectively not great, but you expected that with their anything-goes curating. That wasn't really the point. Untitled outflanked the tiny local art establishment and revealed just how irrelevant they were. People don't like that. Ruby Green was showing installations that were formally challenging and exhibitions with intense content that bothered people.

CHRIS CAMPBELL: At least twice that I know of, Ruby Green offended or turned off so many people they didn't come back. The first time was the postcard. The other time was when my second show was Greg Pond. He had these machines on pedestals, these like loud mechanical machines covered with deer skins. They were so violent and when they came on it was so loud and then the hair was flying. Some members from VAAN saw it and they never came back. I thought they'd appreciate it. The shows at their space were more like undergrad-conceptual. They'd have been totally torn apart in a critique at the Institute of Art.

LANDRY BUTLER: Ruby Green was a nonprofit art center. And some of those things Chris exhibited were installations that you just can't sell very practically—very conceptual type work, you know? Shows like sound installations and things. It's like, you can't put this out on your patio. That was great because nobody else was doing that. And she was not only doing it, but she was taking it seriously. Those of us that are creative, one of the things we like to do is to go outside of the lines, and it was great to have a place where you could do that or see somebody else that's doing that. That was also a great place for meeting out-of-town people. There were a lot of out-of-town people that would come to Ruby Green. I introduced myself to a woman at a show and she said, "Hello, I'm here from Paris." People from New York or LA or whatever would come in. I'm guessing that they were in town for other reasons, but Ruby Green was known enough that if you were plugged in, that was the place you would go in Nashville.

CURE BOARD ILLS

JOE NOLAN: There's a Destroy All Monsters song called "Bored." When the conversation about nonprofit boards comes up I think about that song.

CHRIS CAMPBELL: A nonprofit is required to have a board. In the beginning we did have those kind of people who put in their sweat equity and who would do a lot to make it happen—show up, get people to come, spread the word, help hang, do all this stuff. Ruby Green lasted about ten years and those people lasted about three.

LANDRY BUTLER: I was on the board of Ruby Green. Chris wanted to do like a regional art center kind of thing. She specifically wanted to bring interesting, independent, and alternative artists from outside of Nashville, like Atlanta or Louisville or Knoxville, just to show Nashville what was going on in these other nearby art scenes. Chris was good at finding people like that. And that was always inspiring because those of us in town, we were just looking at each other's work, and sometimes it's nice to have something a little fresh, and something that the mainstream galleries are not turned on to.

CHRIS CAMPBELL: The original board members were always replaced with somebody saying, "What can Ruby Green do for me?" We even had a couple so-called board members learn what we were doing and then try to replicate it with their own galleries. Like this woman who joined long enough to figure out how to do it. She had a whole gallery of paintings that looked like Wacky Packages bubblegum cards.

JOE NOLAN: Ruby Green earned an outsized reputation by equally upsetting and inspiring. In the meantime it was a little struggling nonprofit gallery. All of that is why they got noticed.

CHRIS CAMPBELL: The Jan Hankins show made a lot of press and I think the Andy Warhol Foundation for the Visual Arts Initiative program had scouts out looking for new recruits. When we joined it was only like twenty-four other nonprofits across America. And I mean, they had big ones like White Columns, Creative Time in New York City, and there was Luggage Store in San Francisco. We were just so lucky to be part of it. I received a letter in the mail asking if I would apply. Just to apply for this grant I would get $1,000. Next thing I know, we got it and it was a total of I think about $125,000. $100,000 of it you were never supposed to spend. It was supposed to be money in reserve that you never touched, and then the $25,000 you could spend.

LANDRY BUTLER: When Chris won that Warhol grant that was amazing. That was very encouraging to all of us, I think. Nashville was always a good place to be creative and to make art, regardless of what form that art is. But because of the music industry that dominates, it's hard to make money at the art here. Artists felt like they had to go outside the city. And so a little bit of recognition like that, you know, the Warhol people saying, "Hey, you guys are doing some good stuff there in Nashville. We want to support it." Well, that's great. Because that gets a lot of the newer artists now doing work in Nashville. And you have more established artists like Omari Booker splitting his time between being in-town and being in Los Angeles based off of a reputation that he made here.

JOE NOLAN: Ruby Green and Terri Smith's Temporary Contemporary series at Cheekwood Museum of Art both won funding from the Warhol Initiative program, and that felt like a win for everyone in the city's contemporary art scene.

CHRIS CAMPBELL: But at this very time is when I was thinking about quitting because I was broke. I didn't have a job. I felt like I had tried so hard and so many different things to bring in money: art classes, screenings, music. Anything I could think of to bring in some cash to help fund this thing.

LANDRY BUTLER: Ruby Green was kind of like a great record store as far as galleries are concerned. You would go in there and you'd see stuff or hear stuff that you'd never find anywhere else. We did some great music performances there: Peggy Snow and the Cherry Blossoms played there a few times. Dave Cloud played there. I was working with a band called 3 Pups Music that was like a jazz improv thing. And we played there a couple of times.

DAVID MADDOX: A lot of the shows I ended up writing on were at Ruby Green. Chris Campbell was really a very good curator. She also brought other people in to do things. Joseph Whitt did a wonderful group show there. And Chris Davis has always had his foot in both the art and music camps. And so the galleries are an obvious place. There's open space, and they're kind of not using it most of the time. And in theory, there's a resonance between, you know, doing something interesting musically and having something interesting on the wall.

JONATHAN MARX: What happens is that you have a de facto connection that exists when you've got sound and visual art in the same space. Sometimes not even intentionally put together. Which means that the spaces themselves become meaningful because they become a place where things happen like that, where the community is built.

CHRIS CAMPBELL: In reality, the crowds didn't combine—the music people never came to the visual art and the visual art people didn't come to music. It was like different people. They didn't respect the art on the walls. In fact, art got damaged during that. I couldn't be there at night too, to watch the space. And so I felt bad about that. I always thought, "Well, I don't have a job. So, I'm going to create my job." One of the things with the Warhol grant is, I actually wrote in there, and they agreed, that I should get paid. That I should have a salary and get paid. Well, the board wasn't having it. They didn't think that I should get paid, but at the same time, this shows to me that the weakness of the whole Ruby Green Foundation was I did not have a board that understood what it took to pull this off. How much it cost and what their roles were. I know several of them have gone on and used it in their resume, and advanced their own careers saying they were on the board of Ruby Green.

EMERALD EYES

JOE NOLAN: I think during that time we were all getting our first lessons about sustainability. It's really hard to start any kind of gallery, but it's even harder to make a creative space that can last.

CHRIS CAMPBELL: And people didn't get it. I think they actually thought Ruby Green had money. It's clean, it's lit up. I did everything. I was janitor. I hung. I fixed the walls. I did everything by myself. And I was proud of it. But it wears you down. I made some great contacts and friendships and I feel like I really helped some artists, like kind of gave them a springboard. But I had pissed a lot of people off in my local community by saying "No" to them about wanting to show. I only had about six to eight shows a year. My view was, if you're showing at Zeitgeist, you don't need a show here. If you've just had a big show less than a year ago or so, I don't want to. I was all about bringing in the new. Trying to make us relevant with the rest of the country. I didn't want us to be just local, feeding off ourselves. And I think I really kind of made some people unhappy. They thought that I owed it to them or something. But I felt like Ruby Green was bigger than that. And I really wanted us to be respected internationally. I believed in Nashville before other people believed in Nashville.

JOE NOLAN: The best artists, the best curators, the best critics, and the best collectors all have great vision. They see a thing and they're creating an expression of it so that other people can see it too. Ruby Green was Ruby Green. None before, none since. That was Chris's vision.

CHRIS CAMPBELL: One of my favorite shows was Adrian Gold's *B Sides*. He is Canadian and he gets big public commissions and stuff. It was a little bit awkward because he thought a car was going to pick him up at the airport—like a limo. But it was just me in my regular car. He had never been to Nashville. He had like country music ideas. He was a conceptual artist and he had created this whole display with graphic vinyl signs that you stick on the wall. So on one side it was like the dates and seismic impacts of all of America's atomic testing. And then correlated on the opposite wall are these dates of Hank Williams's B sides going up and down the charts. And he thought because Hank Williams was country music, classic country music, that there would be a lot of people here. It was one of the least attended shows we ever had. But it was great. He was a real interesting guy. Donté Hayes was a Black man from Roswell, Georgia. His show was called *The Gingerblack Man*. He used the shape of a gingerbread man, but it was black. It was like a kid's dress-up paper doll. So he had stereotypical Black man's costumes, like jail stuff, Louis Farrakhan outfits, and rap gang thug stuff. You could mix and match the different components of these outfits and stick 'em on these Black men. It was like giant dress-up dolls on one wall, and then on the other side he had paintings. I bought one of the paintings and it was called "Middle Passage." It was like a grandmother fitting all these Black men on a cookie sheet. The editor from the *Tennessee Tribune* came and she was livid, she was mad. She was kind of yelling at him because he was playing with all these stereotypes. The Sunday that we had Donté's talk was the first day they did a Super Bowl in February. They've all been in February since then.

EVERY NEW DAY

CHRIS CAMPBELL: In 2006 or 2007 I was pregnant and I decided I wasn't going to write any more grants for that year. I wasn't gonna do it. And someone from Atlanta had said, "Why don't you just make studios just to hold onto the space till you can get back?" I said, "Okay. That's what I'll do." Well, during that time, the money just wasn't there. We got broken into, and the landlord died. His daughter took over, raised the rent, and then just expected so much more with no kind of leeway or conversation. She went in there because I was late on rent. She just took the money directly from the artists renting studios and locked me out of the space. We had a pro bono lawyer. His response was to go to the board chair, which was a guy who didn't know anything, didn't do anything. And then the board fired me. And they didn't even tell me I was fired. So I got fired.

JOE NOLAN: Nonprofit models are one of the norms in the art world, but they can be a lot riskier than people know. You can break your back to make a gallery or an organization happen and then fundraising as a nonprofit can look like a path to sustainability. But once that board is in place you lose all of your autonomy. You can find you're on the outside looking in even though the whole organization might have been your mission and your creation.

CHRIS CAMPBELL: I had to declare bankruptcy. It took me a couple of years to pay it off. When my house burned down in 2011, I used the money to pay off my bankruptcy. It's been a slow slog ever since. I'm like a mile from Ridgetop now. I've got a couple pet sheep. I've got fifteen acres. I love it. When I bought the place in 2020 there was this old oak tree in the front. But this year it died. It was like three hundred years old and an ambrosia beetle got it. It's sad. But it's OK.

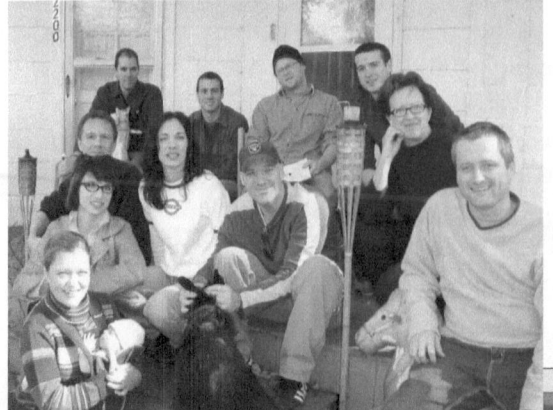

C. 2004 The Fugitive board meets on the front porch of the artists' house on Grantland Street. Pictured left to right, (back row) Mark Hosford, Greg Pond, Patrick DeGuira, Hans Schmitt-Matzen, (middle row) Bob Durham, Julie Roberts, Lain York, Carol Mode, Bryan Hunter, (front row) Iwonka Waskowski, Lesley Patterson-Marx with her son. Megan Walborn and Donna Tauscher are not pictured. *Credit: Bryan Hunter*

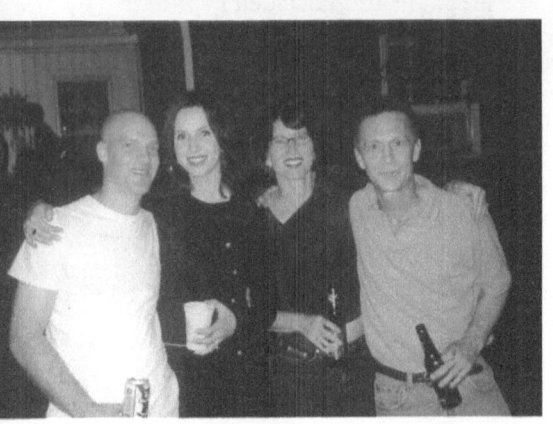

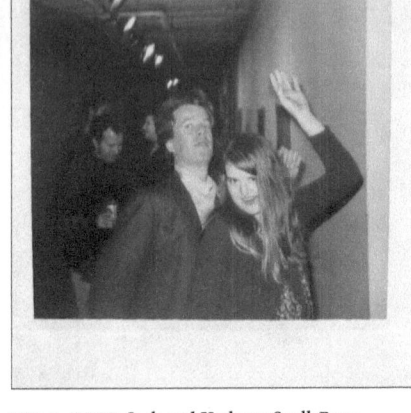

C. 2010 Artists Lain York, Iwonka Waskowski, Carrie McGee, and Bob Durham at a get-together in the backyard of artist and gallery designer Todd McDaniel. *Credit: Terri C. Smith*

FEB. 1, 2003 Jack and Kathryn Snell-Ryan boogie down at the opening reception for Steven Thompson, Pam Pecchio, and Erin Weckerly's exhibition at the Fugitive. The after-party featured DJ Cut-A-Rug and the Big Nasty. *Credit: Lori Paluck*

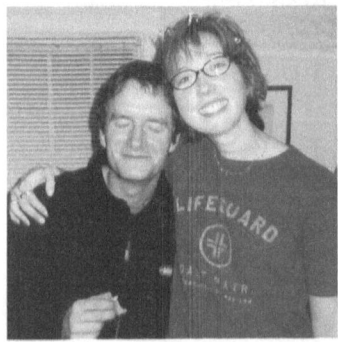

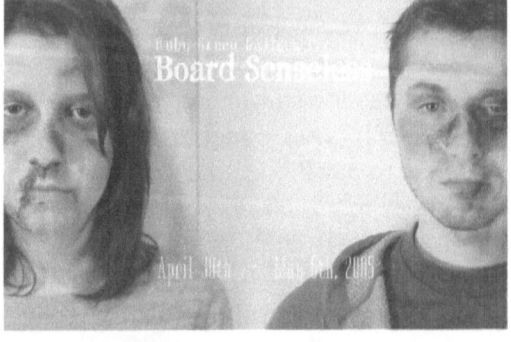

C. 2005 The author with curator Terri Smith in Smith's kitchen in Nashville. *Credit: Terri C. Smith*

2004 One of Mark Hosford's eye-popping exhibition posters for The Fugitive Art Center. These big, bold three-color prints on chipboard became collector's items on the coffeehouse and record store bulletin boards where the Fugitives promoted their shows just like local bands. *Credit: Mark Hosford*

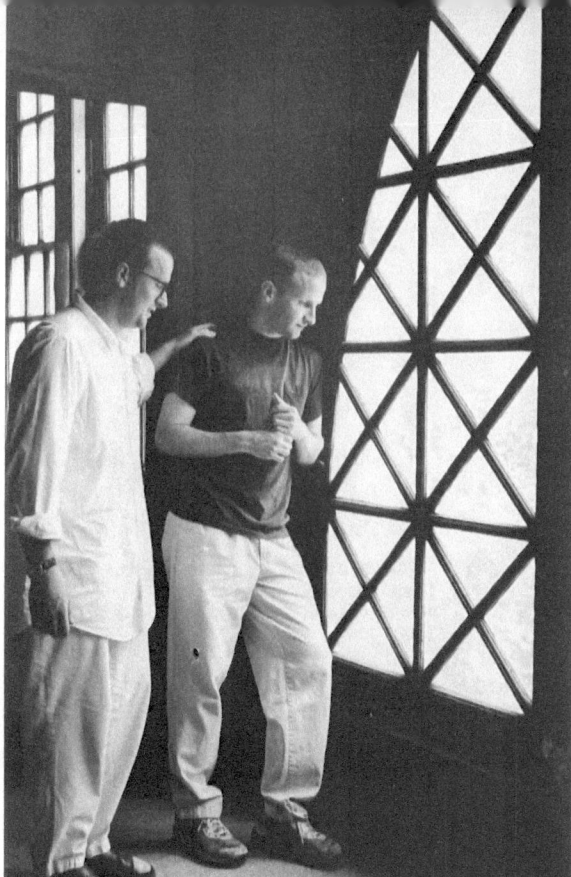

C. 2003 Todd Greene and Andrew Harding were among the first artists-in-residence at the Downtown Presbyterian Church. The studio program is noted for its historic architecture and light-filled spaces. *Credit: Andy Harding*

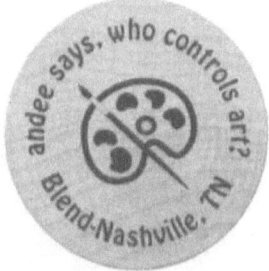

APRIL 2011 Andee Rudloff challenges the gatekeepers with her printed "wooden nickels" at the *Floats Like a Butterfly Stings like a Bee: Who Controls Art?* exhibition at Blend Studio. *Credit: Ben Vitualla*

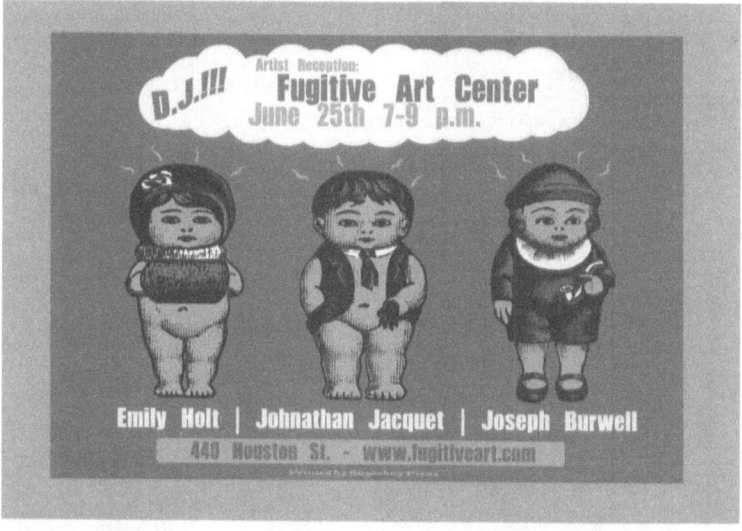

2004 An exhibition postcard announcing a Secret Show at Ruby Green gallery. It features Secret Show group members Jaime Raybin and Jason Driskill. No artists were injured in the making of this postcard. *Credit: Jaime Raybin*

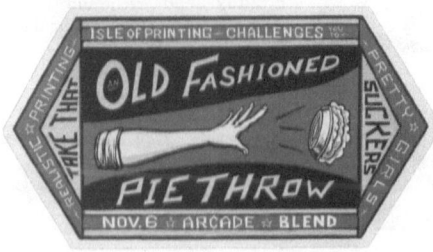

NOV. 6, 2010 A Bryce McCloud poster for his *151th* [sic] *Annual Old Fashioned Pie Throw* performance at Blend Studio. *Credit: Ben Vitualla*

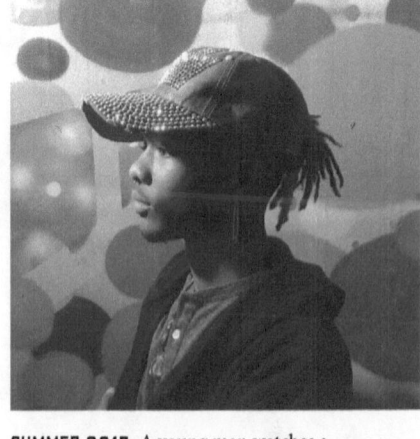

SUMMER 2017 A young man watches a performance at Brikolaj in The Arcade during the Downtown Art Crawl. *Credit: Jared Brennan*

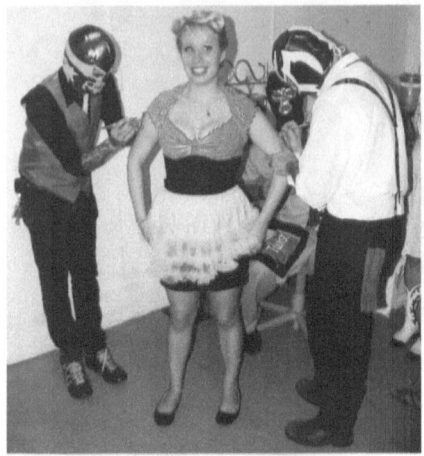

AUG. 7, 2010 Elizabeth Streight volunteers for an art performance, receiving temporary Sharpie tattoos at Mitch O'Connell's art opening during First Saturday Downtown Art Crawl at Twist Art Gallery. *Credit: Beth Gilmore*

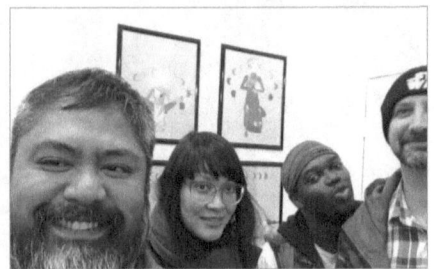

2017 Blend Studio founder and curator Ben Vitualla with (L to R) May Hwen, Quintin Watkins, and Jason Hargrove at the Downtown Art Crawl. *Credit: Ben Vitualla*

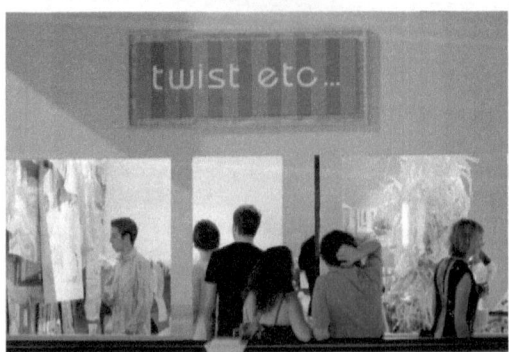

C. 2010 Gallerygoers crowd the balcony outside of Twist Art Gallery during the Downtown Art Crawl. *Credit: Beth Gilmore*

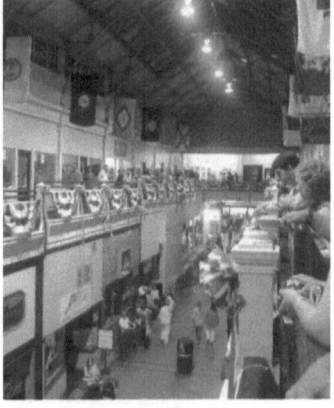

C. 2010 Gallerygoers crowd The Arcade at another First Saturday Downtown Art Crawl. *Credit: Beth Gilmore*

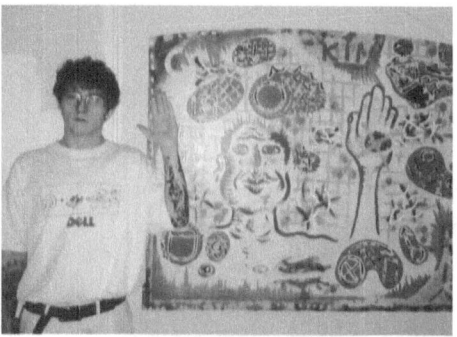

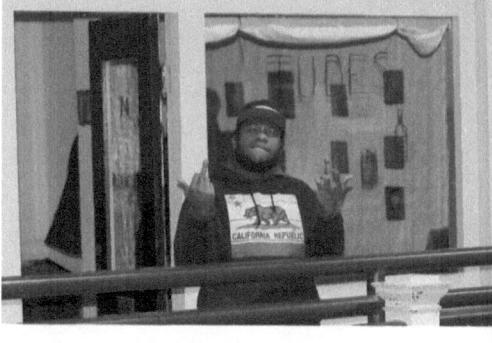

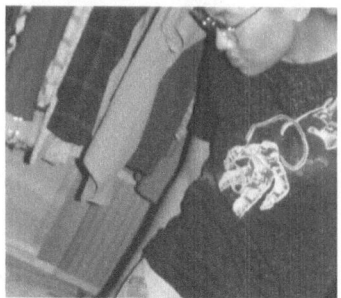

2017 (clockwise from top left) Artist Daniel Lane at his debut solo painting exhibition at Brikolaj. *Credit: Jared Brennan*; Comedian Brad Sativa hanging out after hours at Brikolaj following an Art Crawl. *Credit: Jared Brennan*; Jared Brennan's Historic High custom vintage clothing debuts at his Brikolaj space in The Arcade. *Credit: Jared Brennan*

2010 The author explores the fourth floor of the Downtown Presbyterian Church. *Credit: Beth Gilmore*

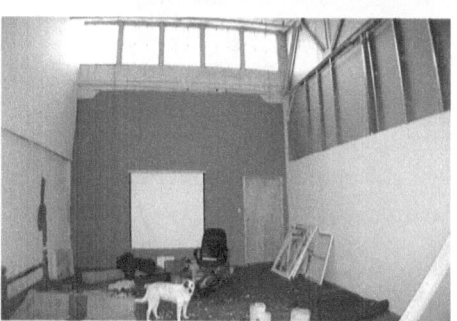

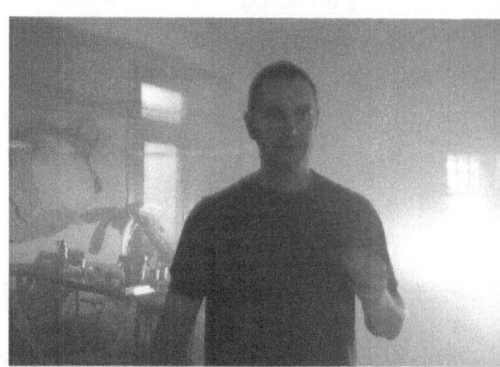

APR. 16, 2007 The Sooplex studio/gallery space at the Chestnut Building. *Credit: Mike Calway-Fagen*

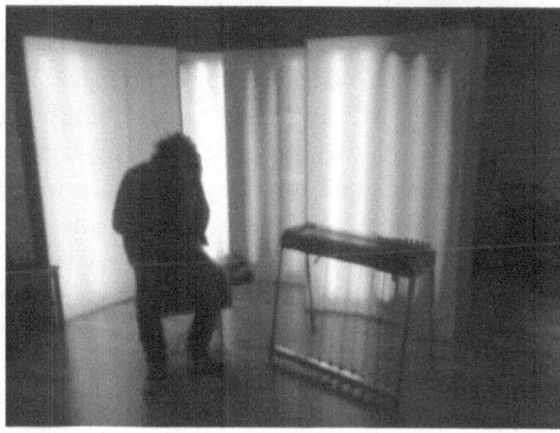

FEB. 4, 2017 Luke Schneider sets up his steel guitar for a solo performance during the Art Crawl. Luke's custom light boxes were built by artist Rhendi Greenwell. *Credit: Jared Brennan*

Art Monks in Little Egypt

1995–2015

THE DOWNTOWN PRESBYTERIAN Church's artist residency program is the oldest creative incubator of its kind in Nashville. It's nurtured the careers of artists, gallerists, and museum professionals, and the program's Browsing Room Gallery is a don't-miss downtown contemporary art destination. It's the birthplace of Herb Williams's signature Crayon sculptures and Todd Greene's groundbreaking Paw-Paw Sermons paintings. And it's an uncensored sacred space inside of one of the few existing treasures of Egyptian Revival architecture still standing in America. There's no place in Nashville quite like the church's artist studio spaces, and this one-of-a-kind program is as unique as it is long-lived and influential.

JOHN HILLEY: It was a crazy, crazy time. And I can't believe all those crazy folks now have kids—some of whom have gone off to college. I'm just thinking about the cast of characters who came into this thing.

DAVID MADDOX: It was completely organic. You know, Tom Wills started it by being a child of the church, coming home from college and saying, "Hey, you think I could use one of those empty spaces up there to paint in?" And people were like, "I don't see why not." "And what about my friend, Todd?" And you know, then the next kid.

JOHN HILLEY: I had all this empty space up on the third and the fourth floor, and I was looking at some synergies, and I was looking at how we might be able to bring in different artist groups that could occupy space there. This architectural space in that back building, with its winding staircases, its incredible light. There were these big open spaces that could become dance studios or whatever. I started bringing in different groups and bringing in architects and asking, "What could this space become?" And there was the beginning of a movement outside of our door, where we had Anne Brown start The Arts Company as a pioneer on Fifth Avenue. And we started talking to one another and then we realized there was an emerging arts community here, and I wanted to go wherever there was energy. We had some people who were starting to drift over from East Nashville—the bohemians. And the big key was Tom Wills. Tom Wills had finished up at Center College and come home to Nashville.

TOM WILLS: So when I got out of college, I was doing volunteer work with the homeless ministries, because that interested me and I was laying out their newsletter, "The Church Mouse" for like $25 an issue or something like that. And I said, "Listen, you got all this space up here, could I turn one of these rooms into an art studio?" And they said, "Sure." I continued to do the volunteer work and I did the newsletter layout for free.

JIM HOOBLER: And so in about 1995, Tom Wills moved upstairs, and some of his friends Todd Greene, Andy Harding, Herb Williams, Julie Lee heard about that space and asked if they could get in. So the church decided, well, why not? We were not using that space, and at that point the artists were helping out with the weekly lunch for the homeless. They did some art for church bulletins, and in return they got some space upstairs. That's been going on now for almost thirty years.

TOM WILLS: Growing up at Downtown Presbyterian church, when my brothers and I were kids, we'd always check the stairwell doors on the second floor of the building to see if those stairwells were unlocked. And when they were unlocked, we would go explore on the abandoned floors in between like Sunday school and church. My memory was there was this room up in the corner that was full of wheelchairs on the fourth floor. I remember having wheelchair races with my brothers around the hallway that goes around the dome of the building. I went to that very same room that had the wheelchairs in it and cleaned it out. I remember it had a bunch of boxes of a book from one of our former pastors, Pat McGeachy. It was called *Help, Lord!* and they were all covered in soot because he had put an air conditioning unit in the window, and I think it got struck by lightning. So I cleaned up the room, but I got locked out of my car. I was living in an old apartment on Woodland avenue near Montgomery Bell Academy. And I was covered in this soot and I locked my keys in my car. And I tried to get a cab and nobody would take me because I looked like I was a chimney sweep. So I just hiked home.

JIM HOOBLER: The building was built between 1917 and 1919 by Henry Strickland. I think he's the early twentieth century's best architect in the city. He did a lot of the buildings at Vanderbilt, Peabody, Fisk. He did that wonderful library at Fisk that's now the admin building. He preferred Gothic revival and Roman, and being a member of First Pres he played nice with the building outside. It's very Egyptian revival. It has cavetto cornices, it has three stone Amun-Res flying over it. The bracket lights on the side of the building have very buxom lady sphinxes flying on top of them—which is very odd. Lady sphinxes were Greek. Male sphinxes are Egyptian. But these are definitely ladies. But there's also a round coffered dome with an oculus patterned after the Pantheon in Rome. So Strickland got his Rome in there, but it's in the core of the building. It's sort of a secret. That's a very big stretch for a Christian Church to do the Temple of Amun-Res at Karnac. But somehow it worked, and I think maybe the reason it worked was Adelicia Acklen. Her first husband had died just a year or two before this was going on. And she hired Adolphus Heiman to build a mausoleum at Fairview Plantation to bury Franklin and their deceased children. It was Egyptian. It had the battered surrounds like the walls of an ancient temple, and the window frames and door frames of the church. It had cavetto cornices like at the church. And it had a huge, stone-carved, three dimensional Amun-Res—the sun god—flying over the front door. So Strickland came up with his very stripped down Egyptian revival design for the church. And when probably the wealthiest woman in the South says she doesn't have a problem with Egyptian, and she can help fund the building, I think that probably swayed the congregation. That's a supposition, but I think it's a pretty good one.

TOM WILLS: The studios are in the Sunday school building. I guess the early twentieth century is when Sunday school got hot and became hip and churches needed to have Sunday school and a space for that. So they built the building and it had a big rotunda in the middle that everybody would gather in before Sunday school probably. And then they would all break off for Sunday school in the different rooms. And then they would gather again for church later in the day. When they were built, the pastor was being courted by the Presbyterian Church to lead the World Mission headquarters for the Presbyterian Church. And he said, "I don't want to leave my church, but I'll do it if you put it on the top floor of this building I'm building." So that's what the top floor was, the World Mission headquarters. In the 1950s, the church split and the congregation had outgrown the property, and First Presbyterian moved out onto Franklin Road. And a small group of elders, including my grandfather, broke off and formed the Downtown Presbyterian Church. I think it was in the 1960s, they redesigned the chapel and abandoned the third and fourth floors to collect dust and be storage space.

JIM HOOBLER: That's the third building that's been there and every iteration, it gets a little bit more particularly defined. The first one, we have no idea what it looked like, but presume that it was sort of Greek revival. That burned in 1832 and they rebuilt, and we've got an engraving of what that looked like. But boy, when Strickland came to town and was hired by the state to do the capitol building, that really was a game changer. He was the first president of what would ultimately become the American Institute of Architects, their professional society. And, you know from the capitol, his preferred style was Greek. So when he did a proposal for the replacement building in 1848, it was Italian. Which meant sort of Italian Renaissance. And I'm thinking these hidebound Calvinists were like horrified, "Oh my God! That means Rome and you know who that means! We can't have that!" So that building had twin towers, like the present building and like the present building, the bottom and middle stage of those towers were squared. It all looked sort of Renaissance revival. I think he went back and thought about a Gothic revival church he'd done in Philadelphia—St. Stevens—which had octagonal towers. So he topped it off, took the square off the top, and put octagons on it and then went "Oh, what the heck" and just went full Egyptian Revival.

TOM WILLS: You sort of walk into this building that is really sort of a conundrum. You can get into it from a few entrances on the side of the building. And it's just, you know, this Sunday school building that you can tell is sort of cut-up and a little disastrous to sort of maneuver because you walk into the middle and you find there's this giant chapel with a giant dome. It's impressive to look at. It sort of forces the rest of the building to sort of conform to it. You have this sort of circuit of hallways going around and it just doesn't seem very useful. You walk up these weird, narrow, steep steps and you come upon a door—it's almost always locked—at the end of these steps. You're on the second floor, you can go into the sanctuary, which you normally would do from there, into the old building, which is an old architectural gem in and of itself. It's an old Egyptian Revival building that used to be First Presbyterian that was built in 1851. It's like one of the only major examples of Egyptian Revival architecture still standing in the US. So, you've got that. And then you've got this building with a dome in the middle that seems to serve no purpose. If you open the doors instead of going into the Sanctuary you look up the steps and see these dusty steps and this paint that's from the 1930s or 40s. And you start walking up and the ceilings get really high. And you come to a landing and, and you step through, and you're suddenly in a giant room that has a big arch on your right that is filled in with Plexiglass circles from the 1960s. And then on your left, you see this big arch window looking out over the parking lot and letting light in. An old chandelier is hanging from the ceiling—it's half eaten away. We cleaned these spaces out and there's three rooms that had had these arches that let light into the chapel and big windows looking out and then there's rooms in between them. They all have like 16 foot ceilings and usually some pretty special light. And then there's another floor above where you actually have a hallway going around this dome and you've got all this 1917 era frosted glass. The window doors with stenciled numbers and gold leaf paint on them, right out of a film, a Bogart movie.

JOHN HILLEY: I came here in 1994. I was a young guy, in way over my head at Downtown Presbyterian Church. I'd wanted to come back to the South and so we strategically looked at Nashville, Tennessee. I grew up in Louisville, Kentucky and North Carolina. Then spent time in New Jersey, also in South Africa, Iowa. Then I wanted to get back closer to home. But I had a quarrel, a little bit, with the South, because of the places where my education had taken me to. Places such as South Africa, where I did a postgraduate fellowship looking at the life of Dietrich Bonhoeffer in the context of South Africa. Before that I was a student at Wake Forest and I took a class with Maya Angelou. That put me on a trajectory that led me in, in that direction. We were constantly asking two key questions in the community. The first question was "What do you know about the Downtown Presbyterian Church?" A lot of people said, "Isn't that that museum on the corner of Fifth and Church?" The other question was, "What do you need us to be?" There had been a lot of concern and wringing of hands because, "Is anybody going to come back?" With the rise of the Civil Rights Movement, there was the exodus out of the city. People who believed in the mission stayed. Spinsters stayed. The architecture lovers stayed. Everybody else left, and they were not coming back. So who's going to come to this church? We were looking in the wrong direction. We're looking at West Nashville when really we needed to look across the river to East Nashville, to the artist types, the creative types.

TOM WILLS: This is 1994. Downtown was a different scene back then. It was before there was an Art Crawl and all that, but there was Watkins College right down the street, basically where the library is now. I took classes over at Watkins. I did some figure drawing classes there that were really helpful to me. We hadn't yet had any redevelopment downtown and there was a little bit of grit to the city still. Downtown was mostly a lot more parking lots and some sort of failed attempts at revitalization. Church Street Mall—the new library ended up replacing it and Watkins. The Arcade had a great smoke shop in there at the time. It doesn't have that anymore. Downtown was pretty much dead on the weekend. Lower Broadway was really just the honky tonks at that time. It was pretty sleepy. As I started to branch out and meet other artists, I ran across Todd Greene. I invited him to my studio and I quickly realized if I invite someone to my studio, they're going to want to move into one of the other rooms. They were sort of like enticingly not being used. It was just a beautiful space to come and work.

J. TODD GREENE: So, I grew up in Nashville and went away to Savannah College of Art Design. I graduated in 1992, and then I stayed in Savannah for a bit, and then went away to Northern Ireland for a year and came back in the winter of '95. When I was in Northern Ireland I actually decided I was going to come home to Nashville and give it the college try. That's like, "I'm going to be an artist when I get home and I'm going to try it as long as I can." And that's when I met Tom Wills who I think was just fresh out of college that same year. His family had ties to the Downtown Presbyterian Church since the origins of the church. It was used as a hospital by both sides during the Civil War. They weren't using large portions of that building. Tom had this idea of like, "Hey, why don't we just kind of squat up there and be artists?"

JOHN HILLEY: There was nothing, no contracts. It was just an understanding that you can have a space. We were running electrical cords up to the fourth floor. We were running undercover of codes. The artists gave their time to help prepare and serve the homeless individuals who had lunch here.

J. TODD GREENE: And it was just such a weird place to be. In the mid-nineties downtown was, it was a real transitional time culturally and population-wise, and it was just really dead for lack of words. I remember throwing a Frisbee on the front steps of the SunTrust building, which is directly across the street from Downtown Pres. Just throwing it wildly back and forth across that open plaza not worried about hitting anyone because there was just never any traffic, barely any foot traffic. We had The Arcade with Manny's House of Pizza and The Peanut Shoppe and everything, but none of the awesome art spaces were happening there. Watkins College of Art was still downtown, and Anne Brown had The Arts Company gallery down there on Fifth Avenue. And Tom and I just kind of pretended to be art squatters in that building and we would just spend enormous amounts of time just painting and just kind of working out our creativity. And it was really, really cold in the winter and really, really hot in the summer. But we just felt like art monks. That's how we would kind of refer to ourselves. We said "This is an art monastery." We could just come and go, and we did a little work trade with the church. We would set up and help take down the Wednesday lunch, which was a free lunch to the public often referred to as the "homeless lunch."

ANDY HARDING: We had to pay some sort of utility fee every month, but that was like, you know, pennies on the dollar for what you would be paying rent for somewhere. And so it was really just an incredible kind of opportunity. And, you know, we gave back, we did a lot of stuff. It wasn't necessarily transactional. We did a kids' art camp in the summer. Even people who weren't members of the church would just bring their kids. And Todd and I and Julie and Tom, and some others were involved in that. We just came up with different stuff for them to do and activities. We volunteered and served the Wednesday homeless lunch at the church. And so we got to know a lot of the guys and the women who would come to that. That was part of the whole experience too.

TOM WILLS: The nicest thing about it was that there weren't any real strings attached. And I think that's what made it work is that it could have so easily have been a meddlesome environment. When I asked for the art studio, the congregation was graying but was curious and interested in things, and they supported me. And our pastor at that time, John Hilley, was a young pastor and he was up for opening the back door and letting in as many artists as we could. The whole miracle was that we were doing volunteer work, mostly with the homeless ministries, but we ended up expanding that and doing other things with the church. You don't have to attend church here. You don't have to be a member. You don't have to really be a Christian. It's pretty loose and the church got more out of it than it could have ever asked for in terms of bringing other people around and making them feel welcome.

HERB WILLIAMS: I moved to Nashville in 1998. I got a little studio. My wife at the time was doing graduate school at Vandy and we found a tiny little apartment, a beautiful little, one bedroom, tiny place for like $750.00 a month, which seemed like a lot of money back then, you know? And I found a storage unit that I siphoned electricity into and kind of made just a little closet into a studio where I would start to make art. I made a whole bunch of just terrible, terrible work for almost a year until I realized like I didn't know how to sell it. I started going to different art galleries to try and get a feel for what the art scene was. I went to an Untitled event and met Lain York at Zeitgeist. I went to Cumberland Gallery, got to see a show of Red Grooms's work they had. I just started hitting the pavement and I decided that I had to get a day job. I knew how to make my art but I just didn't know how to make a living. I eventually found a job at The Arts Company working for Anne Brown. I walked in the day of Artrageous and she was like, "I can't give you a job, but we have the biggest AIDS awareness charity event and if you want to volunteer tonight, we could use your help." It was kind of a trial by fire and I did whatever they needed me to do and met thousands of people that night. They eventually hired me. Through doing that I met Tom Wills and Todd Greene and they told me about their studios over at the church.

ANDY HARDING: Around 1997, '98, I was kind of finishing up school and beginning to think about abandoning my degree in chemistry and trying to become an artist. I had taken some courses from Lanie Gannon who's a mentor of mine and friend. She taught sculpture at Belmont at the time, and I'd taken a couple of classes from her and she was just so encouraging. And I was just super excited about this whole thing. I hadn't taken an art class since middle school. So I got super interested in this and started hanging around with Tom and Todd. And they invited me to do a show with them at the DPC. They were doing a two-person show in the Fellowship Hall of DPC in fall of 1998.

HERB WILLIAMS: Tom and Todd were like "You've got to see the church. It's like the only existing example of Egyptian style architecture remaining in the US." I made good friends with the pastor and I liked what they were doing. John Hilley was such a cool guy. He said "You should come by and volunteer for our homeless lunch on Wednesdays." And I was like, "That'd be great!" And I got to know Todd and John and Tom Wills. Tom is such an unusual dude, you know? He's just quirky and he lives in his own head so much. And if you look at his art, it totally explains him and it's just the wildest, coolest art. He was doing these landscape paintings of interstate exit off-ramps.

ANDY HARDING: I was working in an environmental lab at the time, kind of a dead-end chemistry job doing soil testing. I asked work if I could go part-time to get ready for this show. And they said "No," so I quit. I quit to do an art show! I showed handmade iron lamps and these books I was binding. We set the exhibition up in the Fellowship Hall—that big room where they have the homeless lunch. It was such a fantastic experience.

HERB WILLIAMS: They found out that I was making art and eventually just invited me up and asked if I wanted to join them in the studios. And I was like, "Man, this is amazing." And the only thing you have to do to pay rent is to volunteer on Wednesdays at the homeless lunch. I was doing that already so it just made perfect sense. It was an unreal opportunity.

ANDY HARDING: As far as I know, that part of the building just kind of sat there and they used it for storage. So it just kind of fell into disrepair and became one of the most incredibly beautiful spaces I think in town. At least for artists, you know? You really felt like there wasn't a space like that in Nashville. When I first went up there it was just gorgeous texture and the patina of age and these huge semicircular windows like you see in New York in 1980s movies. Bright lights, big city, you know? Gazing down on it. Of course, from there you're only three floors up.

HERB WILLIAMS: I had a beautiful big space facing Fifth Avenue, and it had giant windows that you could open up. Man they were gorgeous, like half moon shapes and they had this thick glass that you couldn't really see out of because they were so old and dirty. It felt sacrilegious to try and clean them. But in the summers you could open them up—the windows themselves had to be eleven or twelve feet tall—and they just split open and pull in and you look out. Being downtown you'd hear all the cars honking and stuff. And there were beautiful ginkgo trees up and down the streets. They were like cherry blossoms. Gorgeous, man, in the spring. On the right day, they would all be in blossom and then lose their leaves at the same time. So sometimes, if you left the windows open, it would hit it, right? And you would get all of these crazy white blossoms to just float in.

ANDY HARDING: It was like, the year 2000 when I finally kind of got up there. Tom had pretty much quit painting at that point and was becoming a heavy-duty 35-millimeter film collector. So he was no longer really up there. Herb was up there some and Julie Lee was up there some. But it was mostly just Todd and I during the day-to-day. Like every day. We didn't have families or anything or a mortgage or anything like that. No jobs. A cool kind of aspect of that era for me was just learning so much. I never went to art school, so that was sort of my education, like just being up there and thinking. Todd and I joked about kind of being art monks or whatever. We were in a church and we would just go up there in the morning. Todd really influenced me in this regard because I was just like ready to get to work. But then I would watch what he was doing and he didn't start painting for a couple of hours after he got there. He would sit and meditate and read, and it's like, "Oh, this is what we're supposed to do," you know?

J. TODD GREENE: Tom and I both started showing at The Arts Company in 1997, but we would also put on weird shows, art shows, and concerts up in the studios. And we also had kind of run over the entire Sanctuary too. And we recorded albums and made up just weird things to do using the spaces in that building.

ANDY HARDING: Todd and I did a show together up in the studios, which I don't think had ever been done before. And was probably against all kinds of codes. In the year 2000, we did a show called *Communion* together. I was doing actual kind of 2D and 3D artwork instead of just doing the books and the design objects. I did these mixed-media pieces for that show, and Todd did paintings primarily. We set up the art all over the studios so that you could sort of walk around. We had those clip lamps everywhere to light the work, and it's still one of my favorite shows I've ever had, because it was just such a beautiful space. And it was really well attended. There was such a great turnout and it was really magical in a lot of ways. I was just starting out. I think one painting was like a hundred dollars or something. One of my professors at Belmont—she was an art historian—she came and bought a piece.

TOM WILLS: Every room was filled with some sort of junk. There were about four sets of doors for every door in the building. Each one had been removed and replaced and stacked in rooms. Or there'd be a pile of pews about six feet high. There were old sewing machines from World War II probably. I found an obscene book of photos in a small suitcase. It had a bunch of Polaroids of a guy and his girl, and a bunch of checks written to cash for a hundred bucks. It was somebody that was homeless who had entrusted the church with his prized possessions to hold for him while he went to the mission or something.

HERB WILLIAMS: There were all these rooms full of all these weird artifacts. All these maps and just weird posters from fifty years, and just all the clutter and detritus of ages of you know, of the church existing. There were old hymnals and guide books. Todd and I both used some of those in some of our collage, like in paintings, all these old maps that they used to have. I was using a bunch of old maps of flood prone areas and it wasn't even related to the church at all. It was just a big stack of different areas of Tennessee and Kentucky that were the topographical maps that surveyors or whatever would use. I don't know what they were from, but just lots of weird stuff like that found its way into our work at the time.

JOHN HILLEY: I remember Herb Williams being up there with his table saw—he was doing a lot of wood projects. And with those half moon windows the light was just incredible. In the Gospel of John, "the light shines in the darkness and the darkness has not overcome it," and you go into that space and it becomes sort of transcendent.

ANDY HARDING: It's a weird place. The church is Egyptian Revival, like there's so many just odd things about that whole theme. When you go into the sanctuary and look up, there's this grid above you, an architectural grid that's three dimensional that comes down off the ceiling. There are these clouds painted so it looks like you're entering an outdoor Egyptian temple. You go in and then you've got this huge organ and all the stained glass. There's a bell tower. And there was this one-hundred-year-old, rickety wood ladder that you could climb up. They've since locked that up. You can still ring the bell, but you used to be able to climb up into the bell tower, like right next to the bell. And it was just super sketchy and old. I mean, it felt like *The Hunchback of Notre Dame* kind of situation. You've got this huge bronze bell, and you can grab that rope and pull on it and then hang on to the rope and the bell will pull you up off the stairs, into the air. And then you float down because it's so heavy.

HERB WILLIAMS: It's so hard to describe to somebody who hasn't been there or taken an art history course. Imagine an outdoor Egyptian temple. The stained glass looks like palm tree scenes you'd see in the desert. There's a scarab beetle on the altar. It's like the most pagan symbols you can think of in this Christian Presbyterian church—these giant columns with painted Egyptian hieroglyphic writing. It's unreal, man, everything in there.

ANDY HARDING: The studio was not a heated space or air conditioned. So we got very hot in the summer and pretty cold in the winter. It was very rustic in that sense. There was a bathroom directly above one of the rooms. And at one point there were workmen fixing the electricity or something. I don't know what they were doing there, but they were using that bathroom and they're flushing, but it wasn't a functioning toilet. The pipe for the toilet emptied into our studio. And so we were like smelling like urine in our studio because people were using the bathroom on the fourth floor. It was just a lot of richness in all senses.

HERB WILLIAMS: I had to move space heaters up there in the winter, man. It's amazing that I have kids at all because I'd just be straddling a space heater up there. I thought I was going to go sterile just to stay warm. Brutal.

TOM WILLS: Everything's covered in dust and lead paint and there was a room full of ranger uniforms. Park ranger uniform clothing, and Smokey the Bear hats that the church used to give out to the homeless. It was just sort of a weird place. There were like a thousand copies of this old record from 1954 when they were trying to save the church and Dinah Shore and the Fisk Jubilee Singers, and a whole bunch of other people recorded on it to save the church. Sometimes I'd present visitors with a souvenir record to take home with them and a Smokey the Bear hat. It was a wonderfully evocative space and still is.

DAVID MADDOX: They were interested in actively building a community for themselves. And they did that. And they did that by getting involved with things at the church, but also doing things in that space. And again—like The Fugitive—it was a pretty unregulated, unfinished space. In the early days they would have shows up there. And they built a little stage. Todd Greene's band, Bulb, would do concerts up there and they would have open houses and the church community would wander through. They did these big kind of crazy invitational art shows, *Dialogue: An Interaction for Growth* (DIG). They filled the downstairs with art from all sorts of people who were not being kind of vetted in any way for some sort of religiously appropriate material. And then there would be panel discussions and a purchase prize and sometimes concerts. And it was just a kind of festival that would happen over the course of a day or two days—a temporary community popped up. It was a different community than The Fugitive community, although there was some overlap.

JOHN HILLEY: There were always people who wanted to see the building and see the sanctuary. But I had to get them to come on Sunday morning. That was the genesis of the DIG art shows. We had been wondering how to foster and support their work—this downtown art community. We wanted to create a juried art exhibition for this emerging scene that would show we were taking them seriously.

TOM WILLS: At one point, our pastor John Hilley reached out to Todd Greene and I and asked if we'd like to have an art show? We decided we wanted to do a show for the community. So we cold-called artists using like the Metro Arts website and Tennessee Arts Commission website and invited them to show art at the church at a suffering-and-hope-themed show. The idea was that we would have one piece we'd purchase at the reception for a thousand dollars. We sent invitations out and people responded, and one piece was a bit controversial. Adam Randolph, who's actually a childhood friend of mine, had been involved in the art scene a little bit—he was one of the original painters of the dragon mural across the street from the Belcourt Theatre. He submitted a painting of four or five naked, male, World War II concentration camp victims. An associate pastor reached out and talked to him and sort of got a sense for where he was coming from. And David Perkins, the singer-songwriter/guitar player came to that show. Later on he joined Downtown Presbyterian, and he told me "I came to your church for this art show. And I saw this painting and I said to myself, 'Either this church knows what it's doing or it's not paying attention.'" I think he was right. I don't think it would have worked if people had been paying attention too much. The way I thought of it was we believe in prophecy, and in a tradition that takes prophecy seriously. The congregation allowed us to evangelize them, not through our faith language, but through our art language. Eventually, every Lent, we would do another show down in the downstairs portion of the church in our fellowship hall. We also screened some films in the chapel or in the sanctuary. And the we started to have open houses in the actual studios.

J. TODD GREENE: And during that time Julie Lee joined us and Beth Gilmore was there for a while. And Jason Lascu. And something changed during that time when we had all this young energy. We had a CD player where you could load five disks at once. I was wearing out anything Radiohead. We were listening to Doves. We had Lauryn Hill killing it for a long time. We had some Beastie Boys in there. There was still a lot of REM. I never stopped loving REM. The Waterboys and World Party. I remember Michael Penn. Constant blaring music in there. Tom Wills always loved The Church.

JOE NOLAN: Tom has literally burned me CDs of The Church.

BETH GILMORE: I got my space at DPC shortly after The Fugitive was shut down. It was like 2005 or 2006. Tom Wills was up there. Herb and Andy were there before me, and Todd was there before me. Herb had already moved—he was making all his Crayon sculptures at The Arts Company.

HERB WILLIAMS: I was in there—and this was right after 9/11—it was such a pivotal time. Such a crazy time. And just sitting in there trying to think like, "Is anything I'm doing worthwhile?" after that event. That was the biggest thing to happen to my generation and I was trying to make sense of it. I was in that church and I would hear little kids from the Sunday school, occasionally making little childish sounds and hearing their little voices sing-song through the halls and echo from downstairs. I was thinking, "Man, how is anybody going to explain this event to their kids and what are kids going to think about it?" And kids use crayons. And you started seeing American flags everywhere. And I've always been a big Jasper Johns fan, and I love the whole idea of the ready-mades. And I started thinking, "What does it mean to be an American now, and much less an American artist?" I was just thinking about the flag and thinking about drawing it in crayons. And I got a box of them and I started looking at it and thought, "How would a sculptor do this?" And I just started playing around with them. I started taking a razor knife and cutting them apart. And I started buying up boxes of the 64, just from different Walmarts or wherever I could go. I think an American flag was the first piece I made and it wasn't that big. It was maybe 18 × 24 inches or something like that. But it was one of those things. I did it and something clicked and it just felt like it had its own voice, its own language.

BETH GILMORE: I didn't see any people upstairs when I was working. I would always be there in the middle of the night by myself, looking out for ghosts, while I was printing something like a thousand times. I was doing the Goose Girl stuff by then. And so that all had to do with Belmont Mansion and World War I, and printmaking, and binary code, and telegraphs, and Victorian stuff.

HERB WILLIAMS: I don't want to say "haunted," but I think it was like a Civil War hospital. It definitely felt pretty strange. It was just eerily quiet—like *thick* quiet. And the walls with the old paint peeling in chunks. It was so cool. Being in there by yourself and creating was really strange. You never had the feeling that you were quite alone, even when you knew you were alone. It would get so biting, bone chilling cold, but you had a feeling like you were surrounded by some of these ghosts. It was eerie and just strange man, but I loved the history and the Egyptian background there. It felt like you fit somewhere in history, you know that there were these people who loved art and making an homage to this ancient culture that's dead? And where in the language and communication of all of it, would your work even fit in? So anything you made, you wanted to think twice, "Is this going to be worthwhile and relevant?" Because you have this strange sense of not being alone, just somebody kind of watching and not judging you, but just being there with you while you're creating this.

BETH GILMORE: The church is haunted for sure. That's my favorite part about it. I never really saw any ghosts, but I wanted to. But I didn't. But they were always sort of around the corner, I think.

HERB WILLIAMS: Jeff Hand was always telling me, "You need to be in New York City." I got Red Grooms's address and I wrote him a letter. I bought a plane ticket and said, "I'm going to be in New York. Can I buy you a cup of coffee or lunch?" And he responded. He wrote me right back and said, "Here's my studio address." And I came to his studio, he let me sketch him and photograph him. And we went out to lunch at a Chinese buffet and had frog legs. It was amazing. And he's like "Buddy, I've got so many friends who are established, you know, New York art names who are dying to move to Nashville. You don't have to live here anymore to make it. You can live anywhere. Nashville is a much cooler place than New York. You're still creating your game in the art world. Here it's so competitive, it's so difficult even to be heard. Try it from Nashville. I've got so many friends who wish they could be there." He's a great artist. He's from Nashville.

RICHARD FEASTER: I did my last two years of high school here at Brentwood High. We moved here from Massachusetts in 1982 or 1983. And then I left and went to college and lived all over the place, and got married and all that. And then ended up in New York for just under ten years. And then, after 9/11, we ended up kind of pulling out of New York and coming here in 2002. My parents still lived here, and I didn't really know what to expect in terms of art stuff. I had a studio in New York and I'd shown my work there and in some other cities, but I'd basically missed the whole 1990s in Nashville.

CARY GIBSON: In 1993, David Dark was living in Ireland and we met through a mutual friend. When he got married to Sara in 1998, a group of us came to Nashville for the wedding—that was my first time in

Nashville. And so over the next few years you had people going backward and forward from Nashville and Ireland. I traveled back and forth, and then, in 2008, I came through Nashville and Joel Dark and I met up and went for dinner and had a very nice time. We started keeping in more regular email contact and we fairly quickly realized that we were a good connection. I arrived November, 2010, and we had a window in which to get married for my visa. And I've been here ever since.

HANS SCHMITT-MATZEN: I came over to DPC around 2014. I had this weird transition period where I moved everything out of The Fugitive to this farmhouse in Gallatin where my wife and I were living near her family. A couple years after that, I was trying to figure out how I could get a studio space closer to town again. Richard Feaster was probably the most senior—still is—the most senior artist-in-residence and he told me that a studio had opened up.

RICHARD FEASTER: Shane Doling was in the space that I think Herb Williams had previously worked in, that looks out onto Fifth Avenue. It had these big, arched windows and everything about that building is pretty special. You walk in and it's an 1850s building. The most impressive entry is through the church, but when you come in the regular side doors, through the back part of the building where the studios and the chapel is, it doesn't blow you away immediately. But then you go up these stairs, and the first set of stairs is just like a regular stairway. And then you open this door and all of a sudden it's like you're back in Renaissance Italy or something. It's like bare stone and a stairway that goes up thirty feet to a set of windows, the light filtering in through the dust. It's very atmospheric. So Shane leads me up there and he was on the third floor. We go in there and then wander and weave our way around the hallway that basically goes around the dome of that chapel. It's pretty unusual architecture. And you can just tell it's old. It feels like someone just shut the place up in the 1920s. It still feels that way. They've got the old push-button lights and all sorts of odd bits of old furniture—some of it's almost Victorian looking. Some of it is Art Deco stuff that just has accumulated up there over the years. And then I walked into his space. I just couldn't believe the light and it was a pretty good size studio space. And he had this amazing view.

CARY GIBSON: I was part of a collective in Belfast called Icon, which was doing something that I think now in academics is called *theopoetics*— it's like a cross between some of the ritual elements that you would get in a church context, combined with philosophy, combined with very interactive theater and performance. That was my entryway into a much more creative world. It was a do-it-yourself group where you become a Jack of all trades. We got invited to go to the Green Belt Festival in England, and they started putting us in bigger and bigger venues until we were at Shelton race course where we were in an indoor venue that held three thousand. We were doing like an hour long installation of ideas and music and stuff happening. People would come in thinking it was worship, but it wasn't. It was exploring ideas and kind of conceptual. And so it was through that, that I got into the visual arts. Moving here, it was really hard to say goodbye to that scene. So in 2011, I started checking out DPC with Joel, and I got immersed into that community very quickly. I was invited to join the Worship and Arts committee, and that was a place where what was happening on a Sunday morning and what's going on in the studios connected. Because of my experiences with Icon, I was most interested in a liturgical context: What can art do in that space?

HANS SCHMITT-MATZEN: I was able to interview with David Maddox—he was the key point person then. He remembered me being involved with The Fugitive and they brought me on like right at the point when they were just starting to talk about transitioning the downstairs library into a gallery. They wanted to do more formal gallery shows there instead of in the big, communal Fellowship Hall. The idea was to take this book storage space and make a white box out of it. To make a space that was a good size where people could try out some ideas and not have it feel like they were taking too big of a risk almost.

CARY GIBSON: I became an artist-in-residence in 2013. I was really privileged to essentially be invited to join the studios rather than going through the traditional application process. That was because I think I had so quickly started articulating this desire to see the liturgical and creative areas come together. I took over Tom's space when he moved out. That room had kind of reverted into a storage space. I moved in in June 2013, but it took all summer to get set up in this filthy huge room with these fabulous, old massive windows that open out onto the parking lot with this ginormous mural. But it was filthy. I mean, it was absolutely grime ridden. I had like a really simple studio set up, but I was doing encaustics and there's only so much dust and grime that medium can take, and everything was just covered in dust. So I spent that summer basically hauling planks of wood and everything sort of carpentry stuff—that studio had become a dumping ground. The third and fourth floors were filled with stuff that people in the church didn't know what to do with. So I had to just kind of try and clear it out, find other spaces, and then make a space for me. I had this huge room, huge ceilings, no heating, no AC, rubbish lighting, and Van Gilmore had a carpet company, and he very kindly invited me to go down to his store-room warehouse. He showed me these rolls of odd bits of carpet and told me to take my pick, and his men would bring them downtown for me. So we were able to get carpet rolled out on the bulk of the concrete and wood floor. That really helped the dust situation.

JOE NOLAN: The Browsing Room gallery at Downtown Presbyterian Church is one of the reasons the downtown art scene is still a scene instead of just an area where there happens to be a few commercial galleries. The Browsing Room doesn't have traditional curators or owners or commercial considerations. Nowadays it's very unique to have a space that large and conceptually liberated in Nashville—let alone in the heart of downtown. It's loosely organized by artists like all the best spots in city have always been.

RICHARD FEASTER: We had been talking about converting the downstairs library into a gallery space. It was sort of in the air for years before somebody got the ball rolling by organizing a book sale. That went on for a while and then a book dealer came in and took stuff. And then finally a volunteer group got together and boxed up the books and I think they auctioned off or sold off the bookshelves. And then it was an empty space for a while. And then someone—around the time that they were redoing the lighting on the exterior of the church—arranged to put up the track lighting in the gallery. It was a couple of years before it was finally like ready to show some art. I want to say the first official show we did was Dane Carder.

CARY GIBSON: I always valued there being a non-commercial space. The church isn't taking a cut if somebody sells something. It's focused on giving space to people and projects that wouldn't necessarily get featured in any other gallery. So there's some focus on students, and up-and-coming artists—quite a few people have got their first solo shows at The Browsing Room. When I was a resident we'd always do an annual group show. They were always really interesting in terms of seeing what the artists in the studios are doing, and seeing the relationship between our work—I always found that really stimulating. Me and Richard Feaster—our work is totally different. Like, there's no comparison. And yet, when our work was hung together, it was so interesting to see the connections. Now I look at those pieces differently.

HANS SCHMITT-MATZEN: I like to think about curation as a continuation of a creative practice in a lot of ways. I'm also pretty hands-off once we've scheduled a show. If people are making interesting work, then usually there's a lot of just trusting them to make the work. And you kind of check-in with them and make sure that you're helping them to get the word out and publicize it. I've always kind of thought that was something that was attractive about the space: it's a place where you can try out some stuff, and even change directions with your work somehow. That's what I mean about having a no-risk kind of space. We've got the space and we'll help and support you, and you can just follow your gut.

CARY GIBSON: I also hoped that the Browsing Room would be a site where art could provoke conversation about things. In the time I was there, that was something that would happen. You know, somebody would do a show that was focused on refugees. Somebody would do something that was focused on the environment. We had a lot of shows that weren't just something attractive to look at or something visually provocative. There was often something with substantive themes you could have conversations about. And so the Browsing Room becomes a springboard for other conversations and to stimulate ethical thought.

HANS SCHMITT-MATZEN: It's been a good way to get introduced to new people. If somebody moves to Nashville, and I meet them for the first time, and do a studio visit or something. They might have some interesting work, but they're not connected to any commercial gallery yet. It can be a good way for them to have that first introduction to a broader swath of the community. Or if somebody is coming back to Nashville the Browsing Room can be the first big thing that gets them reacquainted with the new scene, and the new artists who are here now. A former artist-in-residence, Cary Gibson, is married to Joel Dark who's a dean in the liberal arts school at TSU. We were able to host one of their senior shows here and give a little more exposure to their artists and their program. It's been a great space to introduce people to the broader community.

CARY GIBSON: It has a different purpose to a commercial gallery, it's a place that's open to being provocative in a thoughtful way. Without telling people what to think, but inviting people to have ideas and to think about the work and to react to it. And that's an important part of art—how it makes us feel, how it makes us think, how it makes us relate to the world. From a curatorial sense it's always been about much more than just aesthetics. We probably also attracted artists who were interested in some subject matter, that might be slightly outside of a lot of the mainstream. That's the thing for me that marks it out as a space.

JOE NOLAN: You can take the most unremarkable piece of work—even a bad piece of work—and add an archival mat and nonreflective glass and a frame cut from high-end molding. Then hang it in a dedicated gallery space at sixty inches on center under the glow of proper lighting. Then invite a dozen random people and ask them to dress for a night out. When they arrive, hand each of them a plastic cup of box wine and show them to the gallery. When they arrive that artwork might have transformed into something remarkable. It's about the art, but it's also about more than just the art. Gallery-going is a ritual, and the Browsing Room's location makes that sublime aspect of looking at art explicit because of its context in a sacred place.

HANS SCHMITT-MATZEN: It's pretty cool that we've had write-ups in *ArtForum*, and people from *Burnaway* coming in from Atlanta. The Browsing Room's made some opportunities for regional artists and writers to come through Nashville. We've found ways we could bring in more regional people. It's mostly been a gallery for Nashvillians, but we've shown artists from Memphis and Birmingham as well as artists who've moved from Nashville to New York and then come back to do a show with us here. We've been able to get these interesting regional connections going on.

RICHARD FEASTER: When I started there the program was still pretty young. I got my space the same time as Beth Gilmore—she was next door to me. We were like in that second or third generation of artists to move in there, the first would've been Tom Wills and I guess Todd Greene and then Herb—there were a bunch of people. Andy Harding was up there, and I took Andy's old space. So when I got in there it was still a pretty young program and volunteer work was how you pay your rent and show that you're a responsible person that can be trusted with the alarm code. They were serving lunch and breakfast at that time to homeless folks, and you could volunteer there. There are any number of projects helping to move things around in some storage space or helping out in the Sanctuary if they needed help there or something like that. One thing that really impressed me is that they did not require us to go to church there. I never felt any pressure about that at all. It was more like we were expected to be involved in the community, and we were expected to be responsible and to contribute.

JOHN HILLEY: I wish I could say it was very intentional and very strategic. Those guys had so much energy and were hungry to engage, but I think there's more than that. I've been deeply influenced by *fides quaerens intellectum*: faith seeking understanding. Our quest for understanding is not always worked out cerebrally and with pen in hand to paper. But that expression happens through a multiplicity of senses, and in different ways. And it could be with a paintbrush. I was looking for an expanded vocabulary of faith in my own time in my thirties, there. I was noticing that people were looking for new ways to express themselves, and that faith was seeking expression in different formats. I'm trying to think if I would be more reticent to let people just kind of come on in and take up space today? Without a memorandum of understanding or some kind of lease agreement? I would probably feel greater pressure to do paper nowadays than back then. But I'm amazed that it still continues.

RICHARD FEASTER: I never really knew how long I would last there or be invited to stay or whatever. People would ask me and I would say, "Well, I'll stay until they ask me to leave," and no one's asked me to leave yet. I think all artists deal with this. A common experience is that you have some very weird studios over the years. In New York I had a studio in Dumbo. There were wild dogs that roamed in the building and the guy that I sublet from didn't want to give me a key for some reason. There was just odd stuff like that, but it was very cheap. The next one was in the East Village. And that came with a giant Rhodesian Ridgeback that would gallop toward you anytime you entered the building—it didn't make for the best studio visit experiences. I'd always have to explain if it was someone, a curator or someone from a gallery or anyone you're bringing into your space. We'd be outside on the street. And I'd have to warn them that this dog—this giant terrible dog— is going to charge us, but it won't hurt you. I'd open the door and this dog would charge, and the curator would melt down—which made it all worse. Every studio comes with some strings attached, whether you're paying or not. So I think artists are used to that.

HERB WILLIAMS: I've always struggled with my faith. But when I was there, it really felt as though you were part of something bigger than yourself and trying to do something real in the middle of a city that was really blossoming. Things back then were still small, you know? The art scene was so small and so fragile, and a lot of emerging artists got a good start at the church.

Old School

1885–2021

WATKINS COLLEGE OF ART WAS a learning center for high school dropouts, retirees, and kids on summer vacation in the early 1990s. The school's transformational, triumphant, and traumatic life cycle winds through the story of Nashville's contemporary art renaissance. During the 1990s and into the new century, Watkins' students and faculty were a part of every important conversation in nearly every corner of the city's developing creative scene. The school's impact on the form and substance of Nashville's visual art community is indelible. This isn't a book about institutions, and Watkins wasn't an institution, until it was. Until it wasn't.

KRISTI HARGROVE: I started at Watkins in maybe '94 or '95. I had entered the Tennessee All-State Art Exhibition. It was always at the Parthenon and they always had a purchase award. I won that thing and then I got a call from Madeline Reed. She needed somebody to teach a drawing class. And I was like, "I've never taught drawing class before." And she said, "Well, I saw your work and this could work out, and I'm kind of in a pinch." And it really was like that. I said yes and Madeline kind of took me under her wing. It was downtown where the public library is now. So I kind of got started blindly. I was probably twenty-five or twenty-six. I'm a native Nashvillian, born and raised here in Nashville. I ended up in Vanderbilt as an engineering student. My dad's side of the family all matriculated through Vanderbilt and it was just like, "That's what you're supposed to do in this family." And I love math—it was always something I was really interested in. So at Vanderbilt, in the engineering school, in my junior year, I took an elective— Marilyn Murphy's drawing class. It just unnerved me. I don't know what it was. I'd always drawn, but I'd never had classes of any kind. And so I took more classes, and took Don Evans's class and my mind was blown. I ended up having this weird degree. At the time they didn't have studio arts. So I have an art history degree and this weird sort of civil engineering thing. Then I did graduate work in Vermont. So, yeah, I grew up here, and anything I've done in art has not been planned.

BARBARA YONTZ: I was born in Tampa. I have an undergraduate degree in fine art from the University of South Florida, and then I stayed there and got a master's in art education. And that was back in the late '70s. And I had a son at that time too. He and I moved to Atlanta because his father lived there. We lived there about five years and then moved to Nashville with someone I was partnered with at the time who was in the music business. So that's how I came to be here. And that was probably the mid-1980s.

KRISTI HARGROVE: I started teaching night classes. I'd teach six to nine. It was more continuing ed and it was also a place for kids who needed their GED or something like that. So there was this mix of high-school-aged students and returning students interested in art. There were a mix of retired people looking to learn how to watercolor and some people that would wander in off the street. At one point I had a student who I knew was homeless, but she would come regularly and I found materials for her. I think that's the magic of Watkins in some ways. It was this magnet for like odd misfit toys that sort of just found their way to this place where you had permission to kind of do what you wanted, and feel supported doing it. People would come take a class there and then they would take it again. So you got these returned students that would take your class four or five times and it sort of built a little mini community of people.

BARBARA YONTZ: I was in advertising, that was my profession, that's how I made my living and supported my family. And it really wasn't until the early 1990s that I decided I just needed to get back into art somehow. There were no MFA programs in the area and I didn't have an MFA, but Vanderbilt had the master's in art history. I took one class and I got a scholarship. So I did that master's program, which then allowed me to teach. I started teaching at Watkins maybe in the early 1990s when we were still downtown.

KRISTI HARGROVE: The kids art program was financially supporting Watkins and keeping the doors open in the early '90s. They had a really robust kids art camp that came downtown. I mean, it was crazy. That's what supported continuing education, community education. I distinctly remember Madeline at one point telling us there wasn't enough money to pay us for the last couple of weeks of class, and what did we want to do? Everybody was like, "Well, that's okay. We'll just keep going, and wait for the next cycle." There were some precarious moments.

JOE NOLAN: Watkins was founded by Samuel Watkins in 1885. He was a self-taught business man. The school left the downtown location when Nashville built the new main library in 1999. They relocated to a temporary location adjacent to the 100 Oaks Mall at Thompson Lane and Powell Avenue in South Nashville. The school began to develop its bachelor's degree program in a ramshackle maze of temporary structures. They secured their last permanent location as an independent school in 2002 when the college moved into the former Carmike movie theater complex at Fountain Square mall on Rosa Parks Boulevard, in the Metrocenter business and retail district in North Nashville.

KRISTI HARGROVE: The way I understood it is we sold the property where we were downtown with the intention to buy land and do something, but, in the interim, we went over to 100 Oaks at the temporary location. We had studios and rooms there, but it was a temporary structure and the walls didn't go all the way up to the ceiling. So, like, you could hear every other class in there. Terry Glispin was there and Greg Pond came on board for awhile and Barbara Yontz was there. Joy McKenzie was kind of running the program. The curriculum was starting to get developed from Terry Glispin and Barbara Yontz and a bunch of the other people that were there like, "Let's go for it. Let's do this thing." But it was also a super exciting time because you could make quick decisions. You didn't have to go through these tiers of academia and committees and approvals. At Watkins, we could decide, "Hey, let's start a photography program!" "That sounds great! What's the curriculum?" "Let's get this going." "Okay!" By the next semester we were up and running. So it was a different way to sort of think about academics. It felt exciting to be in a space where you had other people who were coming from different types of educational models. Terry and Jack Ryan and Greg—they all had master's from the University of Georgia. So they had a certain idea. And then Terry was the one who really set the tone for what it became, and I'd say Barbara Yontz was right there with him.

BARBARA YONTZ: When we moved out to Powell Place, that's when Terry Glipsin came. And then there was a full-time position for art history, and I applied for it and I got it. At that point, Terry and I were the only full-time people in the art department besides Madeline Reed who was still there from back in the day. We built the BFA program and then we moved over to Rosa Parks.

LAIN YORK: Right around the time Fugitive gets going, Watkins was hiring. And there's this wonderful synergy there. Nashville had this free-wheeling independent artist scene, and then all these young professionals started showing up from out of town with MFAs. They're being taken on by academic programs and in '99 Zeitgeist started doing the *Switchyard* shows. *Switchyard* was all about reaching out to these people who had shown in the independent scene and giving them a shot at showing at Zeitgeist Gallery. Let's see if they can deliver three consistent pieces of work. Let's see if they can show up and let's give them a shot. So now these independent artists are showing in galleries, and taking faculty jobs. The colleges and universities started spending money on their programs—Watkins in particular. Everyone else followed very quickly. Cheekwood Museum was doing its Temporary Contemporary exhibitions. Everything kind of started working together.

JACK RYAN: About a year after my exhibition at The Fugitive I was teaching in New York and Terry Glispin reached out and asked if I wanted to teach a class. I was working as a journeyman doing carpentry and painting, and as a 3D animator for Donald Trump who was just kind of a real-estate doofus. Terry was just like "Listen, Jack, come to Nashville. I've got a job for you. I've got a place for you to live." He was really generous in terms of like me paying rent at the house on Grantland. And at some point I went to Watkins for my first term and one of my classes didn't make in terms of numbers. And so they were going to cancel it. And he just went to the director at the time, and he said, "Look, this guy came from Brooklyn. He just arrived. He needs this teaching job. I promised him this, and we can't cancel this class." And so, you just have a group of people that really go to bat for you. I'll never forget that.

CHRIS DOUBLER: Jack comes to class with a spray-painted briefcase, sits down, opens up the briefcase and he goes, "Oh! I've uh . . . pardon me. I have forgotten my documents." And then he leaves. And people are like, "What's in the briefcase?" And it's all just like crumpled-up paper. No syllabus, there's no agenda or anything. And he was just basically like, "Excuse me for a second," and just left the classroom. And everybody's like "What just happened?" That was a great introduction to that class because it was a fun sculpture course. He would come up with these great, engaging projects—simple projects to get people to think big. I remember we did these little line sculptures, these brazing projects. You've got five pieces of sticks, but you need to put them all together and then make something interesting in the round.

JAIME RAYBIN: Jack was one of my professors. He always used to carry this briefcase with him to school. And I just always wondered, like what was in the briefcase? And then one day he dropped the briefcase and it fell open and it was full of these toys. I remember there was a plastic rose. I was like, "What?"

JOE NOLAN: The art critic Dave Hickey spent some time living in Nashville in the 1970s. He called the city the "plastic rose capitol of the world."

LESLEY PATTERSON-MARX: I was dating this guy, J. D. Wilkes from the Legendary Shack Shakers. They were playing on Lower Broadway and that was my connection to Nashville when I was living in Western Kentucky. After grad school, I went to work on a project with Judy Chicago in Bowling Green, Kentucky, and my stipend fell through so I needed a job. J. D.'s friend Doug had a conversation with his old professor, Kristi Hargrove. Watkins was becoming a BFA program and they needed MFA people to teach. And so, basically my job at Watkins started with a conversation at a bar. And so I called and Terry said, "We really need a printmaking teacher, but it has to be nontoxic because we don't have ventilation." I said, "All right, I'll figure it out." One of the participants in the Judy Chicago project was my good friend Frieda Fairchild. She just happened to be a really experienced non-toxic printmaker. And so literally just hours before class would start, I'd be at Frieda's apartment. She had her press set up in her living room, and I'd be learning what I was going to teach the students that afternoon. I taught myself nontoxic printmaking and I feel like I built that program with the students. We all kind of did it together and that's how we became so close.

ARMON MEANS: Terry Glispin was very connected to people like Greg Pond and other teachers and artists in the area who were thinking more broadly about what contemporary art was, instead of being grounded in the traditional idea of what the arts were. It was this kind of heyday because it was the explosion of all that stuff. I also think Watkins had a good plan forward at that stage. We were building the programs that made sense for us to build, and really trying to attach to this explosion of the arts in Nashville. All the galleries and the Frist and all these things that were really beginning to take root and take hold in the city.

LESLEY PATTERSON-MARX: I was usually the youngest one in the classroom. I think I was twenty-five when I started teaching there. It put me in a mindset about teaching that we're all at different skill levels, different phases of mastery at different ages. If I went to go study guitar, my guitar teacher might be twenty-one, but that guitar teacher has had a heck of a lot more experience than I ever have at guitar. So it put this thought in my head that knowledge and experience really don't have a whole lot to do with age. And so I'm still a lifelong learner, and maybe that was influenced by my seventy-year-old students back in those Watkins days. And I'm getting to where some of my teachers are quite a bit younger than me as I've been learning sewing over the years. So, I was just a kid. My student Lee Ann Hawkins was seventy years old and in my 2D class and pronouncing that she just got her first tattoo because she felt like she was old enough to not change her mind. Those older students in the classroom really raised the bar for the younger students. And it was just this amazing intergenerational community. I remember this kid, Carl was like eighteen and Lee Ann, the seventy-year-old woman, were just like so tight. They were just like such good friends and it was just beautiful. And I just sort of wished that all educational experiences were intergenerational like that.

ARMON MEANS: We still had a number of nontraditional students who filled the night classes, whether it was like an older student coming back for a second career transition, or whether it was just somebody who'd been out of school for a few years, and just kind of delaying their start. We saw a lot of those, but we also did start to see a lot of students who were coming straight from high school. So a lot of the classes were a really broad mix, which I think was a real positive for the students because it meant they had such a broad perspective range.

AMANDA DILLINGHAM: That was one of the reasons I think my mom was freaked out when she visited because it seemed like older students, like a career school. But I liked it because there was a lot less BS, a lot less drama. It made everybody take it a lot more seriously because a lot of people were coming back to school with a purpose. So they weren't trying to bullshit. We all partied and did all that too, but it wasn't a traditional campus.

BETH GILMORE: We were all—technically speaking—grownups. It made a huge difference. Also my children were always allowed. It could be like a snow day for the kids, and it's like "Everyone's going to school." And Watkins, and everyone at Watkins, anywhere I had to go, and I had to bring my two little girls with me, they were like, "Jasmine! Grace! Awesome! We're so glad you're here. What do you think of this painting?" I remember Grace objecting to some of Jason Driscoll's work. But, you know, Grace was always really sweet about it.

JOE NOLAN: That era of the Watkins scene happened because you weren't dealing with classes full of traditional freshmen. They didn't require that kind of supervision and nearly everyone could legally drink and socialize away from campus.

BETH GILMORE: Lesley, she was crucial. She was—and is—so kind and nurturing. I'd just seen some lecture at Watkins and I was just like, "Lesley, I feel like someone's just taken out my brain and reassembled it and put it back in my head because I didn't know any of those things. I hadn't even thought about things like that." And she said, "Well, have you thought about going to school here?" And it was like "Okay. Fine." But it was totally not, because I already had children and I was already out in the world, and going back to school would be difficult. But she made it totally un-intimidating.

CHRIS DOUBLER: Lesley was a very good teacher. She's really good at showing you the process and engaging you. She can go over a project with you, and you're watching and engaged because she brings such a calm demeanor to a classroom. And it just encourages a creative mind.

LESLEY PATTERSON-MARX: I think that Terry Glispin really set the tone and I feel like it worked and it allowed us to have a certain kind of dialogue with the students to help them, help each other grow. I feel like there's so many ways in which he was a brilliant leader and educator. He provided that space for us as educators to have those kinds of conversations with the students that would break down barriers and allow people to dig deep into their work without fear of being judged or ridiculed or censored. That was one thing that I thought was really wonderful—that people didn't feel the need to censor themselves. They would just try random stuff. If it didn't work, it didn't work. But when it did, it was really amazing.

BARBARA YONTZ: After we got into that building at Metrocenter we had this amazing few years when we were kind of running under the radar. Terry was hiring people that he had gone to grad school with that were really vibrant and contemporary. Jack Ryan, Greg Pond—all these people. And then Armon and me. People in the community were thinking, "What are these wacko guys doing over there?" It was fun and exciting and vibrant, and I wasn't really thinking that much about what we were building or anything. It just happened.

JOE NOLAN: Watkins was an inspiring place because they focused on the creative, subjective, conceptual side of art over the objective, technical side. Traditionally art schools focused on technique because it's easy to quantify if someone has become a noticeably more accomplished painter, et cetera. And that's a result you can sell.

BARBARA YONTZ: Terry and I were both looking at more contemporary programs and seeing that this could be something that was more conceptually based. The students still had to take foundations. They still had to take drawing. They still had to take art history. But then instead of them coming out and saying, "I'm gonna major in painting," it was more interdisciplinary in terms of what they were doing. Some of the administration was never on board with that. So there was always this rub. The truth is, a lot of people in administration in academia don't seem that smart. They don't have a vision for anything, really. Even when the students were so energized by their work and what they were doing: developing their own collaborative groups; making their own shows. To us it was crazy good. They were inviting faculty to be in *their* shows. But other people thought this was something that students did in grad school and that it had no place at the undergraduate level.

BETH GILMORE: My sister went to Boston University and every once in a while, she would talk about her college experience versus my college experience. I'd say, "My friend is the chair of the department. We just had a party at their house." She'd say, "I've never met the chair of my department and there's three hundred people in my class, and I've never spoken to my teacher face to face." But at Watkins we just all went to school together. And then we all went and had a show together and there's no "titles." Everything was just all a big group of people and we happen to be able to use a school to facilitate.

BARBARA YONTZ: So there were certain things that had to be taught. Like if you're teaching welding, you have to make sure people don't get hurt. And if you're teaching wood stuff, you have to make sure people don't get hurt. But then the idea was to try to give projects and assignments that would make people think, and to bring in contemporary artists. It's just the normal way that I teach now. I don't think anything about it. But it wasn't like that before. And so there was this kind of almost an atelier sort of sensibility. And so when the decision was made to build this different program, what really ended up happening was contemporary artists, contemporary ideas infiltrated into every single classroom. And then, once the students got to their sophomore year, they were in special courses called seminar courses. And so in seminar we would give studio prompts. And I mean, these are things that I do now, but it wasn't the way things had been before. If you had been at like MICA, you know, or someplace like that, they were maybe doing some of these kinds of things, but most art schools weren't.

ARMON MEANS: I went to grad school with a guy named Anderson Williams. He's from Nashville. He grew up in East Nashville, and I had come down over a spring break just to visit with him and his family. I moved down and got picked up to teach a class or two at Watkins. I was teaching photo. Watkins was my first introduction to the Nashville arts community. It was maybe three years after they got their full accreditation—I think that was around 2000. At that point we had studio which was like painting, drawing, photography. Ceramics as part of sculpture. The film and video, and then illustration, graphic design, and interiors. It definitely was a more robust program than I had anticipated. I kind of did the adjunct-everywhere thing: Nashville State, Vol State, MTSU—kind of a broad spectrum. Watkins was the one where the students were really pushing beyond conventional ideas of media types or a major. They were really beginning to look at the full spectrum of possibility for the work that they were making, and the directions where they could take it. I think a big part of that was Terry Glispin who was definitely an outside-the-box thinker.

DAVID MADDOX: Watkins was a big deal. If you want to talk about Golden Ages, you know that was the Golden Age of Watkins. Watkins students, at that time, were mostly people who were from here—it wasn't people coming from all over the country to go to art school. But then there's Terry Glispin and Kristi Hargrove. A lot of energy was coming from them. They all got involved very quickly with pop-ups at various times and non-commercial stuff. There was always something worth looking at in their gallery. And you had some really strong social practice people like Shaun Slifer and Ally Reeves. I think Terry was encouraging a lot of that.

SHAUN SLIFER: When I first shifted away from being a graphic design student, it was because of Terry and this requirement Sculpture 101 course that I took. And Terry was this whole other character than I was used to. He just talked about art in ways that I think I was aware of, but hadn't maybe been given permission to think about. And I had Barbara Yontz teaching art history and I'm starting to understand things about more fringe movements and whatnot. I was very interested in Dada, the Fluxus movement, stuff like that. And those things had an impact on me in relation to understanding how art does, and can, and cannot interact with markets. Because as a graphic design student, I had been funneling my energy into figuring out "How am I going to get a job out of this?" It sort of sounds funny in retrospect. I think this is also how I convinced my parents that this was a good idea. That I was going to take out loans to do this. But then Terry was a part of ruining that path for me. So people were very clear with me about what it meant to work in the arts as a designer. And then here's Terry providing these methodologies for making things and these examples for what's happening in the world.

CHRIS DOUBLER: So I think I was the first class to start at the Metrocenter location. I was kind of on the fence between Memphis College of Art and Watkins. So when I was touring Watkins to see whether or not I wanted to go there, it was toward the end of the 100 Oaks facility. They had this interim location right next to a Home Depot. So I toured that, which was totally insane. They also gave us tours of Metrocenter where the new location was still being built. I started Watkins in 2001. My graduating class was three students: me, Mike Bielaczyc and Jaime Raybin.

JAIME RAYBIN: Watkins was my second attempt at college. I started at Hampshire College in Amherst, Massachusetts. I was twenty-one. I'd dropped out of college and I was doing zines. I was just traveling around and stuff and feeling like, "I'm not ready to be in college. I have to get life experience before I can, like, concentrate." I'm glad I did. It gave me stuff to make art about. Then I was waitressing, but I was making art all by myself. I didn't have a community. I'm originally from Nashville and when I was visiting my parents we went on a tour of Watkins. I met Bob Durham and I talked to Terry Glispin for a long time and I showed him my portfolio and I just felt, "I need to be here." During the first long chat I had with Terry Glispin he told me that the *Cremaster* movie was playing at the Belcourt, and I should go see it. And it was *Cremaster 3*. So I went with my mom, and the movie was three hours long. And when we got out of it, it was unexpectedly dark.

There was a power outage and all the lights were flashing. And I was feeling like, "My life is changing!"

JOE NOLAN: The faculty at Watkins was deeply involved with what was happening in the independent art scene during that era. They were interacting with the faculty at Lipscomb and Vanderbilt. They were assigning local exhibitions for students to go look at and analyze. Lots of folks graduate from art school not knowing how to approach a gallery or how to properly install their own work. Those Watkins classes were seeing all of that up close. They were learning everything.

AMANDA DILLINGHAM: I am from Nashville. I grew up in Fairview, but I went to school mostly in Nashville. I was going to go to college, and I went to the Art Institute in Atlanta with these big dreams of what that was going to be and it turned out to be mostly a scam. There were some really good teachers there, but there were also a lot of bad teachers and overall the school administration just didn't care. I went there and I didn't have a great experience, and my parents were focused on me getting a degree that would make money. The only way they were going to agree to an art school was if I was a graphic design major. But I hated these graphic design classes. The only classes I liked were the ones that were real hands-on, like experimentation with media and things like that. I left school in Atlanta and decided to just go to Watkins. It was kind of a weird plan because I never wanted to go to Watkins. I didn't even know what Watkins was, but I always had the impression that it was a lesser school in my head. I thought I'd go to Watkins for just a year, while I figured out my next steps. I didn't even go view the campus or anything. I just filled out the application and my mom was freaked about it. She insisted that I had to go check it out. So she took my sister to open house day and it was at the Staples store building. It was when Watkins was over at the 100 Oaks mall when it was transitioning from downtown to Fountain Square. She called me, like almost in tears like I was making a big mistake. But Watkins moved that summer, and I started the first semester at the new location at the movie theater.

ARMON MEANS: I came out of two really strong arts programs: Cleveland Institute of Art and then Cranbrook Academy of Art. We had students who were amazing in both programs, but there was very little impetus for the students to really like attack the city with their work—beyond just the gallery space in the school. Or maybe like one other gallery space in town who were really friendly and seeking out opportunities to connect to the school. Whereas what happened here was really the students kind of going outside of the walls of the school themselves and finding these ways to either connect with local spaces or create their own opportunities to exhibit and put up work. I think part of that was the influence of the instructors at Watkins.

AMANDA DILLINGHAM: Terry Glispin was the chair when I started in 2002. Barbara Yontz was there and she was my advisor. I had 3D design with Jack Ryan that semester. So it was 2D with Lesley Patterson and 3D with Jack and they were awesome. I kind of went behind my parents' backs and only signed up for studio courses. I needed those studio courses anyway and I wanted a semester where that's all I was doing. I took 2D design class with Lesley and I loved her class and just loved everybody in it. And I talked a lot to her about why I had to be a graphic designer because of my parents. And she encouraged me to just talk to them, and she even volunteered to talk to them. I was prepared for them to think I was crazy, but I went home at Christmas and told them I was changing my major. And they were totally cool. They just gave in.

JOE NOLAN: All these kids who were still in art school were raiding the gallery scene with these spontaneous installations in these random settings. They were carrying on that Untitled tradition, but with a more conceptual aesthetic and a more curated style.

ARMON MEANS: The professors were encouraging students to go to exhibitions, they were taking students to various places to look at work, they were active and thinking about how the space outside the school could be part of the educational experience. That also meant bringing in artists to talk about their work and what it was they were doing—people who weren't doing just traditional kind of work in a limited medium. So I think the students really saw that as an opportunity to think about how they could begin to tell these stories that spoke to a broader audience than just within the walls of Watkins. I think that they also felt like personally responsible for carrying on this tradition of the arts. That it was kind of their place to step it up and see what it meant to bring the arts to the city in a very direct way.

ART STUDENTS ATTACK

AMANDA DILLINGHAM: There was Jason Driscoll, Derek Gibson, Will ClenDening, Heather Spriggs Thompson, Eve Peach, and Jaime

Raybin—we had the most classes together. Jaime was a year behind me, I think, or a semester behind me. And then I was a semester behind all of them. But Watkins had a few groups that just happened to end up in all the same classes and getting along well.

JAIME RAYBIN: Jason Driscoll and Amanda Dillingham were the two main co-founders. Secret Show grew out of a Seminar 1 class all these artists shared. Seminar 1 prepares you to do your Senior Show so their class decided to do a curatorial project. Secret Show was all about peers curating peers. The original board members were Will ClenDening, Amanda Dillingham, Jason Driscoll, Derek Gibson, Eve Peach, Heather Spriggs Thompson, and Kristin Burton-Work. And then around 2005, I think, they added me and Iwonka Waskowski.

AMANDA DILLINGHAM: Originally the Secret Show group was Will and Derek and Jason and Kristen Burton-Work and me. We were the moving force. We were the ones that got obsessive, I guess. So at Watkins you had to take a seminar class, you had Seminar 1, 2, and 3. And so Seminar 1 was these exercises, conceptual exercises that you had to do. And then 2, it was more about developing your own ideas. And then 3 was your senior show type thing. And Jason had a studio in the Chestnut building. He had a big studio downstairs, it was the first door on your right when you entered down those stairs. Across from Dane Carder's studio. But Jason and Kristen and I did a lot of collaborative stuff together too—like drawings where we pass drawings back and forth. And so I was going to show with them because of that. And then I had some other work and Jason asked me to just show with their seminar class. And so the idea of the seminar class was that Terry Glispin would bring in all these people like Terry Thacker and Barbara and Kristi Hargrove, and they would do critiques. They'd walk through, one by one, and give you a critique on your work. So it was really graduate school level. When I got to graduate school it was the same shit we'd been doing since our sophomore year. They had critiques in the morning, and we were going to have it up anyways. So we decided it should be an actual art show. But then Jason said we shouldn't do an art show in his little space, and we should do it in the hallways upstairs. And he knew that the landlord went home on Fridays at four. So if we waited until Friday at four to set it up, we could have everybody come in at six and do this big show. So we just happened to tell David Maddox—we sent out a little press release and he put it in the *Scene* that week. And then we were terrified that the landlord would find out because we didn't ask permission—we were just planning to throw it up and take it down, and they would never know. And then all these people came and Yazoo brewery donated a keg. All of a sudden we're doing these shows and we had such a good time. It became this like thing that we decided we would do quarterly-ish shows. And that's how it got started.

JAIME RAYBIN: It just seemed like there was this energy with Secret Show. Like something was happening and these postcards would appear around the circle. They were just so cryptic and cool. And you would go and like all the teachers would be there and people thought it was interesting and just felt really alive.

JOE NOLAN: I remember those shows as the "Secret Show Series," and it got less secret as they went on—it became kind of an inside joke. Too many people were interested in what they were doing next. It's kind of unheard of for students to play such an active role in bigger cities with more established scenes. But there was a gap for them to fill in Nashville at that time—there were lots of gaps. The surprising part was how those students with the Secret Shows and Off the Wall created those opportunities for themselves, and then delivered consistently creative exhibitions for months and even years.

JAIME RAYBIN: I wasn't part of the first Off the Wall show. Originally it was a one-time pop-up thing by Michelle Anderson and some students: Quinn Dukes and I think Jen Ramsey and some other people. And then they decided, "Let's keep going." I joined them for the second show. The members changed a little bit through time, and—like the Secret Show—it was more of a curatorial project, even though the curators did include their own work in the show. Off the Wall was more like a band, it was five or six people over various times. And we met every few weeks, and we talked about our work with each other and we kept having these shows and we would each have an area of the room for our individual work. Although sometimes we did some collaborative projects. Then we always had a guest artist—a person that would be part of the group for that one show. And then we usually had a charitable element, a piece that we auctioned off in support of something. Quinn was real into activism. And she wanted that to be part of it from the beginning.

JOE NOLAN: The Secret Show group made a splash right out of the gate and then, as they developed they started to stabilize in a few different locations. For those of us who'd been in the scene since the 1990s it was like watching the evolution from groups like Untitled to something like

The Fugitive happening all over again. Their first sort of semi-permanent location was a big space on an upper floor in the May Hosiery Building.

AMANDA DILLINGHAM: There were all these little cubicles and we had cleaned it up and everything. It was like trashed up there. The Tennessee Rep used to rent some of the spaces up there to make costumes. So that's when we started doing the Secret Shows up there. My family didn't really come to anything because we didn't even think it was going to be a thing. And then they started coming and the guy that owns Pizza Perfect, Amir, was like my second dad because I worked there for around fifteen years—like forever. He's this funny Iranian guy and then the guy that got him into restaurants was this Irish Catholic guy named Bob Patterson. Bob was like my adopted grandpa. The two of them became part of our family, and so they decided to come to one of the Secret Shows because they didn't really know what I did. They had never seen any art ever. And there was this one video of Jason projected on the ceiling, and he's nude and the camera was underneath him filming through glass. So it's like the equivalent of looking up a girl's skirt, but it was Jason—he was like in a shower or something. Like they walked through the hall and they were like, "What the hell?" And then they got to my piece and I had done it in Jack Ryan's class. It was a drawing class and I did a series of drawings on the ways women have always chosen to have abortions without a pill or the medical procedure—putting a lemon up in their crotch and you know, all kinds of stuff. So it was all these illustrations about contraception kind of. And Bob's super Catholic and he's just looking at me like "What?" And then there's the party going on. And it was just these worlds colliding that I maybe wasn't a hundred percent ready for. Bob was super, super Catholic. And I made all these images of like abortion. "OK, Bob. You need a beer right now." My parents had never really been exposed to contemporary art until we started having those shows. Now my mom loves contemporary art. She sees more stuff than I do. She'll save me magazines. She saw something about James Turrell in the *Times*, and she saved me the article. It was an education for them. And I think that the shows being more casual made it more accessible too. So it was easier for them to understand it and not feel this pretentious gallery environment.

JOE NOLAN: Off the Wall was super aesthetic and often collaborated with the guest artists they invited into their shows. It was also an all-woman art group, and the guest artists were women. They never really

portrayed themselves directly through that lens, but there were feminine and feminist works naturally emerging from those shows. Off the
Wall was emblematic of a wave of strong women artists, and their exhibitions connected directly to the kinds of works that Lesley Patterson-
Marx was making or that Adrienne Outlaw or Vadis Turner were making in Nashville at that time.

JAIME RAYBIN: We supported each other and we tried to do what we
did for each other in school. We tried to keep the support and stuff,
and dialogue about our work going even after we graduated. We were
involved in each other's work as though we were in a tight-knit class
together. A lot of the work was really personal. So it was sort of an artist
support group. We were all friends and I'm very shy, and it was easier
for me to promote my friends than to promote myself. It was cool and
it lasted for, I think, seven years altogether.

AMANDA DILLINGHAM: We really took advantage of Watkins at some
points with those shows. We were all in printmaking three together—
Lesley Patterson-Marx's class. And we would use that whole time to
plan the next show or you know—we weren't doing anything related
to the class. I felt bad at times. And we would steal a lot of resources. If
we needed like wire, we'd find it in the 3D room and then quietly put
it back. We'd borrow all the tools for the night and then return them
like it never happened. We were careful not to get caught, but I think
they wanted us to do that. We had a lot of faculty take turns showing
in the Secret Shows too.

JAIME RAYBIN: Off the Wall had a lot of donated spaces. Somebody had
a connection at Marathon Village and we showed in their big events
space upstairs, although they wouldn't let us turn the air conditioning
on when we were there so in one of those pictures from that we're all
like dripping with sweat. We showed at a coffeehouse and we started
showing at galleries. We had a show at the Renaissance Center in Dick-
son when Jason and Amanda worked there after graduation.

AMANDA DILLINGHAM: Eventually, people saw the May Hosiery building
and saw how awesome it was and all the spaces started renting out for
studios. All of a sudden it was like people started to know about that
building. We got kicked out of the upstairs because all the space that
we had been using got rented. So we did the next series in the back
stairwell of building. It was like all in the stairwell. You'd walk around
the stairs as you're going down these stairs there was like just random
art. It was really weird.

JAIME RAYBIN: I became a part of the Secret Shows right before they decided to get the 310 Chestnut space. When I joined it seemed like they needed fresh energy, especially with how laborious running the 310 Chestnut space ended up being. I was fresh energy and they wanted to grow the series and have a gallery. And the original plan was that Jason would have his studio in the upstairs part. It was an old record plating facility and it was just covered in rat poop and it was this building that someone owned and was just sitting on.

AMANDA DILLINGHAM: So we found the space across the tracks that we called 310 Chestnut. That was our gallery space for our last year. We let other groups like Off the Wall come in and use it. I don't even remember if Jason just paid for it. Or like, I don't even know how it happened if we all paid for it or what, but it was a shitty building and it had all this toxic waste in it that we couldn't figure out how to get out. It had been used to make records and Jason and I and my dad did some demolition, and we found these like giant bins of toxic waste. I think we literally just like put it in a corner and built a plywood divider in the corner.

JAIME RAYBIN: We did all this work. I can't remember how much the rent was, but it was really low. But they escalated it a little bit every month as we renovated it. We put in a handicap bathroom to make it ADA accessible. And I remember me and Derek Gibson, we went to Home Depot and we bought all this stuff to build a staircase because the one that was there was rotting out. And there was this old safe that was like a million years old. And we were always like, "We can open the safe, and maybe there'll be treasures inside." We were all paying a little bit of money every month to rent the space. And then as the rent started to escalate, we started working with different groups doing noise music concerts and dance parties and stuff. We'd rent out the space for a night for money so that we could have the space to do our shows. I was the liaison when there was somebody renting the space for music. And somebody said "Oh, the lead singer for Ass Chapel just threw up in your bathroom. Now you've made it!"

JOE NOLAN: We miss the possibility of affordable space in Nashville. But I also used to resent the conditions I'd see artists trying to work in— these filthy toxic spaces.

JAIME RAYBIN: The thing that kind of destroyed the momentum for the building was when we got broken into. My other group, Off the Wall, we were either renting or they were letting us use the space for a show. I was there by myself and I had the key and stuff and I walked in and the door was open. All they took was Derek's tools, but it just felt so scary and violating and I didn't know what to do. Will ClenDening came and sat with me just so I wouldn't be alone in the space while I was freaking out. And we waited together for the police to come. And beer was a big thing at the shows, and I always had like this empty keg in my car and it was always really gross. I have all these photos from an opening where it's my dad and an unhoused person drinking a beer together, looking at the art.

GOOD WILL

AMANDA DILLINGHAM: Jason and Will and I all applied for graduate schools at the same time. So that whole semester we were all doing the same thing. You had to have the applications in by midnight at the state, so Jason would take our applications to the airport postal service to get them postmarked. And Jason and I both got into our schools, but for some reason, Will didn't. That was crazy to me because Will was such an interesting thinker. But he also shot really high, for big schools. I think he got into one, but he didn't really want to go there. He didn't know what to do. So one thing led to another and he bought a motorcycle, which, to me, was the nail in the coffin. I was never a fan of motorcycles in the first place. I had a classmate in high school who passed away on one, too. But, that's what Will was going to do. He was going to get a motorcycle and figure out what's next. He was talking about moving. I think he talked about moving to Australia at one point.

CHRIS DOUBLER: Will needed a roommate. Trent needed a roommate. I needed a roommate. On a cigarette break I'm like, "Hey, do you need a roommate?" And they're like, "Yeah." So we all move in together. It's Will, Trent, and me—we're all two years apart. Will's four years older than me. We were in The Nations. Fifty-First and Michigan. And it was insane over there at that time, total chaos, right out of *Gummo*. Our next door neighbor had like a pond in their front yard, but it was built out of railroad ties and like a tarp over the top. And then it was just full of water. We're next door just like smoking cigarettes on the front porch. Like it was total chaos. That would have been 2002. Will is kind of a keystone figure in my life just because of that roommate introduction into independent living. I think he was working with Joe Nolan at the time at Cheekwood. I was still working restaurants and retail. Will was probably one of the more integral figures in the Secret

Show Series crew, for sure. I had like, I guess five, six big years of my life that he was in, and then he passed away. It's just interesting to have this person in my life that I'm involved with almost daily, and then he's gone. And then to have all of these similar interests and parts of my life that I kind of go down that road a little bit, kind of in his footsteps, but he's just gone. It's just an odd way of looking at things sometimes. Losing him was especially tough just because we were pretty tight. I just think of him as like a good friend, but also as someone I really would have liked to have had around creatively in my life. I can look to him as like a keystone figure or a genesis figure of things that I'm interested in and I can easily pinpoint back to "Will exposed me to this." All kinds of things in pop culture or higher thinking. It would be nice to see what he would be like today.

JOE NOLAN: I met Will when we were both working as preparators at Cheekwood Museum of Art. Artists are often analytical and intellectual or they're more intuitive. Usually it's one or the other. Will was both. He would deconstruct machines and then re-build and re-purpose them—very curious, conceptual stuff. He did some sculptures where he poured molten metal over books. But then he also made these amazing videos where you saw his knack for writing and his gift for performing. He was very aware of that line where something very serious becomes ridiculous, and he had a great feel for pushing right up to that limit.

CHRIS DOUBLER: I remember he was making these interview videos in our living room. He would just straight up be like, "Hey guys, you got to get out of the house" or, "I need to interview myself." He did a lot of video work. He did some sculptural work. I guess like most kids going through school, you're getting a little bit of everything and trying to figure out what it is. I remember his videos being really interesting and I think what he wanted to stick with for a little while, at least. His video work seemed to spark something in everybody. Everybody seemed to always be kind of interested in gravitating toward that. But, I also remember his works on paper too. They had an intensity about them. A quiet intensity—that's kind of like his personality, too. The videos had a lot of personal stuff like in your face, but some of his prints had a certain intensity to them as well.

JOE NOLAN: I was at an artist's wedding when Shane Doling sent me a text saying that Will had died in a motorcycle crash. One time, Will and I were installing a piece at Cheekwood. We were putting the lid back on an empty crate and Will handed me three bolts. I said I needed one more—one for each corner of the lid. Will just smiled and refused saying, "Joe, symmetry is so twentieth century." Ever since then, many local art handlers will use either 3 or 5 bolts to pop the lid onto an empty crate. We all do it that way because Will was right.

AMANDA DILLINGHAM: When Will passed away in that motorcycle accident we were all so close, and I think it was hard for all of us. I feel like I dropped out. Like the art scene started giving me social anxiety a little bit, because it was too much trauma. That sounds cheesy. It was just hard for me to be there because everybody had split. And then I was in graduate school—graduate school was good, but I didn't enjoy it. It really threw me and I didn't know what to do. And I became really jaded to the art scene because when Will died I felt protective. This was like one of my best friends. And everyone feels like they have to do something and I'm like, "No! Fuck that shit! Will wouldn't have wanted that." I just had to get out of it. I've just never been somebody good with death, like funerals and things. I'm not a good person with that. It was like an end of an era in a weird way for all of us.

INNOCENCE AND EXPERIENCE

AMANDA DILLINGHAM: Terry Thacker became the chair my last year there. All that drama happened. We had this student show and two filmmakers Scott [Phelps] and Elvan [Penny] entered some pieces. Elvan did one based off of a Mapplethorpe thing. And it was basically just a guy masturbating. It was a black-and-white photo. And then Scott Phelps was the other film student and they did a video that they put together using footage of this American that was beheaded. And somehow the local media got wind of that. And they went and talked to the dead man's family—it became this huge thing. So between the masturbating photo, and this video, and the family was all upset, that brought down the fine art department. It was really conflicting. It was when Dean Hinton was there. And when all that stuff happened, he just blamed it on the fine art department. But these weren't even fine art students. It was the student show, you know? The student show could be any major, because everybody had to take those foundation courses. And Elvan always had a flair for the dramatic.

BARBARA YONTZ: One of the students was super sincere and the other one was a little bit more, I don't know—rogue. Their idea here was that they wanted to use film for good. And so the idea was that they would have this space at Watkins called "the node." It was just a little empty space that was set up for exhibition and they blocked it off. And the idea was that you would go in one at a time and one of the artists would be there with you with his hand on your shoulder or whatever. They had put together film footage and some of it was very violent and negative about things that were actually happening in the world then. And then they edited that with things from sitcoms and advertisements. So there was a point they were trying to make that we're living in this world where all these really bad things are happening and that we just want to watch stupid TV or whatnot. They knew that it was going to be disturbing to people because the images that they were showing were disturbing. And so that's why they wanted to be there to sort of be comforting or whatnot.

JOE NOLAN: The video was called *Fearful Symmetry*. That title's about these juxtaposed images of consumerism and violence. It's a phrase from William Blake's poem "The Tyger," which questions the existence of god and the intentions of god given the terrifying violence embodied by a fearsome predator. The edit featured images of terrorist hostages in Iraq including the beheading of an American engineer named Eugene Armstrong.

BARBARA YONTZ: One of the pair had also done a photograph that he had submitted to the exhibition that everybody was calling the "masturbation photo." And all I kept saying is "It's a still photo." I don't know that I ever even saw it because it got scurried away really quickly because "What are we gonna do with the masturbation photo?" and all this controversy in the administration and whatnot. All I kept saying was, "Who cares?" So these were the two pieces, these two controversial pieces. And I believe what ended up happening was during the exhibition the decision was to cover it with a cloth or to take the masturbation photo and put it in the hallway so that only adults or somebody could go in and look at it. But then the other piece actually happened, and that was the piece that won the student award. So Alan Bostick from the *Tennessean* came over to the college to do a story about the exhibition. Well, David Hinton then made a kind of big deal about these two pieces so that he really paid attention to them, probably more so than if he had just, you know, been allowed to go and do it. And he wanted to talk to the two students. And apparently then it was his article that was published that alerted everybody else. So they got picked up and that's when I got phone calls on my phone at Watkins of just irate people who are like "How could you do this? This is so terrible!" It was all blown up.

AMANDA DILLINGHAM: I think one of them won a jury award, and people felt like the fine art department celebrated that. And then all these questions of censorship came up, which was really interesting at that school. I felt, "Just leave our program alone! It was really good and you guys are fucking this all up!" They were trying to put paper up so that they couldn't see into the glass gallery and it just got out of hand. And then one thing led to another and basically Terry Glispin kind of took the fall. I don't exactly know what happened, but he had to leave and that sucked.

ARMON MEANS: I know that one of the things that surprised me so much was how the students really like came and wanted to stand up for Terry. That was a really great thing to see. They had been so active all over town and now they had this chance to be active within the walls of the school. So I thought that was a really great response.

AMANDA DILLINGHAM: At one point everybody was doing a bake sale to raise money to help pay for Terry's position, because the school tried to tell us that they couldn't afford to keep him. It just became a huge mess. And then Barbara started to leave, but Barbara stayed, and I like to think Barbara stayed to help see me through, but it probably wasn't really me. I was terrified of losing both of them. It's like, so the end of the world for me. I wanted to fight the censorship and stuff until I realized it was going to tear the department apart.

KRISTI HARGROVE: I think he was really wounded. He really poured himself into the students there. I mean, he worked endlessly and tirelessly with them. There was controversy from a student show that was really blown out of proportion and the administration, I thought, dug in on the wrong side of things. And Terry and the students kind of went to bat for this show and it pretty much got blamed on Terry. He became the scapegoat for that whole situation. Barbara Yontz actually left because of that, she left Watkins and took a job up in New York.

BARBARA YONTZ: When I look back and I think about that event and how it happened and all of the fallout, it was a really, really rough time for everybody. The emotions were running really high in the administration and among the students. And the decision that was made to fire Terry just seemed like it came outta nowhere. And yet maybe they'd been looking for an opportunity where there might be something that could justify firing. Even saying it right now, like, I can feel this in my chest. Terry and I had worked so closely together for a number of years, and I love that man. He's the hardest working person I've ever been around—and I'm a pretty damn hard worker. I couldn't believe what he was always willing to do for the students. So I was just floored. Watkins president Jim Brooks made the decision not to fire Terry, but it was never the same. He had put so much of himself into that school, and he just felt completely betrayed. And then I left. I think it was just dumb luck that I ended up there when I did, and Terry ended up there when he did. I'm so grateful for it. It changed my life to be part of that. To be in the room when it happened.

CHRIS DOUBLER: Hanging out with Terry are some of the best moments of my life. Outside of school he exposed me to all kinds of stuff. He'd encourage you to go out into the city and see shows and exhibits. And as a student, I would be hanging out with him in Twelfth South. There was The Mirror and there was Mafioso's at the time. And everybody's hanging out in that world. Those are the only things staying open late at that time in Nashville. Terry would have functions at his house and people would hang out. And so there was a real social aspect to everything. And I went overseas with him to Italy, to Spain. We went to the beach, the Denali Bilbao. Barcelona. So yeah, I consider Terry a teacher, but way more of a friend.

KRISTI HARGROVE: Terry Thacker was teaching down at SCAD I think for a bit. Barbara called him up and said "Hey, you're the man for this. You need to come back and you need to be in charge here for a while and get things back on the road for everybody." And he did. He came and did that. He hired me full-time and then, after about six years, he was like "I don't want to be chair anymore. You need to take over." And, again, I was backing into something. It wasn't a plan.

AMANDA DILLINGHAM: Terry Thacker was the best case scenario for covering for Glispin. When he came in, I was not very nice to him at first. I didn't like him just because I was going to be suspicious of anybody coming in and taking Terry Glispin's spot. But I still use some of the stuff he talks about in the filmmaking classes I teach. Thacker talked about how the Cohen brothers use line, and like they are always drawing. When a guy dies in one of their films, they're dragging him through the desert and it's leaving this line of blood and Terry was like, "That's a drawing." I tell my students, "You can see drawings everywhere," and they think I'm a psycho, but it's just some Terry Thacker-ism.

He was really awesome in that he didn't come in and try to make a lot of changes to how we had been doing things.

SCHOOL DAZE

NICK STOLLE: Terry Thacker stressed the importance of recognizing and challenging institutional expectations and commercial expectations, so that period was not especially object-based. We weren't about making products and thinking about how to get those products marketed and recognized. It was just about finding that space and then filling that space, like a gas, and that turned into kind of gaseous works—you couldn't really buy them, necessarily.

MATT CHRISTY: It's funny how little we were concerned with it. I don't know why. We were also just like true believers in the arts. I mean, we were not concerned about careerism.

NICK STOLLE: Yeah, we didn't see a model. We didn't live in New York. We didn't know people who exhibited in legitimate, blue-chip galleries. And it wasn't yet an era where I follow Matt on Instagram and I also follow David Jordan on Instagram. So they're kind of equal in that way. You didn't really see that then.

MATT CHRISTY: I became really close with David Anderson. And David having a career like he has. I think in terms of just being a Nashville artist, it didn't seem like an option during the Watkins days.

DAVID ONRI ANDERSON: I think when I was there, it felt like a golden age because the people in front of me were really good. And the people that were younger than me were also really good. And the people that were teaching were like Terry Thacker, Kristi Hargrove, Brady Haston, Ron Lambert, and Tom Williams. There were some really good gen ed teachers, too. Willie Stewart and Zach Raffuls and Mika Agari and Earthen Clay were a lot of good friends. Everyone was doing a lot of stuff. There was also like the May Hosiery building—we were putting on our own shows there. And I had my first show there in like 2012—it was me and Zach and Brady. We put it together ourselves. And that was the first time that I realized there's an art scene where people put on their own shows and the work is actually good. And people are thinking critically about it.

MATT CHRISTY: I don't want to overemphasize Terry [Thacker], but having gone through grad school in Oregon and Nick going through a New York grad school, there's not a lot of people like Terry Thacker and I think he has single-handedly raised the bar. I think he's kind of like a secret weapon in terms of raising the level of conversation that people are okay with having around the arts in Nashville. I wonder if other people feel that way or if I just glorify Terry, because he's been a close friend of mine for so long. But I think he has been extremely important for the scene here.

NICK STOLLE: When I think about Terry, I think about how his enthusiasm for experiencing art was massive. That's something that I see in him that I didn't necessarily see to such a pure degree in a lot of my grad school professors. I feel like their involvement in the system and the structure in New York soured them just a little bit. I think Terry, being in Nashville, he was just so legitimately enthusiastic and open that he just devoted himself to it. Devoted his life to it and like the whole of his mind. And I think maybe that enthusiasm that he instilled in others makes a case for his huge impact as an educator and a mentor.

JOE NOLAN: In the Terry Thacker era, new groups of Watkins students formed and became active. The work was just as conceptual, but more raw. I remember lots of natural materials and recycled materials coming into play.

NICK STOLLE: I do vaguely remember a conversation when we were talking about the group name. There was an underscore. It was very late '90s, 2000s: "_nym." Obviously the name was arbitrary as hell. I don't think anybody had a strong case for why that was the one.

MATT CHRISTY: I think our first show had something to do with language. We all agreed that we were interested in language. Alison Boyd was making work she felt was related to that. I had that in my head. We were all pretty conceptual that way. So syno*nym*, homo*nym* that's where it came from.

NICK STOLLE: I remember like two or three shows, but it weaves together. I know there was a sex show, the one that was sex scenes.

MATT CHRISTY: That was in the basement of this raw house. There was a basement that was kind of unfinished. I think it was a house that Adam Nicholson's family owned, and they were redoing to rent out or something, but they hadn't got there yet. I remember a painting Nick had upstairs.

NICK STOLLE: It's probably still there! I remember Ken Nakamura's video projection.

MATT CHRISTY: That's right. So he actually went into the bathroom of this place and projected a video of himself taking a shower. So you walk outside on this deck and see Ken taking a shower. It was pretty cool. Nick had a piece where I think it was a painting of a tiny guy fucking a rabbit.

NICK STOLLE: Yeah! It was a weird little painting of a guy, a tiny little man, fucking a bunny,

MATT CHRISTY: Adolfo had his ceramic animals that were half human.

NICK STOLLE: John Whitten was in that. He had a kind of tender portrait of his girlfriend, at the time. It was pretty PG, considering.

JOE NOLAN: Nashville artists had made a tradition out of showing work in unfinished spaces, but a lot of the art coming out of Watkins at that time also had an unfinished quality that seemed at least partly inspired by those exhibition environments.

NICK STOLLE: Terry is very much a guy who—formally—is very interested in like the idea of finished versus unfinished. And he'd look at a section of wall where it's partially painted and partially drywall. I'll always remember Terry talking about the nature of sheet rock green and purple, and looking at that which is generally overlooked but still informs the overall text. And so that finished versus unfinished tension is very Terry. And so it's very me and Matt just by the nature of education.

MATT CHRISTY: And Nick and I both wanted a level of unfinished-ness or a level of rawness. I think that was something that we all wanted in the work. I don't know if "punk" is the right word for it— something that was not refined. I mean that in a sort of conceptual way—something that was delightful in that it didn't have its business suit on. Big galleries have their business suit on and we wanted art to be naked.

NICK STOLLE: Yeah. And that was very Terry as well, like kind of a humility and a pathetic-ness. And he's such a devotee that I feel like there was a humility that got instilled in us, directly from Terry. The human part of the humility and the impoverished-ness seeped in, in like a rigorous academic way from Terry and from the environments we were working in. I made some graphic tissue art. I had a series of tissues. And I printed out lines to a poem on each of them. I had written each line and crumpled them up. I called it "Cumrag Millionaire."

SCHOOL'S OUT

KRISTI HARGROVE: We didn't get accredited maybe until 2000. Around 2004, 2005, 2006—somewhere in there—Mel Ziegler and Terry Thacker and Carlton Wilkinson over at TSU were in this research about starting an MFA program in Nashville. If we figure out this triad could we make something happen with a master's? Trying to have that many voices was tough. We did a ton of work, a ton of data gathering for a couple of years, and then it just kind of fizzled. But, we continued to talk about a master's program, and in 2014 or 2015 we decided, "You know, let's do it. We're the independent art college. We're the institution that can move things through, right? What if we can build this thing?" I had been through a low-res program. Jodi Hays had been through the same one. Barbie Yontz had been through it. Patrick DeGuira had been through it. There were like ten of us here who'd been through the low-res program at Vermont College. We knew what worked about that program and what didn't work about that program. So we just brainstormed and we did a shit ton of research. It's a huge amount of work. We went through it all and we got accredited in 2016 while we were still at independent Watkins. We had our first incoming class in 2017. We do a twenty-three-day residency in the summer, and then we come in winter and we do a four-day intensive over the MLK holiday.

ARMON MEANS: This was that time period where you saw Watkins build out all the dorms and like really dump this money into this huge campus redevelopment. That was at the same time period that like Memphis College of Art has started to shut down. So I don't know if there was this thought that they could draw those students, and like they were going to be the Tennessee art school and this kind of home for artists from the Southeast? I just don't think that ever happened because of poor recruiting. I think that really hurt them, and I think they took such a huge financial hit there that I don't know if there was that chance to recover. I think that made them vulnerable for that buyout.

JOE NOLAN: In January 2020 it was announced that Belmont University was absorbing Watkins as part of a real estate deal for the school's Metrocenter property. When the First Saturday Art Crawl events opened in February, Watkins students held a protest. They rented a moving van, covered it in signage, and parked it outside The Packing Plant in the middle of the Wedgewood-Houston art happenings. They hung an exhibition inside of the van that included a video installation of a compilation of news clips about the Belmont-Watkins merger. The interior walls of the vehicle were plastered with photographs of life at Watkins and slogans aimed at Watkins president J. Kline: "Don't consult faculty and staff; hire outside consultants." "Fake cry when confronted with your failures."

ARMON MEANS: I want to say it wasn't until I think 2021 that Belmont officially took over. So when I came back we were still fully at Watkins for those first two years, but I think you could kind of see the writing on the wall at that point. The grad program was really starting to get some legs under it and having its first crop of students come through, but there were always concerns about what was going to happen next, and what we were going to be able to do or not going to be able to do, financially. You could already see those things kind of starting to boil over. The thing that you noticed the most was just the shift in the antic- ipated enrollment versus like the actual enrollment, and how the school was handling recruiting and trying to rectify those things. It was just this complete fail and it got to the point where there was no saving it. And I think probably some of the people who are at Watkins proba- bly saw it coming way before the rest of us did. When I came back at Belmont and at Watkins teaching adjunct it was strange to be the one person who was on both sides of the coin. That was weird. And a lot of it was because I knew the changes that had happened at Belmont since I was there originally in 2004. I had been there like right after the Southern Baptist split happened and when the push to open up Belmont's recruitment happened and when they really began thinking more about how to be a diverse university and not just a traditional conservative Christian institution. So I had seen a lot of the changes in that program and realized that the art program was not this place that people should be scared of. Like it wasn't this big bad wolf that people were making it out to be. But I also knew that Watkins was this gem that needed to be handled in a very specific way because those students felt like they had such a home there.

KRISTI HARGROVE: I have found Nashville to be more cooperative than competitive in the arts. And so when I think about Watkins and this sort of reaching into a community where all these little things are pop- ping up, I think it's because of that. It's because there's support, not competition. Maybe it's just a perfect storm of people who kind of got their teaching feet under them at that place because it was also a place that didn't pay well. And so a lot of times people came and only stayed a few years, but when we talk they say "Those were some of my most fond memories of teaching." There was freedom to sort of explore in a syllabus, freedom to create a class. And freedom to say, "Hey, we need a space downtown. What if we go to The Arcade? Let's go get a space at The Arcade." There were just people who were eager and excited to extend not only what they wanted to do personally and professionally and you know, creatively, but they found a way to do that through the classroom too. In a city where a lot of the creative people can intermingle we had guest critiques all the time for juniors and seniors. So we're always bringing in people from the community. It's like there's a noncompetitive thing. Even with Austin Peay, their faculty would come to Watkins and critique, or people from MTSU would come or Vanderbilt would come. To me that was the magic charm: it was community, not competitive.

ARMON MEANS: It's strange in that you can now see where there's a legitimate foothold for the arts in the city. You don't feel like there's a tenuous thread that it's hanging on by anymore. Now it's like staked into the ground. But at the same time, it's unfortunate there aren't as many opportunities anymore for students to create their own thing or for emerging artists in the city to find a place to kind of do those pop-up shows and some of those things that they did in the past. Those spaces are in such high demand now. I think that's the biggest shift.

KRISTI HARGROVE: I was at Watkins when the big tornado came through. I had just parked in the garage on 6th and I literally stood in the garage and watched it come by. I guess that was 1998. I mean, there's been so many. I feel like there's one every two or three years now.

Print City

1848-2019

THE ROOTS OF NASHVILLE'S VISUAL CULTURE can be found in the printing industry of the nineteenth century when the city's music business legacy began with sheet music publishing. Nashville's print artists are a unique community that connects the city's earliest visual practices to its contemporary art renaissance. Nashville is one of the top letterpress printing centers in the nation. Here you find printing in museums and galleries as well as on kickass band posters. Art hierarchies and boundaries between various genres and forms have dissolved in the postmodern age. And Nashville's printmakers have lead the city's creative scene through those changes, erasing the divisions between art and craft, and demonstrating how a visual language from the city's past can speak in a new way to its future.

JIM SHERRADEN: It started in 1848—there's a historic landmark that's still downtown. A gospel hymn book titled "The Western Harmony" was the very first sheet music published in Nashville. So Nashville was really well known for its sheet music. And there is this incredible statistic: Nashville's within 500 miles of nearly 80 percent of the entire United States population. So it's regionally very, very practical. I think that's why the Confederacy wanted to get the city back during the Civil War. I've always said in a thousand Hatch Show Print talks, I think where Nashville sits logistically in the continental United States is why Hatch survived. If you're playing Little Rock on your way to Cincinnati, whether you're Bessie Smith or the Beach Boys, you're going to play Nashville. So you always needed posters. And I think that was true regionally for the sheet music.

BRYCE MCCLOUD: My uncle was a historian of industrial technology for the Tennessee State Museum. What that really meant was printing—that's what he focused on. So as a teenager and in college, I was sort of watching over his shoulder as he was running around Nashville—and the region—collecting equipment and stories from these old timers. Nashville was an industrial printing center from the 1800s.

JIM SHERRADEN: The sheet music was published here and then the microphone and the radio is invented. Where are you going to put these stations? Well, put them where the sheet music is. And then the studios start. Where are you going to put the studios? How about the same city as the radio stations, and the microphones, and the sheet music? And next thing you know, you've got a hell of a music industry here in Nashville. And as you know, the Grand Ole Opry was one of many radio shows, but it had that extra power, that clear-channel—it was the gold standard and that's why Hank Williams wanted to get on it.

BRYCE MCCLOUD: I was born in Nashville, raised in Hendersonville. That's important because the suburbs to me were like a cultural desert. There wasn't anything except the library—and this was pre-internet—so you could only explore through National Geographic. There weren't working artists around me that I knew of. I really thought that there were three jobs available to artists: You could be a cartoonist, like a political cartoonist for the *Tennessean*, or—if you got lucky—*The New York Times*. We didn't subscribe to *The New York Times*. You could be an airbrush artist at the mall. Or you could work as a caricature artist at Opryland. Those seemed to be the three careers where one might have a creative outlet. I just didn't even understand what the art world was. So that's where I started.

JIM SHERRADEN: I remember picking up the Grand Ole Opry on WSM in Kansas. I grew up in Kansas. I was a wrestler that wrote poetry. And when I heard "Bennie and the Jets" for the first time in 1974—it's one of those childhood moments—I looked up Elton John and saw that he had a lyric writer and I thought that's what I wanted to do. I went to college out in Western Kansas because they were one of two schools that offered a four-year wrestling program. And Waylon Jennings was playing a show. I remember thinking he had a weird voice because I grew up on my parents playing Barry Manilow and The Carpenters in a ranch style, middle-class house, going to church three times a week. Anyhow, Waylon's playing and he has to go through the wrestling room to get to the stage. So I followed them after the show to the Holiday Inn where they were staying. And I gave my lyrics to the lead guitarist, Gordon Payne, who called me from Austin three days later and said, "You're not a bad writer. If you ever want to move to Nashville, look us up." I left the phone hanging in the air like a cartoon character. My parents drove me down. We went over to Waylon's office there on 16th. Hazel Smith was there. Captain Midnight was in there. Tompall [Glaser] was in there. And I moved to Nashville to start my terrible career as a waiter of tables at Pizza Huts. But Waylon's office was always a base. And then I got hired to be the gopher for Audie Ashworth and J. J. Cale. I went back to college in Kansas. In eight months I had outgrown all of my friends, you know, living in the big city. They were like frozen in place. I moved back to Nashville. I got hired at Waylon's. What an adventure, 1978 and 1979. I was a trusted kid because I had good work ethics and I did not do cocaine—which was a huge asset back then. My Dutch girlfriend and I moved to the Netherlands, and I learned Dutch. Waylon called me twice over there to check in on me, gave me a Guild guitar as a thank you gift. But when we got back to Nashville, my girlfriend was going to school at MTSU and I thought if I was going to stay in my family I needed to get back to college. Education was highly, highly treasured in my family and my dad was the first in his generation to go to college and so I went. I went to college carpooling with perfect strangers. I asked one of them what subject was easy? He said he was in printmaking. That seemed pretty simple. And I fell in love with printmaking. I got an English degree but I did this rinky-dink show at Midtown Cafe. A Vanderbilt University art teacher saw this show and said I had to see this dying old show poster print shop in downtown Nashville before it goes out of business. And that was Hatch. So I asked to run the place—it was being poorly managed. And in the meantime, I was still writing for a Scandinavian band that was being recorded over at Audie and Cale's place. We won two Scandinavian Grammys and that was great for a writer. Robert Keen was my roommate. He and his wife ran Hatch while I went back over to Europe to write more. And when I came back, the shop had been sold. I was penniless. I was living on a $452 income tax check when the new owners at the Country Music Hall of Fame call me to come back to Hatch as a curator. So I started printmaking. I started putting all of my time into Hatch and making art through the print shop.

BRYCE MCCLOUD: Letterpress printing overlaps fine art and commercial printing. You could either print parking tickets or fine art prints. There's these folks who have and run this equipment, they're real masters of the technique. Printmaking is an interesting craft because it's part art and a lot of technical skill. People kind of skew one direction or the other, and, usually, it's just the smaller subset of people who are interested in doing technical things as artists. When I got into printmaking in college, I just remember having this really distinct feeling of going to the Southern Graphics Association and the men and women that were teaching me, it seems like they'd all come out of like the Tamarind Institute—that school out West. And printmaking for the generation previous to them was a very technical pursuit. It was about fidelity and making a perfect edition and really being in control of the tools. My professors were taught by this very strict drill sergeant team. Printmaking—whether it was relief or intaglio or litho—this is all fine art printing, but it was still reproduction. It was almost as if a painter would come in and make a beautiful image and the printmakers would then reproduce them with high fidelity. My teachers were taught that way, but I think they were like baby boomer rebels against the authority who were open to other things, but they were still kind of locked into that mindset.

JIM SHERRADEN: In the 1950s here comes offset printing. It doesn't hurt Hatch because everybody needs a poster. In the 1950s and 1960s, Hatch is still very busy. The 1970s is when the shop first started failing because Hatch was in competition for advertising dollars with primarily FM radio, and the country music stations start blowing up. I don't know exactly what those numbers were, but in five years I think the poster jobs went down two thirds. It was all but closing in the late 1970s. I get in there and start trying to resurrect this thing because I was as interested in the history of the shop and its influence on Southern culture and the entertainment industry as I was in the printmaking. So I started at Hatch's fourth location, which was directly behind the Ryman Auditorium. Everything up and down Deadrick there by the capital, it was all printing, all printing supplies. There was no white flight yet to the suburbs. Everything was printing downtown. And after I got off the print floor at Hatch, after thirty-four years, I got to go upstairs and do the archives for two years to literally go through piece of paper by piece of paper, all these boxes that we protected for all of these decades. And it became so clear to me: Hatch probably only has one out of every ten or fifteen blocks ever carved there, as large as that archive is. And all the supplies that Hatch needed, everything they wanted, was downtown. Even the horse glue for the bill posters, the brushes for the bill posters. All the paper companies were downtown.

BRYCE MCCLEOD: And that's kind of my memory of downtown. Printer's Alley was a real thing, and it used to extend over into the neighborhood where my shop is across Lafayette. So you just have this whole world of like old print shops and printing, and businesses that were ancillary and supported printing. When I moved into town, my first shop was surrounded. I could walk a hundred yards and get to a commercial paper supplier, a place that manufactured ink, a place that would make metal plates for printing. Down the street there was a place that did photo stuff for mostly silk screen, they would make films and negatives. And then right across the street from me was Griffin Art Supply, which turned into Plaza. Not to mention the hardware store, the rubber tubing place, motor repair, sheet metal. Yeah. I bring it up because if you wanted to be a printmaker, it was kind of like Nirvana. But, because that's how I started off, I didn't even know how amazing that situation was. Everything was literally here. Not to mention Hatch Show Print. When I moved in, it was like starting to fade. The commercial print places were still there and the buildings were there. But you could see the tail end of this golden era of commercial printing in downtown Nashville. Hatch Show Print was a very specific thing and it had a siren call to a lot of us, but that basic technology was echoed in a bunch of these print shops. Through the early 2000s, they all had letterpress equipment in them. And they had people who ran them and their dads probably taught them how to run those pieces of equipment. Nashville is unique in that regard, because the stuff was literally just laying around.

JOE NOLAN: Hatch Show Print moved to Broadway in 1991 and I moved here in 1992. I had lots of posters made there before I realized it was a breeding ground for all of this printmaking culture in Nashville and in Tennessee—all over the region. So many of the artists making prints in Nashville today have interned or worked the floor at Hatch. It's a rite of passage.

BRYCE MCCLOUD: I just remember, in the '90s, even before Hatch Show Print posters were ubiquitous, even when people were designing photocopy posters to put up for a show, they used the Hatch format. I just think it was in the air. And moving back here when I was fishing around trying to figure out how I was going to make a living while I was trying to do this public stuff, I thought that I could always make rock and roll posters. That would only make sense in Nashville because there was this readymade example: Hatch does it. I can too. And my uncle had encouraged me to go get a job at Hatch when he was still alive. I laugh at the experience because I was kind of shy and Nashville seemed like the big city to me—which is pretty laughable even back then. But I remember going in and it was probably somebody that I ended up working with, and I didn't know how to get a job. I just remember going up to the first person who came to the door, which would've been like a twenty-two-year-old or eighteen-year-old kid. I said, "Are you guys hiring?" or "Can I have a job" or something like that. They probably said no, and I didn't ask any other questions. I just like left. Fast forward a few years and I had this plan to gather my uncle's equipment into a shop, and I didn't know what to do. So I decided to go back to Hatch Show Print again. And maybe I had a little more chutzpah. I don't know how, but somehow I got past the front desk and talked to Jim, and he wanted to get together. Our first meeting was at Hooter's on First Avenue with his wife, but I don't think they were married at the time. Jim was like, just wonderful. And we had a conversation. He thought that I was trying to get rid of the stuff and I was explaining that I was trying to do this shop. And he told me to stop by the shop and hang out. I had just started a job at the Hard Rock Cafe, which is right down the street from Hatch. I was living out in Hendersonville with my folks and came into town for the day. I would work at the Hard Rock at night. But I would drive in early and park on Broadway, which is impossible now. And I would go just pester, just stand around Hatch and see what they were doing. So I'd been around it and I'd seen my uncle do it, but I didn't have any direct experience with it. I'd done relief, like wood cuts and lino cuts, but it's a slightly different thing to run a letterpress than to do those things. I needed to figure that out.

JOE NOLAN: There were lots of posters everywhere and I remember racks and bins where you could just buy a cool poster you liked. I was usually stopping in to order posters for my own shows or to pick up. That place smelled amazing—all that old wood and ink. The printing was happening in its own space, but in full view. You were immersed. There were always musicians coming and going and you'd always run into somebody and shoot the shit about your next gig or a new band or whatever. You'd tell them the info you needed on the poster and they'd fill in your design to fit your show. I did a lot of singer-songwriter gigs at this place called Jamaica and we were always throwing in this palm tree print block.

BRYCE MCCLEOD: I don't think Jim expected me to start showing up every day. But I did, and I didn't have any purpose. So I would just stand around and like start telling jokes and shoot the shit with the other kids that were like the same age as me and distracting them from their work. I was just excited to be there, and finally Jim's like "Well if you're gonna be here, why don't you like sweep or something?" I would start sweeping and then I started putting the type away or whatever. Whatever they didn't want to do I would do it. And I was picking up stuff and after a few months of that, it became "Why don't you start making posters?" And then, after a while, it became "Well, you're working here. Why don't we start paying you?" It all plays back into my inability to actually know how to get a job. It worked out because at that time, that place was impossible to get a job at. I became the person on the other side of the counter and all day long people would come in, "Can I work here?" And we say, "No." What really needed to happen is you needed to grow up in Cheatham County. The Country Music Hall of Fame had bought Hatch. And the folks that I worked with, most of them started off in the gift shop at the Hall of Fame. The folks who eventually became my friends and peers and buddies—brothers in printing—they had started off as like clerks at the Hall of Fame selling t-shirts and magnets to tourists. And because there was that connection, they could move over to Hatch. And so these were kids that were all from Cheatham County. Hatch was the Normandy beachhead of the Cheatham County invasion. When I moved back to Nashville, I thought everybody was from Cheatham County, because when I got in at Hatch everybody was from Cheatham County. I don't think anybody had gone to college. Nobody was technically trained or like went to art school. They had just picked it up as a skill, but there was a lot of care and devotion. We were all learning this craft together, kind of like in a really old way. It was like becoming a tradesman, if that makes sense. Like an on-the-job apprenticeship. That's important because it wasn't like a steady stream of RISD graduates.

MARK HOSFORD: A lot of the print scene was based, obviously, in Hatch and the residue of Hatch. It was mostly artists that were here because of Hatch or artists that stayed around post-Hatch. A lot of them got their chops working there and then did their own thing. So it's an interesting city because we have multiple universities, so there's an inherent number of people that do the same thing because of different universities. So someone might be able to teach at Belmont versus Watkins versus Vanderbilt. You've even got MTSU and Austin Peay. TSU and Fisk. There's not just one school in town that's got one printmaker, and then that's it. So there's enough positions that there can be a little bit of an academic scene. But then you have just massive amounts of printmakers that came through Hatch in the music scene doing poster work. Bryce McCloud is the first printmaker I knew well.

BRYCE MCCLOUD: I feel like Jim became kind of my older brother in this craft. A different sort of person could have seen me as like the young upstart competition. He had the opportunity to run me out of town. I'm pretty persistent. I don't know if it would've worked. But instead he gave me a place, a safe harbor through Hatch. He introduced me to the art scene of Nashville. Just a zillion cool people were coming through Hatch all the time back then. It was like a beacon for people who were interested in letterpress and posters and printmaking. I credit that time with really expanding my universe and taking me from the theoretical of art school to the practical understanding of making a living as an artist. My community really began there.

JIM SHERRADEN: We moved to our current location in 2013. Celene's been running it for ten years. Thank God.

CELENE AUBRY: I was living in Chicago and hand-cutting stamps out of erasers and things like that—doing hand registration, making cards. I was doing a lot of mail art. It was an excuse to create something that I could send out to friends and family and people that I felt needed a weird card in the mail or something like that. And I was talking to a graphic designer and he said, "You know, there's a slightly faster way of doing that. It's called letterpress printing." I looked into it and found the Columbia College of Chicago Center for Book and Paper Arts. I met Jim Sherraden and Brad Vetter at a workshop that was hosted by Columbia College in 2000. I fell in love with wood type and Columbia College had a pretty spectacular collection of wood type. And so I loved the literal practice applications, but also the figures and the texture and all that. So when I took the workshop with them I couldn't believe that there was a place in the world that still existed where you could actually earn a living, working with wood type and mixing ink and making posters or whatever customers wanted. I'd see Jim or Brad or somebody from the shop, you know, once or twice a year and we'd catch up. And one year Jim mentioned that the shop was going to be moving and it was going to be expanding. And I said, "If you need help with that, let me know." I moved down here in June of 2012, and started working in the shop on July 2nd. I learned everything from front to back, bottom to top. I worked the retail side, made tons of posters. Worked with Dan, who was our like eighty-something-year-old, cranky press operator who worked on the big press in the back. And then we packed the shop and moved it to the Country Music Hall of Fame. And when we opened shop here, Jim transitioned into his master printer role so he could focus on that. And I took over running the shop.

JOE NOLAN: Now that Hatch is operating out of the Country Music Hall of Fame, it feels so elevated and ensconced compared to their scruffy little shop on Broadway. When I first came to Nashville part of what made the Hatch prints so desirable was that they felt like they were about to disappear for good.

BRYCE MCCLOUD: When I got out of college, my uncle had recently and unfortunately passed away young, and he had been collecting equipment for the State Museum, but those places were going out of business so quickly and it was a huge volume of stuff, and there's just only so much budget or need for or space at the state museum. But once you love this stuff, if you don't rescue it, it's gonna go on the scrap heap. He was just dragging this stuff home. And I remember helping him push type cabinets into their kitchen—it was just everywhere. Kinko's didn't exist in 1950. What would you do if you wanted your church pamphlet printed and you didn't want to go to a big commercial joint? A lot of the guys who worked for these large commercial printing houses would have a small press in their garage or their basement. They would fill that role and have a little side hustle. But around the 1990s that generation of people were getting old and dying. So there were all these families that were kind of going through the same thing that my family was going through. There was this beautiful and wondrous equipment that weighed like thirty tons sitting around the couch. What do you do with it? That's how my story was transformed. I got out of college with a sculpture degree, scratching my head, wondering what in the world I was supposed to do next. I moved back to Nashville and the family made the decision that I would take over that stuff, which meant I had to find a shop—like a place to work and that's what I did. I just found like a semi-abandoned upstairs of a warehouse to rent. It wasn't a plan on my part, but I landed smack in the middle of the former heart of the printing industry of Nashville. I got into doing rock 'n' roll posters for a long time. Honestly, anything that anybody would pay me to do that involved letterpress printing. But in the back of my mind, I was always working on this public street art, and trying to work out how to do all of these different things at once.

MARK HOSFORD: I would go to Hatch all the time and that's when the Gill sisters were there. There were three different Gill sisters that all kind of ran the show for a while. Back then you just drove down and parked right in front of Hatch because during the week no one was downtown. You could just park anywhere down on the strip. It was easy.

BRYCE MCCLOUD: My uncle had taken copious notes as a historian. So he was kind of like sitting there with me, on my shoulder as I was reading his notes and then I would go to Hatch. And at that time there was an old fella who was kind of the master printer named Kenneth Hinson. He taught Jim and he taught us all. He worked at Hatch for I don't know how long, like fifty years. When I was there, he was more or less retired, but I would go and sit with him at his house in East Nashville. He had a printing press next to his bed and we would just talk about stuff. So that's how I was learning through trial and error, and through my friends from Ashland City, and from Jim and my uncle and Kenneth Hinson. And then of course I had these technical skills from Oscar Gillespie, my professor at Bradley University in Peoria who taught me my background of relief printing and litho and etching.

JOE NOLAN: Bryce has this education and this family tradition of print-making. He was always entrepreneurial but he also has this street/ community art thing happening. When I lived in the Belmont neighborhood I went to a gallery show that included some of Bryce's stuff. This was a *fine art* display: mats and frames and track lighting and box wine—very fancy. I was working as a framer and art installer with Gene Sizemore at Museum Support Services, downtown at Cummins Station. I'd always drive in on Franklin Pike. The Monday after seeing this show I'm driving under the bridge at Division Street and there are all of these wheat-pasted posters of these figures that are obviously Bryce's designs on all the columns. It's like there's a whole group of people hanging out under the bridge. They hadn't been there the previous week. So over the weekend he'd opened a luxe gallery exhibition and also snuck out in the middle of the night to poster bomb this bridge in time to shake people up on the Monday morning commute. He never really separates his fine art / street art / retail design work / community art. It's all just one big thing for him.

BRYCE MCCLOUD: I think art, of course, exists in everybody's life and is such a powerful force in how we define ourselves and think about the world and discover new things both internally and externally that I wanted the people around me to feel that same way that I did. I've always felt that—for whatever reason—our culture makes art feel like something that is closed-off from a big group of people. So I always had this desire to break out of that pattern of pursuing a gallery career with the aim of getting in museums. I really wanted to put my art where regular old folks hang out. That's not to disparage museums and galleries—I love that realm. But I just felt like I could be a bridge between those two worlds. I started at the same time that people like Shepard Fairey were starting to do their thing and street art was becoming a thing. Years later I watched *Exit Through the Gift Shop* and I remember thinking I had gone totally the other direction. They were all photocopying stuff, and they really prioritized being out on the street and wheatpasting stuff up. I'd gone and learned this whole weird ancient craft of letterpress just to produce the images, and then trying to also get it out on the street. And so I was putting like 90 percent of the effort into making the thing and then 10 percent of the effort getting it out. It was generally the same thing, but the approach was exactly the opposite. And so early on, the idea of street art and public art really appealed to me as this do-it-yourself way to open people's eyes to the magic. I was doing public sculpture, but with printmaking you could disseminate. I remember dragging a one ton sculpture home from college one year and it's a real hassle. But prints—like a hundred prints—can be rolled up in tubes and you can send them everywhere, like all over the universe. I realized it could be the same thing. This is public art, but instead of writ large, sitting in a city center, it's posted all over and it's in people's houses and it's on some street corners. It occurred to me that there was this wonderful opportunity with the multiple prints to reach many more people a lot more efficiently.

MARK HOSFORD: Historically there were two kinds of printmakers: You have people that are printmakers that learn the medium to make work themselves. Then you have ones that become master printers to start a shop that prints for known artists of the day. Even back then it created this weird duality of printmaking done for the sake of the craft and printmakers as artists who used the techniques in order to expand their practice of what print could do. But it's weird because the artists who were artists first, who didn't start as printmakers, didn't suffer from that, right? No one looked at a Rauschenberg's screen printing and said, "Well, that's based in craft, not fine art," right? It's a weird world in that way.

BRYCE MCCLEOD: I feel like the generation that I'm part of saw print-making as a really interesting way to make marks. The images that you could get out of a print were so different than a painting or drawing, and that was really appealing. I know the thing that really pulled me in was just the idea of multiplicity. Instead of having one painting or one sculpture, you could have a hundred of something. That just blew me away as a concept. So I feel like the reasons that we used the tools were changing over time. Of course, we also grew up in that era where mechanical reproduction started coming through computers and pho-tocopies and so just getting something made was less daunting. When there was a really fast, cheap offset printing press that could print park-ing tickets, letterpress no longer had to serve that function. And so we could daydream and have more flights of fancy. The renaissance of letterpress has been based in some part around the prevalence of automated and quick printing. In one way it killed the industry, but in another way it freed it to be a means of artistic expression.

JOE NOLAN: In the 1990s and early 2000s, during the initial Untitled era, the Fugitive era, we were always trying to define what we meant by "contemporary art." First of all, we had to differentiate the art scene from the music scene and get out of its shadow. But some of us were super strict about it all. We saw printmaking as a craft connected to the music scene. We saw it as something that was in the way of the contemporary art we were trying to encourage then. I think we had good intentions, but we were off. In the end the creative printmakers in town helped to lead the contemporary art charge. They were always a part of that movement, and maybe even a few steps ahead. Print is high and low and fine art and craft and pop all at the same time. And the more familiar aspects of that work helped to draw new people into the art scene in a way that video installations or formalist painting never could.

CELENE AUBRY: This is fascinating. This is an ongoing conversation because Southern Graphics Council —one of the largest organiza-tions that gathers printmakers—is finally coming around to the idea where somebody who is a letterpress printer can be considered a fine art printmaker, which I think is great. That to me is just very rela-tively recent. What's craft and what's art, and all of that question—I'm fascinated by it. I think one of the things that is interesting to me is regionalism and how that feeds into art and what is considered art. I think there's a lot of crafts. A lot of people dub things Southern crafts whether it's fabric art, quilt making, or making instruments by hand. Whether it's for domestic purposes, bowls that you use in your kitchen or woodworking or things like that. The further we get from everybody having time and access to the tools and materials to make things with their hands, the further we get into the digital and technology, and everybody's using screens and pounding their fingers on pieces of glass all day long, the more afraid they are of working with their hands. When we work with the public, it's fascinating to see how fearful people are of trying something with their hands because nobody works with their hands anymore. I think everything that is handmade becomes that much more rare, and then it becomes, not just craft, then it becomes an art form because we're losing all of the connections to our past, and to our history, and to the beauty that fed into making a beautiful Gee's Bend quilt, for instance. We're losing that the further we get away from it. Redefining what is art and what is beauty is an ongoing thing. And I think the further we get into ways of working so directly and heavily with your hands, and even your body, I think that makes things that were once just strictly craft or process more interesting and more rarefied.

BRYCE MCCLOUD: I don't know if this is just like kids being kids, but when I was in college, painting and sculpture were like "real art" and printmaking was not. And I feel like a lot of people like me wanted to root for the underdog. So we sort of took up the mantle of this thing and I loved it. It was the place where folks without raging egos went to just make art. Maybe that's too much? I just feel like in Nashville there was room for people to innovate and do new things because it felt like there was such a spotlight on the fine arts, and no one was paying attention to what we were doing over in the corner. So we were able to move without drawing attention. There just wasn't that pressure. It felt punk rock, and I think that's part of why people got into doing it. I started doing letterpress because I saw this *Star Wars* saga where all the Yodas had disappeared and there was no one practicing The Force. My uncle had died, and it felt like if I didn't do this stuff it would just trail off into eternity. It'll be just like the wagon wheel sitting outside of a Cracker Barrel. My impetus to do it was preservation of the skill and the craft. When I started doing this, it was sort of considered a lesser art form and a craft or a trade skill. The cost of entry was just right: Come and get it! A lot of my equipment came from places that were closing down and some of it came from universities that were making way for computer labs, which I was just laughing about as I would haul away their stuff. Now the circle has turned again, and all those places want letterpress equipment again, and they're buying, and they have university budgets. So they've jacked up the price of all this equipment that they gave away to people like me for free twenty-five years ago. Folks like myself and Jim, and a hundred of my other friends who are doing this same sort of work have elevated it. When I started, no one wanted it. To get someone to pay a hundred bucks for a run of posters was like magic. I was literally competing with Kinko's. All the things that I did to make a poster had zero impact on the value of the thing. Whereas now you can charge a premium for that, because people realize what it is now.

CELENE AUBRY: One of the great things about it is you're working here in the shop with seven other fellow creative people, you're not toiling away alone. We're all sort of pushing toward one goal and we all have different ways we'd solve a problem. We all bounce ideas off each other. It's kind of nice.

BRYCE MCCLOUD: People have gone out their way to help me and I would do the same for other people. I don't know why that is true of Nashville, if it was like a reflection of the collaboration of the music scene or if it's just Southern hospitality. But I feel like that has attracted all these people. It was the confluence of location, opportunity cost, and the way everything works. I can't explain it. It's just like magic. And I'm so glad that I happened to dumbly be from here.

MARK HOSFORD: In other cities there was the kind of idea of "Who's on top? Who's getting the best gallery spot?" There was a kind of cutthroat nature of getting the sales. The bad thing in Nashville was that there weren't a lot of sales. There was not a lot of people buying. And that's what kind of saved us in a way. We didn't have the big shots and the little ones that are trying to like get all the money from the big art collectors. Everyone was just kind of finding their own way at the same level. Everyone wanted to know everybody and everyone wanted to help everybody. Everyone just wanted to honestly enjoy everyone else's art and to make sure that everyone could be incorporated and could continue to grow the scene collectively.

BRYCE MCCLOUD: If I would've gone to New York City, I would've just been another, like drop in the bucket. New York isn't a place that needed me to do anything for it to continue to thrive as a city. But I felt like in Nashville, I felt like I could make a difference. Like it was small enough or like the need was apparent. There was already opportunity to do something. I could do work here that would be meaningful and directly impactful to the community, like immediately. So I decided to stay and do my thing here.

M KELLEY: I was at Western Kentucky University. When I was getting out of school, I was thinking about where I wanted to be. Because I'm a huge nerd, I did a comprehensive breakdown of all the cities within about a five-hour radius. I was looking at Louisville, I was looking at Lexington, I was looking at Cincinnati, I was looking at St. Louis. I was looking at Atlanta and looked at Nashville. I did this huge breakdown of like what all the cost of living was. What all the job market was. What the art scene was like? How much of it was institutions? How much of it was on the ground? And then, with all that detail and all that information and like everything I could get my hands on, I did a huge forecast to see where I thought the city would be in about ten years. So I took that and I did the preliminary rankings. And then I started blindly reaching out to people in cities, just to see if I could talk to people about what their journey had been like, what their experience was, how they liked their neighborhoods. I called some places, I never got answers back. I called some places, people were too busy. Every place I talked to in Nashville, even if they were too busy, they would say, "Oh, maybe you should talk to so-and-so." Or they would say, "Well, I could answer some quick questions over the phone." And it just felt like people were genuinely interested in connecting. It looked really good on paper in terms of my forecast. I could have never anticipated stuff like the TV show *Nashville*. That totally skewed my numbers. Something I found across the board is that people were very communicative. They were happy to talk to you. They were excited about what they were doing. Even if it was something small—a weird pop-up somewhere. People were really enthusiastic. And they were genuinely welcoming. Nashville just kind of ended up coming up on top. That's how I ended up in Nashville.

LESLEY PATTERSON-MARX: Platetone started when a lot of my students, once I was at Watkins long enough for people to start graduating, they were wondering, "Where are we going to print?" And Leanne Hawkins and Patricia Jordan pooled their resources and bought a press. And then several of us chipped-in some money and rented a space at the May Hosiery building, but back then everybody just called it the

Chestnut building because it was the building on Chestnut Street. So we had a little space in there right across the hall from Adrienne Outlaw. We had a show in that space and it was really a great little place for people to work once they graduated.

M KELLEY: I guess Platetone started around like 2004 with Jaime Raybin and Patricia Jordan and Lesley Patterson-Marx. It was the three of them basically deciding, "We need to buy a press." Printmaking presses are prohibitively expensive for someone who's just coming out of college. They were all going to buy a press together and then just book time to use it. Then it just snowballed from there. And they ended up getting spaces and by the time I caught up with them at Charlotte, they had maybe three locations because they just got more members and they needed an actual place as opposed to, "Here's the key to my back door, even though I don't know you."

JOE NOLAN: The art printmaking scene in Nashville has these deep roots in industrial printing and in music publishing. But that community grew and evolved for all the same reasons that the so-called fine art scene grew and evolved: artists need spaces to work in and communities to interact with and learn from.

M KELLEY: I came down to Nashville and I moved into a fairly small apartment. I did a lot of mail art at the time because I wanted to make art, but I didn't have anywhere to keep art. One thing they don't tell you in college is that in order to actually make art as an artist, you have to move the art out of your house so you can have space to make more art. I was also doing that thing where I was just talking to anybody I could: people in the line at the coffee shop; strangers in the supermarket; just trying to get a conversation started and just getting to know people. I ended up having conversations with folks that eventually led to a space at Open Lot in East Nashville. I needed space to work. Real estate in Nashville was more affordable then, but for any kind of space you were typically going in with a group of people. Those early conversations were around 2009. I was sharing the studio with my partner at the time, Steven Zerne. I was the painting and printmaking tech in college, so I ran those studios and I took a fair amount of printmaking classes also. I was making some work, but it was all like mostly block print and it was all like printing-by-hand kind of thing. I have distinct memories of me and Steven with a really big linoleum cut, we were stepping on it trying to make sure we were getting as much even pressure as possible. Open Lot was good times / bad times. In the end the whole thing kind of imploded around 2011, which is what tends to happen when you don't have clear guidelines about money. I think one of the most important things I got out of that was you learn really what not to do as an organization and how to better have transparency among all the people involved. It really affected the spaces that I would go on to work with later. There was a very strong emphasis on transparency. A very strong emphasis on making sure agreements were written down. No matter how well intentioned I think people can be coming into something, there's a certain amount of fame and power and money that can turn even the best intentions into giant cluster fucks.

LESLEY PATTERSON-MARX: We lived on Montrose Avenue in the 12th Avenue South neighborhood, and there was this little pink building that used to be a grocery store. And it came up for rent and the rent was super reasonable and it was bigger than the space we had. This was after I married Jonathan and Abraham was a baby, and it was a couple blocks away from my house. And so I talked everybody into moving over there and I had a studio space there. The other half was a practice space that we rented out to Lambchop for awhile. So they were practicing amidst all this printmaking equipment. My friend Colleen McCormick rented a little spot there. So did Sue Mulcahy and Carol Mode—we just needed a little extra money to afford it, and so we always had somebody else and myself renting it.

M KELLEY: When everything kind of imploded with Open Lot, I was working strictly out of my house for a while. I was very disillusioned by the experience that we'd had there. Then Steven and I started doing more silk screening type work. That's something else I'd been doing since back in college—the world is your oyster when you're young and don't ever need to sleep, apparently. I was burnt out working with other people. Of course we worked on our own for about three months or so and then I was like, "I miss artists." I think I saw something about something about Platetone. They had started doing open houses. So you could come in, you could make something. You could spend some time, you could get to know people. Somebody would lead a demonstration. And I thought, "Well, maybe I'll go check it out." At some point I realized I'd committed myself to leading a demonstration. Before I knew it I was putting in for a membership to be able to work there around other people. I was probably in Platetone's second generation.

LESLEY PATTERSON-MARX: Jenkins Hardin, a local realtor, purchased our building and raised the rent. And so we couldn't afford it. And so we moved over where Thistle Farms is now on Charlotte. We moved into a very small space. We went from this wonderful old grocery store into a tiny, tiny space.

M KELLEY: When Platetone was off Charlotte it was also really convenient to my house, which was great. I didn't have to drive all the way to East Nashville across the river during a Titans game to get to my studio anymore. So while I was still doing some painting at home, having access to the printmaking studio allowed me to really focus in on that. I apologized to my former printmaking professor. I actually didn't like printmaking when I was in school. I liked the medium, I liked the concept, but I hated the traditionalism of it. It was steeped in like, "This is the way to do things." I apologized to my old professor because I do recognize that it was a, "You've got to know the rules before you can break the rules" kind of thing. I wanted to experiment with doing all kinds of weird things. I wasn't worried about my print being archival and lasting till the end of time. I wanted to print something that was transient and fast and an interaction. And that had that aspect of decay and degradation to it. So going off being in a space on my own, without the pressures of grades and midterm critiques, I was able to start addressing some of those conversations. Figuring out what I wanted to say, how I wanted to say it, and seeing how much of it actually was feeling true and necessary to the work I was making. Sometimes you wonder, "Is this actually valid or is this just bullshit?"

LESLEY PATTERSON-MARX: Thistle Farms wanted to take that space over so we moved again. And I think from there, we moved to our best location ever on Fourth Avenue along with Turnip Green Creative Reuse and Recycling. Kaaren Engel was such a huge force in making that location happen for us. We had a little gallery space in our hallway and we hosted the Nashville Print Revival there.

JOE NOLAN: Platetone was sort of similar to the Off the Wall group at Watkins. They weren't explicitly a printing center for women, but it mostly worked out that way. It wasn't really something anybody remarked on. Women have always been a leadership force in Nashville's art scene. It's always been that way since the 1980s.

M KELLEY: When I came in, Kaaren Engel was the president. Patricia Jordan was the secretary. Carrie Cox had been doing a lot of the community engagement. Lesley was still doing stuff with them, though I know she had begun to really focus on her home studio. There were just a handful of other members and people involved. Jaime was doing some stuff, but had not been doing a ton there—a lot of the equipment that was there in the Charlotte space was still hers, I think.

LESLEY PATTERSON-MARX: There were a few guys that came through, but none in leadership. I have this great memory of this one artist—his name was Santana. He was silk screening there and doing some really great prints. And he would just work at all hours. And I took a field trip of University School of Nashville students there, to the Fourth Avenue space. And it was an early morning class and we walked in and there's Santana in his tighty-whities. And the students were, "Oh my God!" And Santana ran out, "I'm so sorry! I've been here all night!"

M KELLEY: I would say the biggest thing I had going for me with the print scene was I was just willing to talk to anybody. I was willing to try just about anything and I really liked connecting people, finding opportunities for them, whether that was figuring out a way to show some of their work or figuring out how to do something to a product or an object. Or teaching them how to do something. As Platetone moved into to a space off Fourth Avenue—over by what is now SoBro— I ended up running the little side office that was in there and having my studio there full time. I just kind of became the person people asked questions. I became the person that people asked if they wanted to tour the building. They could count on me being there, and I really loved teaching people how to do things.

JOE NOLAN: The Open Studio events at Platetone were unique because they felt like an opening reception—people talking, eating cheese and crackers, drinking wine. But they were organized around activities instead of exhibitions. They'd have a facilitator who walked you through making some kind of simple printmaking project. It was a great way to show people what made printmaking different from painting. Folks walked away with a handmade souvenir and a new appreciation for the art. Our regional printmaking and collecting culture didn't spring up over night. It was cultivated and nurtured by places like Platetone, one print at a time.

M KELLEY: I really tried to organize more of the open studios. We ended up doing those monthly. And it wasn't always me teaching everything. Other people had amazing, wonderful things that they do. So a lot of times I was making sure that there were drinks, making sure there was cheese, making sure the doors were locked when everybody was done. We had a traveling bookbinder and papermaker who came through. They had this little tiny house wagon thing where all their studio was.

And they were just traveling from place to place. And so we hosted them and they did one of our open studios and then they got to talk to people about their little traveling studio. That's when the whole conversation around the Print Crawl happened. I think at one point we may have had like ten or twelve shops on the map. It ended up almost being like a whole day event by the end of it. People would go to each of these shops and they would get one part of a poster printed. So they would start a print, they would see a shop, they would get to talk to people—a lot of artists would have stuff for sale, whatever. Then they would go to the next place and get the next piece of the poster printed. The idea being that when you went to all the places you had a finished poster. It was a huge, huge event. We did one around Halloween one time, and I think we had like 500 or 600 people come through the shop. People were there before we opened and it was the kind of thing where at a certain point I was like, "Y'all have to go home." We ended up doing after parties just to give people a place to funnel to. Otherwise, none of us were leaving our shops until like one o'clock in the morning.

LESLEY PATTERSON-MARX: I think every time we had to move, it was a hit—other than that move to the Fourth Avenue space which was very energizing. It was hard to pick ourselves back up every time we moved.

M KELLEY: The space moved to the Fourth Avenue location. And then fairly quickly, Patricia Jordan died. She was the secretary and her death was very sudden, and there were no contingencies in place. Me and my partner Steven, at the time, we had been doing a design firm. We were tech savvy and I got tasked with trying to recover all of our digital assets: the website, all the documents, all those ownership transfers. I ended up becoming stand-in secretary for a couple of months just to make sure all of our stuff was taken care of. It was definitely a wild time.

LESLEY PATTERSON-MARX: And the thing about moving to Fourth Avenue is we had Kaaren Engel and she was a force for good. She put so much energy into growing that organization. She helped us get nonprofit status. She was a former lawyer and she just put her whole heart and soul into growing this. And I think at that point, there was a point when we were up to like twenty-five members and, then she got cancer and passed away. And nobody really wanted to step up and put in that same kind of energy that she did. I certainly didn't. It just hit us hard. We all had a hard time after we lost her.

M KELLEY: Jennifer Knowles was our vice president at the time, and Jennifer ended up stepping into that interim role for a good while. And then Megan Lightell, I think, was the president for a while, and then I was voted in as the president when Megan moved to back to Canada for school. I was the last president.

LESLEY PATTERSON-MARX: I think dealing with the grief of two important people within, I think it was like within three years or something— we just couldn't really recover from that. And I feel like, for myself, I feel like I lost touch with the young folks in Nashville as the community became more spread out. And so we moved over to East Nashville and shared a space with Make Nashville. I can't remember why we decided to move. Maybe it was money again. I don't remember. But then we moved over to Nolensville Road across from InterAsian Market, next to Casa Azafran. I think from there, we were just sputtering along. We just sort of really fizzled out at that point. You know, we were just hanging on by a thread.

M KELLEY: When COVID came through it devastated our membership in a lot of key ways. We had been doing pretty good, but the problem with our membership model was that our dues were how we paid our rent, our bills. And when COVID happened, in addition to putting a lot of artists out of work for the unforeseeable future, we lost a lot of members that way. We also had a lot of members who had health issues, who were older and were being super cautious. And so we tried for a while, like wiping things down between people being there. Booking space between stuff being open. We didn't do any more public events, which had been a big draw for donations, a big draw for sales, a big draw for more members. I have had the distinct displeasure of having to dissolve a nonprofit. We were around for about eighteen years.

LESLEY PATTERSON-MARX: About a year and a half ago we decided to dissolve our nonprofit and Turnip Creative Reuse and Recycling took all of our assets and our supplies. They're going to revive Platetone as a reuse-themed printmaking studio when they move to their new space. A former Platetone member Laura Young and I are going to start teaching printmaking classes with a reuse theme.

M KELLEY: The concepts behind print are pretty fundamental to how I think about artwork. Print is about multiples, print is about the voice of people, and it's produced in a way that does not typically require outside mediation to do. It's very direct. It's the same reason I like indie comics or Xerox copy zines. I like mail art. I like street art. All of these things are speaking without the lens of another institution deciding what is passing through. Print is such an accessible medium because you can do relatively low-cost prints that make it affordable for anybody to be a collector. Art should be meaningful, it should be something that you really care for, that you want to invest in, in the sense that it has importance to you. But, to me, if you pay $30,000 for a painting you don't look at, that's not an investment. Art's something that you should look at and enjoy, and that asks questions or answers them for you every time you look at it, every day you look at it. Sometimes that's as stupid as a little print postcard. It could change their whole life or their whole perspective on something. So, I kind of come back to the accessibility of print, and the ability of print to allow people to speak and connect.

The Arcade Game

1998–2016

IN THE EARLY 2000S, the upper floor of The Arcade in downtown Nashville became a hive of artist studios and artist-lead gallery spaces that helped to pioneer the Downtown Art Crawl. The monthly event found the art scene breaking into a citywide phenomenon beyond its self-contained community. New interest in the visual arts scene brought new faces into these new spaces as well as national news notices mentioning Nashville's art galleries alongside its restaurant boom and perennial music tourism. The Arcade galleries and studios—along with the commercial galleries on Fifth Avenue—solidified downtown as the hub of the city's contemporary art scene in the early 2000s. And the throngs that packed into The Arcade every First Saturday were an elbow-to-elbow testament to the resourcefulness, ambition, creativity and resilience of Nashville's contemporary art renaissance.

JOE NOLAN: Sean Dudley was the first artist I knew of who had a studio in The Arcade. This was way back in the late 1990s. Being an artist in The Arcade back then was like being the first man on the moon. He was a contemplative guy who was painting these small multimedia portraits and doing these really meticulous book-binding projects. He was there for about three years and then he split in 2001. Later, after everything exploded, I knew he was the true first pioneer who saw the creative potential there. He just didn't tell anyone about it. I think he liked the quiet.

DANIEL LAI: I was a graduate student in New Jersey—my partner and I lived there. He got laid-off and then he launched another job in Nashville, in the pharmaceutical industry. So, we had to move to Nashville. And I hated the idea. I was so depressed. But it turned out to be one of the best moves I ever made. This was in 2006.

BETH GILMORE: In my artistic process and in my life, I just get myself in over my head and then work my way out—as an art process. I just remember being really tired of having to go and keep finding another bar to let us have an art opening. It seemed like it would be so much easier if we just had one place we can go to every time. We could get a space then we just won't have to keep setting up every time and moving everything in our cars every time. I had been doing every Untitled show that was around at that time, and most of the Plowhaus shows. And so there was just the whole process: let's go to this storage space, and get the walls and bring them, and then let's talk to this new place and get them to let us come in. I was just tired of convincing people to let us do what we wanted to do. And I thought "If we just rent a space, and it's cheap enough, we can just do this all the time."

DANIEL LAI: If you're going to move to the city, you're going to have to go visit the city. And here's a very interesting thing—the whole concept of the city was so different back then. I lived in Bergen County in New Jersey. When we say "the city," we meant Manhattan. We could hop onto public transport or whatever. We go to the city, right? So everything is in the city. You want anything, culture is in the city. So when I went to Nashville, obviously I had to go to the city. I walked around downtown. At that time, Nashville was not at all like what it is now. At the time we only had a handful of galleries, less than a handful of galleries, a handful of hotels. It was almost like a dead town to me, especially after five or on weekends. So I walked around downtown, which, you know, you can accomplish in one afternoon, and The Arcade was quite literally in the center. If you've done art shows in New York City—unless you come from money—we had to find alternative spaces like in a basement somewhere or in a parking garage somewhere. So you've got to find all these weird places. So this wasn't that. It wasn't too weird—it wasn't a stretch at all. And then I check the rent and it's like a few hundred.

BETH GILMORE: I was also a student at Watkins at the time. And so the wonderful, insightful professors at Watkins were just like, "What you need to do is you need to get a space." And so I met Caroline Carlisle at Joe Hardwick's photography studio. And we both started talking about getting a space.

CAROLINE VINCENT: I had been doing the airport art program for like four or five years, and I had decided to do something different. I was just trying to find my way and Lain York introduced Beth and I—I think it was at an opening or something. He said Beth was looking into opening a gallery, and I don't know if I had said that or spoken that into the universe, but we started having this conversation and both Beth and I were like, "This is mystical! We must do this thing!" And she had already started looking at spaces in The Arcade, and we had just started talking about the possibility because it was so cheap. I think at the time it was like $250 a month.

JOE NOLAN: The Arcade was built over a few years from 1902 to 1903. It cuts between Fourth and Fifth Avenue North in downtown Nashville and it's enclosed beneath a glass skylight roof. It covers almost an acre and—in it's heyday—it featured two floors of stores and restaurants. It was advertised as a one-stop shopping destination—the Walmart of its time.

DANIEL LAI: So we had a lot of cheap restaurants and there was a shoe-shine place. There was a peanut store and a pizza place. You won't find Sephora—it's the opposite of Green Hills. It was owned by a family, but they didn't have a whole lot of interest in fixing up the space because it's been working for them. It has a lot of character because architec-turally it has a series of metal arches that hold up the whole building, I think. And then it's divided into units. People rent space and run a restaurant, or a deli, or a retail space, or a gift shop, whatever. I remem-ber that each unit is so different and so inconsistent. It's not like today when you have a retail space that you rent out—the floor plan's basi-cally the same from one unit to another. It was so inconsistent. It was a very interesting space.

CAROLINE CARLISLE VINCENT: So The Arcade was mainly restaurants. Business people from downtown would come in and get sandwiches or there was the pizza place. From like 11 to 2 basically is the only time, really, that anybody was in there, and that was on the bottom level. So they just thought we were kind of crazy. Like, "What are you doing?"

DANIEL LAI: When I found The Arcade the upstairs was basically empty. So you have a couple of hair salons, a watch repair shop and a pho-tographer, and there's nothing there. All of the units were completely empty. So, when I first visited the space, I got first dibs so I could find the best space needing the least amount of work. There were two units upstairs facing Fifth Avenue, and the other side was Lori's Hair Salon. So I picked the other side overlooking Fifth Avenue. And then here's the thing—I'm upstairs. You have to let people know that you're there. And I knew no one. I felt like there were artists because I started to make friends with people in Plowhaus, Untitled, and Jerry Dale at TAG. I met people like Lain York and I learned that there was an artist community. There were people who were actually making art in Nashville. If that was the case, if I could get the numbers, I could probably win the battle of us getting people to come to The Arcade for the arts. So the first step was to let people know that we have cheap places upstairs. I started to network with different people. I met Beth Gilmore and I started to tell her about these places, about how cheap it is, and it's totally affordable. I said "It's a fixer-upper, you're an artist, you're resourceful enough to do that, to achieve that." And the word got out. And sure enough, Beth moved in.

BETH GILMORE: And I don't know how we found that spot—Caroline might've found it. But there was almost nothing up there. There was one gallery in the corner space next to the hair salon. No one had been in our space for years. It was crazy.

CAROLINE CARLISLE VINCENT: Our space had been empty for like fifteen years. Nearly nobody had occupied spaces on the second floor. There were a few small businesses up there. I remember a jewelry repair and the hair salon. I don't remember the sequence of events, but Daniel Lai had his space there at the end that faced right out on Fifth Avenue—Dangenart Gallery. He moved in right around the same time. He may have even been there like right before us, but I do remember feeling, "Oh, this is like a movement. Something is happening."

DANIEL LAI: This Arcade was what, a hundred years old? It was filled with asbestos, and it's more than just a hole in the wall—it's like a hole in every freaking wall. It was very run down. You could see that the roof is almost caving in. It was like a glass roof and it was not maintained at all. There were a lot of homeless people hanging out on the ground floor.

CAROLINE CARLISLE VINCENT: It was really hot. There was no air conditioning. It looked terrible. It had weirdly pink walls or something and maybe some bad carpet or something. I can't remember. We spent a lot of time fixing it up just enough to hang stuff on the wall. We had big plans to put some drywall up or something, but I don't think we ever did. We were just hanging stuff on what I guess was the original plaster. The back was just like this black hole of terrible wires hanging down and it did not look good at all. It had like a stairwell that went nowhere. I guess it would've gone down to the bottom floor at some point. It was such a raw space. I think we built out—sort of—the front room, and we had paid Todd Greene and somebody else to paint it. They did a really good job. They patched everything and put the walls in some sort of semblance of looking nice, and everything got a fresh coat of paint. It looked good! The first room was sort of a storefront, and then in the back there were like wires hanging out at the walls and it was dangerous. At one point, Tom Wills was standing back there with me—we had a bunch of stuff back there. We were trying to do more affordable art items in the back—artists designed retail things to make money to pay the bills. The wall just caught on fire because it was like these electrical wires were just exposed and some of them were just sort of taped together. I don't even want to think about it. We're just standing there and it just like spontaneously combusted. Tom helped me like put the fire out and I go get the maintenance guy from The Arcade. And he's like, "It's your space. We have no responsibility for this." I was like, "Dude! The wall is on fire and it's next to the rest of the building. So I just feel like you should care a little, maybe?"

BETH GILMORE: We were getting our space ready to open, then Tag across the street was about to open. And then we were like, "Maybe we should just have our openings at the same time? That'd be cool." And then it just turned into the Art Crawl. I don't remember anyone saying the words "Let's have an art crawl." It just happened on its own. It's like, it's a creature and it was born, you know? No one was in charge.

JERRY DALE MCFADDEN: I'm originally from Texas and Oklahoma. I moved from Oklahoma to Nashville in 1983. I moved here to go to Belmont—it was Belmont College at the time. They had one of the only music business programs back then. So my interest was music and I've always been an art fan. I was always blown away by art. It was something that I marveled at. But music was my love and what I wanted to do for a living. I pursued my music career and once I started traveling and touring and things, I took advantage of seeing art: going to museums; going to galleries; befriending artists that I like. And I was buying things directly from artists and started collecting because I was making money. And all that is what led me to try to do something in Nashville. I was originally over in 12 South before they called it 12 South, you know? We were upstairs in a little house right on 12th Avenue. That's why it was called The Attic Gallery, and that's how it eventually just turned into TAG. I collected a lot of folk art and a lot of outsider art. I was doing the gallery with my wife at the time, Julie Atherton. We opened in 2000, and then Julie and I moved from the little attic to Hillsboro Village in maybe 2002. We were just down from Zeitgeist Gallery in a huge space above the shoe repair shop. Dave Powell and Patrick had their architecture office up there. But they had so much space and they said, "You guys should just do your gallery over here." So for a long time we didn't even pay rent. They just let us use space. They had this whole top floor of this giant old building, and it was so much fun. And being close to Zeitgeist was wonderful too because I was a fan of the things they did there. We changed our name to TAG because even though we were upstairs it wasn't an attic anymore. When we did the first Mark Mothersbaugh show we got some great press for that. And then I remember the turnout was just insane. We sold like fifty-five pieces of art, which we've never done, ever. Even Mark said that we sold more art than any other gallery he'd ever worked with. After we lost the space in Hillsboro Village, Anne Brown offered me a spot in The Arts Company building downtown. After that we spent a year in the space on Fifth Avenue where Tinney Contemporary is now. We were there for a year before we moved to The Arcade.

DANIEL LAI: At that time, there was already the First Saturday Art Crawl, but in a more scattered way. So all the galleries will open on the First Saturday night of the month and have a reception. And then I think "So they're all scattered. They're not within walking distance." So I wasn't trying to kill the First Saturday Art Crawl. I wanted it to be more Fifth Avenue Art Crawl. I wanted it to be Downtown Art Crawl where people could park their car once, and not have to drive different places. So I befriended Jerry Dale. And then I found out that Beth was going to move in and Twist would be ready for the first Art Crawl. The Arts Company agreed to be on board.

CAROLINE CARLISLE VINCENT: The real spark was the sort of moment when Jerry Dale across the street at TAG was having an opening on this particular Saturday night. It might have been like in August—I know it was really hot. And Beth wanted to do our first opening at the same time as Jerry, on Saturday night. But that was strange because The Arts Company was just down the street from TAG on Fifth Avenue and they always did afternoon events because no one went downtown on Saturday night. Back then it would have been really weird for locals to go downtown to an art event on Saturday night.

JERRY DALE MCFADDEN: Well, the Art Crawl thing is an interesting one because I had TAG in the space where Tinney Contemporary is now, on the ground floor on Fifth Avenue when we started the Art Crawl. I would say it was Daniel Lai's idea because he had his gallery and TAG was down there, but Anne Brown wanted nothing to do with it. She refused to be a part of the Art Crawl because she thought it was a waste of time to be open late at night downtown. But then all this other stuff started happening in The Arcade. Eventually Anne Brown came around and I think she claims that she started the Art Crawl now, which cracks me up, but that's alright.

CAROLINE CARLISLE VINCENT: We had just furiously, got everything ready, and put up a show. I think it was Todd Greene's work actually, our first show. And we thought, "Is anyone going to come? Maybe no one will show up?"

DANIEL LAI: I was downplaying it. I mean, I was downplaying it. I didn't expect it to be that big of a deal. I told The Arcade that we have to remain open after six, we'll close at ten. Twist had their grand opening at the same time as Jerry Dale who was starting the new space. He was moving out of the Arts Company. Then the whole thing is to keep the First Saturday crowd to make it a success. And then my friend Brooke told me, "You know what? I better go there and help you."

BETH GILMORE: Everyone said, "You're going to do what? Why would you put a gallery up there? No one will come, you know?" But then everyone came.

CAROLINE CARLISLE VINCENT: Like hundreds of people showed up. It just became this monthly event almost immediately. It was like all of a sudden, without even really planning it, the Art Crawl was a thing.

BETH GILMORE: I remember the first opening. There was no air conditioning up there, but there's also no heat except for the radiators. In the summer it's hot and the winter it's cold. We had popsicles at the opening. And people would be like, "I can't believe we're standing here. It's so hot in here." I'd say, "I know, but don't worry, in the winter it will be freezing."

DANIEL LAI: I did not expect it. I was mobbed. I couldn't believe it because I couldn't even move from one place to another. It was so packed with people. I knew then I was right. People at that time were starving for an art event, an art reception. So that was the first one that we had.

And the following month I was like, "OK, we need to have a meeting. We're onto something very important here. Very big. It's definitely bigger than we thought."

BETH GILMORE: We built a little table that was like a counter where people could come and check out. It looked like a receptionist desk or something on the corner. The building was falling apart and it was held together with paint. I think the walls got thicker. The space is smaller now because we painted it so many times. And I remember at some point we were able to paint the ceiling. We'd been able to paint, you know, the walls and the floor. The water issue was difficult. The bathroom, the tiny thing was across and around from the gallery, you know, to the other side of The Arcade. So it was really hard to get water in there to mop the floor. So I just painted the floor every month that made it cleaner and quicker. When we finally painted the ceiling, everyone's like, "Wow! Did you get your hair cut?"

DANIEL LAI: Twist and I were the only two galleries who were able to sustain a regular schedule of business hours for the galleries. Most other artists, they had a full-time job somewhere else, so they couldn't keep their space open during business hours. So we couldn't really generate a steady stream of art shoppers. Almost everybody was by appointment only. So we had to count on the Art Crawl to survive. So we had to make it happen. Otherwise, what's the point of getting the space there? In the beginning there was a novelty in the space. In the beginning it was new. Everybody was excited about it.

BETH GILMORE: My time in The Arcade was all when I was at my studio at Downtown Presbyterian Church. Those two spaces, those worked together really well. I always needed somewhere to put my stuff and unload and park. And then I had this little wagon I would put things in to take over to The Arcade. If I needed something from my studio, I can just go downstairs, walk through the alley across the street and walk through the other alley into the Downtown Presbyterian Church back door and go upstairs to my studio.

DANIEL LAI: It's just such a crazy pace and it's a lot of work. It's absolutely a lot of work. I had a huge space. I had three rooms. So I had one small room, one medium size room, and then a big room. There's a big gallery. So what I did was rotate half of the gallery because I couldn't possibly change the whole gallery monthly. In the beginning I did that. And then I was starting to feel quite burnt out so I split it in half and rotated bimonthly. So at least every month there was something new to see.

BETH GILMORE: So the great thing about it is like I can go and park in the alley at night. And if I needed to work on the show to get it ready at night, I could stay there as long as I wanted. There were no hours we couldn't be there. We had a key to the building, so we'd go in and if I needed to stay up all night, that's fine. And what people didn't realize about the Art Crawl is that the Art Crawls started for me at like nine o'clock in the morning. We were there all day. There was always something that had to be done all day. I would just bring everything I needed with me, like what I'm going to wear that night. I'd get some food downstairs at Manny's House of Pizza or Mexican at La Playa. I was raising two young daughters at that time and I'd take them down to The Peanut Shoppe to get some chocolate-covered peanuts or some other snack. By the time six o'clock rolled around, I'd already been there all day.

DANIEL LAI: Everything has to be clean and pristine and white walls and good art, and you dress up. So that it's a positive pretty look. But behind the scenes you pull your hair out. When you have a gallery you're everything. You're everyone. You're the janitor, you're the curator, you're the installer, you're the administrator. You're the salesperson, you're the tech support. It really is a lot of work.

CAROLINE CARLISLE VINCENT: I just really loved working with artists and sort of being able to give them this whole space to do anything they wanted. That approach meant that we hosted lots of installation art and performance art that really had no commercial viability, but the space was so cheap and I think we just loved that idea of just letting artists do crazy stuff. And we did some crazy stuff. We did off-the-wall performance things and installations that were interactive. And there wasn't a lot of women artists being shown in galleries, in my opinion, at that time. I mean, there's this idea of like the male painter in the tropes of art history. I was wondering where do women have a space to do what they want to do? I think that kind of became a thread, even though I don't know if it was wholly intentional. But I think we did end up showing a lot of female artists who did some interesting things.

BETH GILMORE: We would look for something interesting that we wanted to exist in Nashville. Pretty often I would just change the whole room around to whatever the artists wanted. If a big sculpture or whatever was going to come in we changed the room around it to be its best environment. We made the room into a world for us. I'd been working at Belmont mansion for a long time, and then I had an internship at the Frist and I saw how museums change all the wall colors and they change everything. They reconfigure everything to make the shows the best they can possibly be. And I didn't know any better. I didn't know how to run a gallery. So I just thought that's what you were supposed to be when you had a gallery. It's also an important factor that the building was old and no one cared. We could paint the walls and the floor every month if we wanted— no one cared what we did. It was unimportant. We found an unimportant space that wasn't valuable to anyone. And that's why we were allowed to do everything that we did. No one said, "Oh, you can't do that! This is really a nice space." It was cheap and no one cared. So that was very important.

JOE NOLAN: Twist became known as a spot for these immersive, floor-to-ceiling kinds of installations. You looked at art at Twist, and you waded into it or climbed through it. They encouraged local artists to think big and be ambitious, and they encouraged all of their artists to make art without any retail pressure. Nearly every show they did was almost completely noncommercial and unsellable in any practical way.

BETH GILMORE: I remember Kristina Arnold and her glass-work flowers suspended over real potted flowers. I remember the whole floor looked like a field and the walls were blue. Lauren Kussro did her cut-paper flower sculptures. And now those artists both had people who bought their work too. They can't take home the whole environment, but we started to figure out ways where they can purchase one of the flowers from that environment and, you know, hang it on their dining room wall. But, most importantly, the space was there to invoke a feeling. And one of my favorite things, one of my favorite kinds of compliments, that I got more than once from different people, was that they were looking for Twist and couldn't find it. And I knew it was because it looked so different than it did last month. It was a whole new space.

J. TODD GREENE: And then actually Beth opened up a Twist part two [Twist Etc.]. And she just kind of gave you the key and then the rent was just like $200 a month for that space. It was basically "Here, Beth. Here's $200. Let me just do whatever I want in this space." And she would say, "Yeah. Okay, sure." But I never had to give her the $200. I owe Beth about $400 right now. That time was very free. It felt very important to all of our growth and development.

TERRY THACKER: On First Saturdays you started to see all these people that you didn't know that were young and engaged, and it was fun. That's kind of how COOP got started. Of course, Beth started Twist in The Arcade and she was also renting the next door space. And Ron Lambert approached them about doing a show and he did a show there. And then Beth was going to close that space and Ron said "Well, why don't we get together and rent?" That's how that started. So it was mostly Watkins faculty, but there were a few other people in on that initial group. And it was largely thanks to Beth because she gave us a really good deal. I think we paid exactly what she was paying to rent that space.

RON LAMBERT: When we started COOP we felt like art was about ideas and just because some ideas weren't acceptable for someone to hang behind their couch didn't mean they weren't important enough to be seen. Maybe that made them more important? Artist-run spaces can be the only place for those unpopular ideas. I think we were helped by the artist groups that came before us. We weren't inventing the wheel, and we knew what we needed to live up to. Not that we felt we needed to compete with the past, but there was a bar set.

BRADY HASTON: Ron was really the lifting force behind that. That's when we had the spaces in The Arcade available really affordably. So that worked for that. And then, it's just taken off. It's been a really good way for people coming into town for the first time, moving here saying, "Hey, what can I do?" Well, just join COOP. That's instant. You start to put names and faces together. You can show there. I mean, there's tons of people involved with it. It's been really good as far as being a really quick way to reference this whole scene and see what's happening.

DANIEL LAI: We were so successful that we didn't even know about it. I took a different approach with my gallery where I introduced a lot of local artists, but my main mission was to bring outside talent and show it to people. So I put out a call for artists nationally and internationally. So we get art shipped to us from California, from New Jersey. One time from Europe. So I didn't realize that the name got out. So one day a woman came into the gallery and we started chatting. And she was so frustrated with a concierge. She was staying at the Hermitage Hotel. One of the most chic, luxurious hotels in town. She came to Nashville to go to The Arcade to look at art. And then she was swearing, pissed at the concierge. Because the concierge told her, "You don't want to go to that part of town." She was like, "That's the reason I'm in town for, I'm going." So obviously it wasn't as bad as the concierge made us sound like. And I said, "How the hell do you know about this?" She said that in *Art News* somebody mentioned something about us. She was very pleased to have found us. And of course at the time there was The Arts Company and Tinney Contemporary was there also. So I had a great talk with the woman and then about an hour later, the concierge actually came to my gallery and said, "Wow, I didn't know that this was all here."

JOE NOLAN: The crawl was a huge breakthrough because it was the first time that regular folks started showing up at gallery receptions. It wasn't just artists and established collectors and museum professionals at exhibitions on Saturday night. It was easier to get downtown then, and if you were a local you knew where to find free parking. The Arts Company's website claims that two thousand people crawled through that block of Fifth Avenue on the First Saturday of every month. Sometimes it was definitely less, but sometimes The Arcade was packed elbow to elbow all the way around the upper floor. Around that time you started seeing Nashville's art scene being mentioned in national press.

DANIEL LAI: Cameron Diaz was in town and she walked passed Tinney gallery, but they were closed—it was like after six or whatever. She was banging on the door. She wanted to buy a painting by Julia Martin. Julia Martin used to do those faces. So that painting looked like Cameron. So she went in and bought the painting.

M KELLEY: One of the shows we did with HAUS Rotations was a pretty decent sized show. I think we had about twelve or fifteen artists for that exhibit. We had a huge turnout and one of the people that came to the show was Duane Arnett. Me and Duane just hit it off. We just had a great conversation. He was one of the two founding guys at this software start-up, FortyAU. He told me about an art show that was at Dane Carder's studio. I ended up going out to that and we ended up talking the whole evening. A couple days later Duane calls me, "I really like what y'all did with the house show. It's been great talking with you. We have an office that we just got in The Arcade and we want the front to be a gallery. We've been trying to coordinate a show for our grand opening and we have no idea what we're doing." We came in and helped them coordinate with the artists. They paid us basically in like food and beers and snacks for the whole week we were doing the install. About a week and a half later, Duane calls me up again and he's like, "Would you want to do this again for next month? We'll pay for any of the materials you need. We'll pay for all the stuff to be printed." We got the show together and it was great. After that we kind of formalized our curating of the gallery at FortyAU. I want to say we did that for seven years.

RON LAMBERT: Jodi Hays and Joseph Whit and I were wanting to open a gallery because the space was really cheap—it was like $200 a month for some of those spaces. One opened up kind of across from Twist and down a little bit. And so I started trying to get together a group of people. We knew if we got like, say, you know, ten to twenty people, we could just split the rent and not have to ask for money and it wouldn't be that much. Joseph was friends with Harmony Korine, and he did a show at Vanderbilt with Harmony's work. Harmony said we can borrow some work from his collection for our first show, but by the time we got enough names together, we felt like we could afford it, that space rented out. So a few months later I had been showing a little bit with a Davis Art Advisory that was next to Twist. And when she closed Beth took on her lease, but it was kind of two rooms. And so I asked Beth if she would sublet half of that. Beth just wanted it because she wanted to be in control of the neighbors so she agreed to that.

ARMON MEANS: At the beginning, COOP and the other spaces at The Arcade were really kind of catching on to that wildfire of arts that was growing in the downtown area. There were these spaces in town that were places like Rymer and Tinney that were these more established art spaces that were still very traditional in the way that they showed work. They showed really great work a lot of times, but they weren't necessarily places where people who had just come out of Watkins or just come out of the area programs or just moved down here to start their arts career could immediately get into. But then there were places like Blend and TAG, and some of those little things at The Arcade that were the smaller spaces where some of them got connected. A lot of the conversation felt like there were places where artists wanted to collaborate and wanted to connect with one another.

BEN VITUALLA: I graduated from University of Memphis and I was looking for an art position anywhere, everywhere. And I started working at the state museum basically. Around 2003 or 2004 I started working with Untitled. The Gill sisters were running it at that time. And that just kind of opened me up to the different artists here, and the community. A lot of those young people, they just cultivated that community really well. I just started working with all those different artists in Untitled. It was mostly for a lot of us a place where we learned a lot of different processes like press releases and promoting the show and hanging the work and installing walls. And then just communicating with other artists. I really enjoyed that aspect of it just because the conversation is always interesting to me. That trickled down to a variety of different things. In East Nashville, Plowhaus, working with Franne and all them was also really interesting. I had the opportunity to show at Dangenart Gallery with Daniel Lai. It was kind of the perfect time because Daniel was about to leave and I was in grad school and I needed to exhibit this work. He mentioned that I should just have a show there. He was leaving and I couldn't afford the whole space. But I was able to afford his smaller space. It was like two or three months with friends of mine working to help me put up the walls, paint the walls, and my electrician friends putting the lights on there. Our first show at Blend Studio [*Home*] was a basically a collaboration with some young people at Millville Elementary. We did projects with them. We talked about family and things like that. Samantha Callahan was a part of that in the beginning. Sam did a lot of marketing—cleaning up the logos and sending emails—and looking at different artists.

M KELLEY: The Art Crawl was already a thing when we started curating FortyAU. It was primarily the big galleries on Fifth. Folks were coming up into The Arcade and there were a handful of galleries that were kind of in there. Not to speak ill of the dead, but I think it was very much people trying to emulate the commercial gallery feel in a space that is very obviously not. There was a lot of emphasis on exhibitions with a capital E. I think we did something really different. We were doing exhibitions, but we were also really open and really hungry for something different. I ended up poaching from so many schools. Working with seniors who were doing stuff that were like, "Fuck it, why not? This is my last year. I'm gonna show some work." And I'm saying, "What you're doing is really interesting. Let's make it bigger. Let's do stuff that's a little bit more experimental." And I think that encouraged schools like Lipscomb who opened a space in The Arcade for a while. Watkins opened a project space.

CELENE AUBRY: I remember going to the crawl in The Arcade. So you have the students who are doing maybe their first public gallery show that they've done, and then you have maybe some established artists upstairs in The Arcade, but some are right across the street in the commercial galleries. And I just loved that conversation and I think that's where the creativity happens. It doesn't happen by just having a bunch of commercial galleries dictating what is art. It's that conversation back and forth.

JOE NOLAN: The best Fifth Avenue galleries walked that line between showing challenging contemporary art and showing more commercial exhibitions that paid the rent. But the spaces at The Arcade were so cheap, and the artist-run galleries were so creative—they were almost always the highlight for me. It would be broiling up on the second floor of The Arcade with no AC in the summertime. Or it would be freezing in the winter. It didn't matter. It was the place to be.

JARED BRENNAN: In my school days, in studying critical theory, I learned about Levi Strauss's concept of bricolage or the bricoleure—it's about building the road as you travel with whatever is in front of you. I just always thought it was the coolest concept for the Brikolaj name. And the musical, the creative process always felt like that to me. But anything in life could be. Like even just remodeling my house with whatever I could find at Habitat for Humanity. I was driving through the alley by Dukes and I saw a couple of really shiny chrome motorcycle parts. And I'd been stashing all these metal parts at my house while I was remodeling, because the previous owner had worked for the railroad and he'd left all these metal pieces at my place, and every once in a while when I'd be working on the house I'd bang on one of them and it was like, "Damn! This sounds good." I built this homemade gamelan [a percussion instrument featuring metal bells like those in traditional Indonesian music] in my backyard and we did a performance—that was the first event at Brikolaj. It was super successful. We were all super high on edibles. We closed down the door. The idea was to just have it be this sound coming out of that room so we were trying to keep people out, but fucking people just kept coming in and opening the door and then they kept coming in and Jack Jones, Kyle Hamlett, and Austin Alexander and I were all banging on this thing, improvising. Austin brought his projectors and we put some video stuff on loops. That was a great event. And then we did it a second time. Kind of rethinking, you know? I kind of enclosed us in canvas. Light came up and shot onto the canvas so you just saw the shadows of everyone playing. It wasn't really intentional, but because of where the light was I was like, "Oh shit, look at this!" It was a blast for awhile. I got to have a fucking store and an art gallery. I did some pretty cool shit for however long that was, a year and a half or two?

ARMON MEANS: Things like the Secret Show Series and Untitled were kind of more pop-up oriented exhibitions. I think those—particularly the Secret Show Series—did a great job of thinking about how artists connect interrelated ideas and start to collaborate on small scale works for short-term exhibition. That really created a space for COOP to think about creating a real collective that wasn't temporary. COOP really caught that idea and grew it into something that was much more sustainable.

RON LAMBERT: It was pretty raw. Terry Thacker and I built a wall along the back because there was so many like pipes and stuff coming out. The lights were there before we got there, but we called an electrician, and there was like one little spot where you could stick your head up and look at the wires. And he just pops his head back down and was like, "Holy shit! Your wiring is just short wires pig-tailed together above the ceiling." It did feel like—at some point—The Arcade was going to have somebody come in and say, "This is not nearly up to code." Reverend Ethan Acres was our first COOP show. He got in a car accident. So we're waiting for him to show up, to do this performance and he never showed up and Rocky's texting him. So I just went back to Watkins and made DVDs of some of his videos off of YouTube. We just projected those because we didn't have anything else to show. And that's kind of how it ran. We were never too-together. We just asked people we were friends with if they wanted to come show, and then we put them up at our houses, if they're coming from out of town. We wanted to focus on non-Nashville artists just to bring new things into the art scene.

JOE NOLAN: COOP was also a great resource for seeing sometimes very uncommercial video and installation work. Whenever the stuff at COOP would remind me of something local it always felt validating. It was proof that the artists in Nashville were up-to-speed with the other Southern artists or the artists in the Midwest or the Northeast. We were all having the same conversation, but COOP put those artists where we could see one another, and share our work and connect.

BRADY HASTON: It just helped spice up the Art Crawls. Something completely different. It was always something new to see. And they worked really well with the scale of the little small gallery. And it was easy for other artists out of town to participate because it wouldn't kill them to ship a small display of stuff there. It was a really reasonable and affordable way to do that. Twist was in there too, about that same time. Beth Gilmore really brought a lot of attention to The Arcade as well. She had some good shows there. And then COOP, they were adjacent to each other. That became a really nice hub.

BEN VITUALLA: In the beginning we were always thinking about how it's important to incorporate the community into a lot of the projects. It's important because the artists are learning something about what's going on outside their studio. So we worked with Oasis Center, for example. We did the bike workshop there and they were really interested and, I really thought that the kids really needed that opportunity. We had a project where the kids were making robots out of bike parts. And then they came to the exhibit, they stood right next to their work and they explained to people what their work was about. It was just amazing. People were buying their work. I mean, it was just a really nice process to see.

ARMON MEANS: I want to say that Ben taught adjunct at Watkins for a little bit. He taught out at Austin Peay for a long time, but was still living in this area. He was somebody who just really was a witness to the transition that the city had gone through in so many different ways, both in his own home community as well as just the city in general. He sought to kind of give back and speak to community issues. I was just lucky enough to meet him early on and I shared some projects with him a number of times at Blend and kind of became a part of some of the first traveling projects that he had ever done. I think Blend reflected his future efforts to do some larger projects back in his home in the Philippines and find how art connects there. So I think a lot of the impetus for the community engagement with Ben comes from his background. And, to a larger extent, both from his home in the Philippines, you know, growing up with his family there. But then also Nashville's willingness to involve themselves and engage with the arts has always been really strong. So I think a place like Blend Studio was really able to grasp onto that aspect.

JOE NOLAN: I was always curious about what Blend Studio was up to, but I didn't always get it. Ben and Samantha were ahead of their time with their focus on art that was being produced in the community, and art that was coming from places like North Nashville. Buchanan Street is one of the most happening scenes in the city now, but Blend showed one of Xpayne's first shows almost a decade ago. He had a bunch of prints and t-shirts and a book of his illustrations. This was back when he was still just a young artist and billed as Xavier Payne. Ben and Samantha both came through that local, DIY Untitled world and they never really looked up. They were out in the community and they were discovering all these local talents before everybody else knew where to look.

M KELLEY: We were definitely doing things really differently and probably people were thinking, "What the fuck is this?" But I think it started some really interesting conversations, just the diversity of work that was there. I feel like that made the Fifth Avenue crawl the place to go for a good while. There were so many different things happening there. You could have the really hoity-toity experience where your wine is served in a little champagne glass, and you're talking to an artist whose work is selling for ridiculous amounts of money. And then you can cross the street and wander around, and this gallery is also an artist's studio, and they're working out of there. Or this is a collective show of weird stuff that's been brought in from somewhere else. FortyAU were amazing and fantastic and really had a vision and were supportive of what was happening in the arts. We couldn't have done some of the stuff that we did without them. We were able to offer scholarships for artists to attend professional development workshops. We helped them with their resumes, we were helping them with writing artist statements, we connected them with the press. At the very end we were able to offer artists a couple hundred bucks to help projects come to life. Matt and Joe Christy punched a couple holes in the wall for their exhibit. Willie Stewart totally painted the entire space blood red. It was like four coats of blood red paint. Everything in there was red: floor to ceiling. He built fake walls to change the shape of the gallery. He did a whole construction project. When he brought the proposal to us, I was like, "This guy is going fucking places." He had it all broken down, how he was going to do it, what it was going to look like. And then the place was turned into a blood red room with a concrete mixer running 24-7. You could end up experiencing a really bizarre range of work. It was really unique. Unlike anything else that was happening at the time.

JARED BRENNAN: On a couple occasions I put like eight or ten really good, experimental musicians in a room together. And it was like, "Let's see what happens." Daniel Lane jumped in one time and painted live in the room while we had all these musicians improvising. It was cool. High energy shit, man. It was rad. That would have been, I think probably early 2018. One of my personal favorite projects was with Roger Moutenot [Yo La Tengo, Paula Cole]. He created an album's worth of music—the first personal music he'd recorded in thirty years of producing. And I made like ten or so videos—psychedelic shit that I put on a loop. Roger had a wall of art in there about thirteen or fourteen pieces of his own paintings. And then we looped the audio of this album and I added the video element we projected on a big wall. So it gave it that extra visual component. We got some props on that.

RON LAMBERT: We wanted to show things that were pushing some boundaries. I don't know that we always did that, but we tried to bring in people that were kind of pushing what was accepted in the city already. We wanted to bring stuff like video and different mediums because there really was no place at that time for like performance and video and new media stuff. It's also just easy to show. If you're doing a video show an artist can send you files and you can have a video show really quickly. So it was kind of cheap to show as well. We just felt like people weren't getting exposed to that and we were hopefully bringing in some new ideas.

BEN VITUALLA: I also was interested in bringing other artists in. I actually had two shows with the 98B collective from Manila. They were just sending me information and documents and photos and I just put it all together here. Also an exhibit with artists from Cebu, which was really interesting. They just sent me a bunch of work and then during the show we had them doing video messenger. The crawlers were able to talk to the artists. So it was a little weird. For how small Blend was it did do a lot of things.

JARED BRENNAN: But what I really liked is that it was a spot where it was equally mixed between Black Nashville and white Nashville. And that was pretty fucking cool. Proximity-wise it's close to North Nashville. So there were like some of the coolest moments, when there'd be like a seventy-five-year-old Black couple, dressed-up on a Saturday night, hanging out in the gallery, listening to a No Wave-inspired, fucking punk band.

DANIEL LAI: Jerry Dale needed a space for the shows that he had already committed too. Yeah. I was running out of steam myself. I was getting ready to leave and I was so sick of it. And I had two more, I think not two, maybe three months left on my lease or something like that. I said, "Hey Jerry Dale, why don't you just take over? We'll worry about what we tell the media later. Why don't you just come in with your art and get it started because I need a fucking break."

JERRY DALE MCFADDEN: TAG spent its last year at The Arcade. I just got lucky that Daniel Lie had that space [Dangenart] and he wanted to take a break. So I sort of took over his lease and he had a pretty decent-sized space compared to some of the other Arcade spaces. We took advantage of the storefront windows that looked out over Fifth Avenue and, and put T-A-G really big on the windows so that people would know that's where TAG was now.

M KELLEY: Twist did a lot of really cool stuff and I think between the stuff we were doing and the stuff they were doing, it was really about making stuff that you couldn't buy, necessarily. It really, I think, made the Art Crawl something that would ripple out in all the other crawls that happened in other neighborhoods into something you had to go to and be a part of. Which I think is what shifted people's mentality. It wasn't just like a reception you're going to, it's a scene. We worked really closely with the artists that we were showing. The people who later went on to become part of The Packing Plant or who opened other spaces or who were doing other collectives, started out showing through our gallery. I've had some of them tell me that the experience they got there in terms of thinking about what a show needed, and what they had to do, and what it was going to look like, and who to talk to, and how to talk about it, helped them feel comfortable opening up their own spaces later. Even though these spaces aren't around, that energy is still here.

CAROLINE CARLISLE: The Arcade was not an easy space to get into or out of. There were all these logistical problems like where do you park? There's no real elevator. Barely a person or two could fit into this elevator to get up to the second floor. Just to unload and load it wasn't so easy. Just to get in and out of downtown was a big factor. It was cool. And it did have this synergy of people wanting to come down there and walk around. But it never worked really logistically. So I think that also feeds into the relentless pace of every month having to put up a new show. It was really hard and you're doing it yourself and artists are coming in and out and doing all this work to make this installation and then we're taking it down like less than thirty days later. One reason I ended up leaving was that I just couldn't keep up with that pace. We would get a ton of people at the Art Crawl, but that was it. You'd get a handful of people the rest of the month. And the crowd at the art crawls more and more became just a party scene. People would walk in and just ask "Where's the wine?" They'd come to talk to their friends and wander through a cool space. Like no one really cared about the art and no one was really buying anything. So we had a very cheap space, but we still had other expenses. We were printing postcards and repainting the gallery for almost every show. It seemed like there wasn't a sustainable way to keep it going. We opened in 2006. I was there four years and then Beth went on for another year or two.

BETH GILMORE: I was just like, "I feel dead inside. I hate it here." It was terrible. Well, my last art crawl at The Arcade, they were trying to find me to take some pictures, because it was some anniversary or something. And I was sitting on the floor behind the counter in the dark and I'd just taken some Excedrin and had a glass of white wine. And I was like waiting for this to be over.

DANIEL LAI: It had gotten so wild. I mean, it was like a party atmosphere. It was more of a party atmosphere than it was about art. I was a little sick of that. It was a whole see-and-be-seen event every month for people to get out.

RON LAMBERT: The artists stopped coming because the crowd was just huge. A lot of drunk people coming up from Broadway. So I think COOP was looking to get back to like the place where the artists would want to go, rather than just the place that hands out free beers and stuff.

JARED BRENNAN: You had crowds of people that weren't necessarily a contemporary art crowd. It wasn't the people who went out that night to go to an art gallery. They were just downtown and stumbled on this scene at The Arcade. And that part bothered me.

DANIEL LAI: After COVID, Andee Rudloff drove me around. She showed me downtown. I thought, "Oh my God, this is unrecognizable." It's just too much of a city to me. We had an identity, didn't we? We had a very, almost grassroots identity. This is what we built and suddenly it's taken over by commercial spaces. Do I want to start another gallery? I don't think so. I wouldn't trade it for anything. It was so much fun. I made some of the best friends I could possibly make. We're still friends and a lot of the artists are still exchanging ideas. And how many artists could say that they're part of a camaraderie within the city? And then, of course, we were twenty years younger. We could drink all night and art all night or whatever. I mean, I wouldn't trade it for anything.

BEN VITUALLA: I think all that was worth it. I think people were interested. I mean, in the end, people were coming in. Artists were upset because people just want to go in there and drink, but I didn't really think it was that bad. When you have new people to look at work, regardless, it's still a win for you.

ARMON MEANS: People weren't concerned about selling work. It was about "How do we make things that we want people to see and want to create discourse about? How do we talk about ideas and issues that are important to us? How do we connect and engage?" And I think that was a real interesting place to be because it was so unlike any arts community I've ever seen.

Alternative Art Zones

1992–2015

NASHVILLE'S CONTEMPORARY ARTISTS have built a culture out of discovering and creating unexpected spaces to curate and show work. Front rooms and front yards, utility buildings and cave-like Tennessee basements are common art display environments. This homespun approach brings a more intimate dimension to the community's socializing and networking. And those connections express themselves in collective creative gatherings, late night dream-scheming, wee hours gallery receptions after parties, and black coffee mornings on cafe porches. Nashville is a place where independent curating and gallery design is as creative as the art-making itself. It's one of the hallmarks of the city's contemporary art renaissance, which has always been an artist-lead, DIY movement.

THIRD PLACES

JOE NOLAN: A sociologist named Ray Oldenburg coined the phrase "third place." In sociology, the "first place" is where a person lives. The "second place" is where they work. And the third place is like a coffeehouse or bar, a barbershop or church where people meet and congregate outside of the home and away from work. The idea is that third places are vital to functioning societies and democracies. I can't imagine how a contemporary art scene develops without coffeehouses and bars.

J. TODD GREENE: I don't know if I kind of developed a reputation as a guy who would show anywhere. And even my pay-what-you-want approach, it's just like, "Yeah, that guy's not serious about this." I'm as serious as the next gal or guy, but I'm just kind of muddling through it. I don't know the right direction to go. I'm kind of making work as fast as I can. And if you give me a spot on your wall, I will fill it. I had shown at a few real galleries in the late 1990s, but I had a really big show at J. J.'s. Paw Paw was my great grandfather who was a Southern Baptist preacher in Tennessee and Georgia. He just never learned to read, so he would sketch out his sermons on these four by six inch index cards. So after he died in 1980 a satchel of about four hundred cards was passed down to my mom. She showed them to me when I was twelve or so. And then, about twelve years later, I remembered them and decided to make a painting based on one of the cards for my mom's fiftieth birthday. I just kind of fell in love with them.

JOE NOLAN: It was a huge deal in Nashville's little 1990s art scene. I knew lots of people who were making art, and some people even sold some stuff. But the Paw Paw show was packed with these big paintings. We weren't seeing big solo shows like that from emerging artists. There weren't any galleries open to that kind of thing. J. J.'s had a high ceiling and these big walls—it was a great place to show art but Todd was the first person to see that potential. It was named J & J, but we all called it J. J.'s. I think that show totally sold out. Todd was a local art star after that.

J. TODD GREENE: And so actually one day I was taking some things over to Local Color Gallery and the front part of the building was J. J.'s Market forever—kind of just little convenience store. But this time, as I walked past, I noticed someone was tearing out the walls between the store and the storage area. And I just kind of pop my head in and I said "Hey, what are you doing?" And it was Won Choy whose family had owned J. J.'s, I think since maybe the early '90s. He's like "I'm making a coffeehouse." I was like, "Whoa!" And he had couches in there, it was just kind of a ragtag, sort of flea market look in there, but cool. It had high ceilings and Won painted the floor red, and I also noticed that there were beer fridges there. I hollered "I'm going to come back and I'm going to drink some coffee here." And Won's like "Okay, you do that." And I remember maybe a month or two later I was sitting at Bongo Java with three or four dudes. And I was like, "Man, it'd just be great if we could be just talking and drinking beer." And then I was like, "I know the place! Follow me!" I drove to J. J.'s and I changed my allegiance over to J. J.'s like that night.

KATIE CONNOLLY: There was just a different vibe at Bongo in the 1990s. You would talk to people that you didn't know. We were all kind of around the same age group—young Gen Xers. Slightly disaffected, kind of jaded. Everybody liked interesting music. And there weren't that many big city options in Nashville at the time.

JOE NOLAN: I was working at the cafe in the Davis-Kidd bookstore when Bongo opened. Jerry Hager and I were in the bottom half of a duplex on Gale Lane down near the S&M Communion Bread building. A Michigan friend of ours was staying with us for the summer and he got a job at Bongo. I'd go there almost every morning during the week. I'd get this Southwestern corn casserole bagel sandwich with tomato and red onion. I'd have that and you could get your own refills on regular coffee. I'd get there early on work days so I'd have time to write or draw in my journal before heading to the restaurant where I was a barista, a server, a prep cook, a dishwasher—a bit of everything. I'd write poetry or song lyrics first thing in the morning eating my breakfast. And then, later, when I was lost in the weeds of another lunch rush, it was easier to remember that I was really an artist.

J. TODD GREENE: I feel like probably we went to Bongo Java on the day it opened. It was definitely the coolest spot in Nashville, and it just kind of brought out weirdos and students. And it was just great for conversation. You knew if you walked in you'd know somebody, and you could just start talking or drinking coffee or studying or whatever. It was something very new. It was the 1990s when you would just drink coffee all the time. And no one seemed to have jobs.

JOE NOLAN: I'm still a fan of coffeehouse art exhibitions, but back then a show at a coffeehouse was the best an emerging artist with no MFA could really do outside of Untitled. The academic-style gatekeeping was ubiquitous at that time. Literally building your own walls was one of the only options besides showing in a cafe. But Bongo had a pretty eclectic crowd and a lot of artists hung out there. David Glick had painted a bunch of the tables there and other artists painted more as they added them. I'd see him and Gadsby Creson and Jonny Silva there all the time. Chris Rubin de la Borbolla was a barista there and he was painting a lot. I met Nick Stolle when he worked there much later. We were on a first name basis before I knew he was an artist.

NICK STOLLE: Many people at Bongo were visual artists, but there was kind of a view of Watkins as like those "pretentious academic weirdos over there." But that's only natural.

JOE NOLAN: Chris Rubin de la Borbolla did a great show there and Beth

Gilmore showed at Bongo when I think she was still wearing historic dresses and leading tours of Belmont Mansion across the street. Craig Brabson and I did a show of these real tough guy assemblages with all these steel tiles and antique nails on wood. We incorporated these images from cyanotypes that Craig had made. And we used spray paint and brushes. I painted a lot of text on the tiles or directly on the images—weird bits of poetry from my journals or just stuff we came up with in his backyard. I remember kind of building the show in one afternoon. We had to work outside to make the cyanotypes and because of the spray paint fumes. I remember it was hot and in the summertime. I used to make packs of those watercolor paper postcards with all the postage info printed on the back. I'd buy a pack and paint them all in like a week. Then I'd show Bob Bernstein over at Bongo. He'd buy the ones he liked. I respect collectors who know what they like.

NICK STOLLE: That time at Bongo was hugely important to me as a person. You know, the friendships that I made there—and like in a huge music way. I got turned on to so much music there that opened me up in a very real way. I got to talk to Dave Cloud every day.

JOE NOLAN: I lived just up on Belmont for years and was friends with lots of that staff during that time. If I was there at closing we'd sometimes walk up to Boscos in Hillsboro Village. That was a first wave brew pub where you had a restaurant with a built-in brewery. They had this English Ale called Olde Fool that seemed stronger every time they brought out a new batch in the fall.

JAYJIT DASGUPTA: What I loved about Boscos was the half-raised platform that they had on the side and you can just have this long table and we'd have like twenty people there. It was like a bunch of people you met, but then other friends would just come in. That was a really good hang. After movies, or even after events, we'd just go directly to Boscos because that was just the go-to. I even remember what Tom Wills would order all the time: he loved the niçoise salad with some tuna on top.

JOE NOLAN: Boscos did a jazz brunch on Sunday mornings. Dallas Starke is such a good singer. The band was the Roland Gresham Trio. Roland was a Murfreesboro jazz legend. He was a big tall guy too. He had a huge hands and he would play this big hollow-body guitar. Just fucking beautiful guitar, just gorgeous. I would sit at the bar and drink black coffee because I had probably been there the night before drinking Olde Fool. I would listen to that music and order the Oskar Benedict, which was eggs Benedict with grilled asparagus and a pile of lump crab on top. It was like ten bucks.

JAYJIT DASGUPTA: Another important spot was Sunset Grille and that late-night menu. That was one of the coolest places to hang out late at night and follow these conversations into the ether. You were getting out of Belcourt or you'd been at an opening at Zeitgeist and you're in the village.

JOE NOLAN: The late-night menu at Sunset Grille was killer. That was a great place to sort of wind up. They used to have lots of Paul Harmon paintings all over the place. He was an established painter in Nashville with this really distinctive pop style. Back then it was a big deal for a local artist to be hanging in a restaurant.

GALLERY GO ROUND

JOE NOLAN: Most of our creative community was still living on the west side at that point. Around 2001 people start crossing the river to the East side to go see music at Slow Bar or eat at Margot. When Plowhaus Artists Cooperative starts, all of a sudden we had people crossing the river to go look at art. Plowhaus established the idea that visual art was going to play a role in the creative evolution of East Nashville.

JANET DECKER YANEZ: If there wasn't a Plowhaus, there probably wouldn't have been a Ground Floor Gallery + Studios, honestly. Credit to Plowhaus for giving me the model, and inspiring me to know that I could do a version of it, and I could do it in my own way.

JOE NOLAN: Plowhaus was a self-contained cooperative that wasn't as broadly impactful as Untitled. But they had their own space where their artists worked and showed their stuff so it was a little easier to track than the Untitled events. It was spearheaded by this great lady named Franne Lee. She had worked in theater and film in New York as a costume designer, and she dressed the Not Ready for Primetime Players when SNL was still funny and dangerous. She won three Tonys before she moved here. Franne was super creative and boiling over with enthusiasm for the art and music that was happening in East Nashville. She was another of the creative women that helped to nurture and shape the city's contemporary art landscape.

JERRY DALE MCFADDEN: There was a display cabinet built into the wall down on the sidewalk that was part of the building that I was in when TAG was in Hillsboro Village. My friend Griffin Norman used to design a little poster for all of our shows and then we would put it in that little glass case. During one of our Steve Keene shows, we just put some Steve Keene paintings behind the glass. Of course somebody broke the glass and stole them. Later on some folks started curating that display case as Nashville's Smallest Art Gallery.

JOE NOLAN: Nashville's Smallest Art Gallery was started by a web designer named Daniel Box. His first official display was in March 2008. The case was 37 inches by 27 inches and 4 and a half inches deep—there was a diagram on their website. It even had a small light powered by a little solar panel. It was attached to the wall right outside of the Peabody Shoe Repair where I always got my leather jackets fixed. The concept and the name were like a tourist trap attraction—which is very Nashville. But they actually did a great job of creating these interesting displays. Local designer/illustrator Rachel Briggs was in their first show, but they also curated artists from Europe and Japan. It was a unique space to make art for, and artists responded to that challenge. We covered their exhibitions in the *Nashville Scene* just like any other gallery in town.

RYAN HOGAN: Gallery F was just a special place in a lot of ways. Just physically where it was, but also the community that it created. I met Sabine [Schlunk] and John [J. J. Jones]. They both had their artistic practices. When they moved here, I think they were just looking for places to live and they came upon Scarritt Bennett Center. I think it was originally like a Methodist missionary school. Don't quote me on that. Now it's kind of this peace and justice organization. They have this campus and one way they make money is they host events—conferences, weddings, things like that. So, they had opportunities where you could work for them and they'd give you space to live. I think that's what they did. Sabine worked for Scarritt-Bennett in other capacities, but there was this house on the property that Sabine had the idea to transform into a gallery. It's an interesting space because it's very naturally lit in the front two rooms. There was still a functioning kitchen in the back, so we would have a makeshift cafe where we would work in exchange for a studio space. That's what I would do.

JOE NOLAN: Scarritt-Bennett started as a Methodist school for women missionaries. It relocated from Kansas City, MO to its location at its historic campus near Music Row in 1924. They built some gorgeous buildings there, and the Scarritt Bennett bell tower is a local landmark.

It was a progressive school that racially integrated and hosted a speech by Martin Luther King Jr. in the 1950s. When it closed in 1988 it became a nonprofit center focused on their ongoing social justice mission.

RYAN HOGAN: The space was special and the work that was showcased there was really good. It became a local staple for a good period of time until the administration at Scarritt-Bennett decided they were not going to allocate that space for an art gallery anymore. So it was kind of beyond Sabine's control at that point. But I think Sabine just had a great way of bringing people together, and a way of bringing multicultural experiences together. Sara Estes, Brandon Donahue, and Erin Plew were all there. I feel like Matt Christy hung out a lot there. I think he ended up getting a studio space.

SARA ESTES: Sabine Schlunk was the curator and it was amazing. So I had a studio space over on the Scarritt Bennett campus. It was just like an old rundown studio building. It was like a basement in one of those buildings on campus, and they gave us these little rooms with no windows. It felt like a mansion. We were all over the moon to get this dedicated space. The residents worked in the gallery. So we had a little coffee shop and we would work there in exchange for the studio space. It was me, Matt Christy, Brandon Donahue—a cool crew of people. That's when I first started getting the curating bug.

JOE NOLAN: Eric Lehning gave Gallery F a Best Contemporary Art Space notice in the *Nashville Scene*'s Best of Nashville, 2009 issue. He specifically noted the homey nature of the gallery and Sabine's welcoming demeanor. They had strong shows and their studios were always packed with talented emerging artists. They were also a great example of a place that made people feel at home and at ease at a time when many contemporary art spaces emanated exclusivity.

MATT CHRISTY: It had a way of attracting people. I remember I was working there one Sunday and this Israeli family stopped in. And I don't know why they picked Nashville and I don't know how they ended up at the gallery, but they were visiting their son who was biking through North America to visit different organic farms. And for some reason that's where they stopped to meet their son. And I had a lovely conversation with them. I also remember meeting one of La Monte Young's assistants from like ten years prior or something. She was saying, "Yeah, I just needed some coffee." I only knew a little bit about La Monte Young before that, but that prompted me to go visit one of his installations in New York. So it was just a weird place. I don't know how people ended up there, but it had this way, this gravitational pull of bringing interesting people to it. I attribute a lot of that to Sabine.

JOE NOLAN: When Nashville's contemporary art scene was coming up, we had to push the music stuff out of our way, because Nashville's music rep was so huge and it cast such a big shadow. But maybe we did too good a job. I'm active in music and visual art and I'm always surprised that we don't see more crossover between them. Julia Martin Gallery is probably the best example of how that can work. Her space is built over recording studios, and the live music on her porch is always one of the highlights at her receptions.

JULIA MARTIN: My gallery was a fluke. I took a two-and-a-half-month-long road trip. I'd come out of like a seven-year relationship that just sort of leveled me mentally, emotionally. I just sort of lost it and I kind of threw in the towel on painting. I didn't pick up a paint brush for almost three years. I started working in the movie business. I even went to beauty school for a little while. I was just trying to pull fucking shit back together. I was working in the movie business for like two or three years. I went to a little pop-up show by Shane Kennedy at Lonnie Hutchins's building on Humphreys. Lonnie and I have been friends for, shit, twenty-five years now probably. And he spirited me into his apartment, which is now my gallery. He brought me in and said, "I'm trying to spread the word. I don't want to rent this out residential anymore. I would like to find a tenant who's not residential, who's not going to make a lot of noise, and won't mind music coming up through the floorboards from time to time."

JOE NOLAN: JMG has been going strong for a decade. It's one of the galleries that helped to shift the center of the contemporary art scene from downtown Nashville to Wedgewood-Houston, and it's emblematic of the artist-lead curating and organizing that's the foundation of contemporary art in Nashville.

JULIA MARTIN: I started it genuinely with the intention of just not having to deal with galleries anymore, and just having a home base that was a little fucking vanity gallery. So it took a lot of fucking work for me to get eighteen pieces together to fill this place and have a grand opening. And then forty-eight hours later to be completely sold out of paintings and thinking, "What the fuck am I going to do now? This is not a business model. I have no inventory all of a sudden." I just started reaching out to regional artists that I had shown with and local artists whose work I liked who maybe weren't under contract at that moment. I don't really think of it as a commercial gallery, but I do think it's become a really beautiful and important cog in the art scene here. We have artists who are loyal that only show with me, but I don't like the idea of cock-blocking an artist from doing anything. I like the camaraderie among all the gallery heads. It's never been like this before. I think that the market was always so anemic that it was crazy tense competition between like Carol Stein [Cumberland Gallery] and Anne Brown [The Arts Company]—oh yeah, dude, that shit was ugly. I love now that the more we lift each other up, we all rise.

ART FIGHT CLUB

JAYJIT DASGUPTA: So, uh, interestingly enough, the Nashville Salon didn't actually start in Nashville. It started back in DC at George Washington University. We were undergrads and so there was a group of poets in DC—mainly Cynthia Saunders who's one of my closest friends— she started it because we had this tendency to all hang out and get drunk all the time. She kind of wanted to counter that a little bit. She knew there were a lot of theater people, and a lot of poets, and a lot of other visual artists and performing artists at George Washington, and she started this program. It was this one-night-a-month kind of thing where everybody brought their work together. And of course we all graduated, we all moved away. I came back to Nashville. I grew up in Nashville, but, back then, my Nashville was not the place to move to. It was the place to get out of.

JOE NOLAN: I found out about Salon through the Downtown Presbyterian Church's art community—Tom Wills and Todd Greene and Beth Gilmore. I want to say they were connected to Robert Myers and that's how I got to meet Jay. It was a party at Robert's place.

JAYJIT DASGUPTA: Salon in Nashville started like all great art happens— out of a big heartbreak. It doesn't matter now, but at the time it mattered. I was pretty much reeling from that break up and one of the people who reached out to me to sort of help me was my good friend from high school, Jennifer Cartwright. She took me to a party and introduced me to Freddie O'Connell and Robert Myers. Robert was at Watkins College of Art with Paul Thompson and they were kind of doing some film stuff. So Paul Thompson and Robert Myers were there. I met Joe Nolan there. Johnny McAllister and Chip Wilder. Beth Gilmore was there. Tom Wills and like the Downtown Presbyterian were part of it, too. There were all these artists sort of in this existential mode of like, "What defines me?" "What is the thing that I'm trying to do in my life?" There were all these artists around, but nothing was exclusively bringing them together where they could show each other their work. We were all hanging out. We were talking, we were drinking and shooting the shit, but we didn't have an event that was just art for artists. We were having gallery openings or whatever else. But artists need to talk with other artists because there's a sensibility that you cannot get from someone who's not an artist. I wanted to build that community of support because making art by yourself can definitely be a lonely challenging road. You have a lot of doubt.

JOE NOLAN: I remember reading a poem in somebody's living room— it was probably at Robert's place. I remember bringing my guitar and debuting a song I'd written. We were all beyond playing open mic gigs, and Salon was a good place to break something in and read it or play it for the first time. The real genius was that nearly everybody shared something—that was kind of the rule. It was like Fight Club where first-timers have to fight. People were mostly generous with each other because they knew they were going to have to read or play or let people look at their weird painting. It wasn't nearly as harsh as our poetry classes in college. It was casual. It was a party, but a party with a focus, and everybody there was making something or doing something artistic or they wouldn't have known about Salon.

JAYJIT DASGUPTA: I wanted it to be a very much like a closed event. You only get there because you know someone who invited you to come. And the thing about sharing real work is you have to trust the people who are around you. Otherwise people are not going to share. That's the main thing. They might share the work, but they're not going to share their early work or like early drafts or even sing songs while they're not in the best of voice or whatever. But if you're with other artists and only other artists you sing the song.

JOE NOLAN: I remember Salon becoming a Friday evening thing—like a happy hour. I seem to remember an absinthe Salon at Beth Gilmore's house. And then we all probably went to Boscos. Most creative projects start with a lot of passion and excitement—otherwise they just don't get started. And at Salon you'd be sharing a lot of that new enthusiasm with other artists, and it felt like Salon sort of fanned all those flames.

JAYJIT DASGUPTA: At its peak we were getting about thirty some people coming in and presenting every month. It was very organic feeling. And sometimes you didn't present, you just wanted to show up. But,

Salon to me—especially when we were in DC—was like a Fight Club of the mind, right? And especially between poets. We were part of that poetry program. It wasn't like competitive bullshit, but it was just like throwing punches. The reason I love stand-up comics and theater is because there's instant feedback to what you're doing. In film, which I'm involved with now, that is not there. There is no instant feedback. And I think Salon was a really good way to showcase work at an earlier stage than you would show it to other people. It made you be less afraid of sharing an earlier draft. You'd see what lines were hitting and what lines were not hitting, and that kind of made you move toward the next draft. Sometimes I would introduce a poem at its very early stage. And then months later I'd come back with a later draft or almost a finished draft you'd see the difference in people's reactions. And the crowd always changed enough that even if you came back later with the same thing there was always different people there.

HOMECOMING

M KELLEY: Well, so I actually started curating back when I was back at Western University. I was really interested in ways to show other people's work. And so, I experimented briefly with little weird ways of doing it through zines or through tiny pop-up displays of like xeroxes of people's art stuck to a wall somewhere—that kind of thing. I felt, "I'm going to work with what I've got." But, what ended up happening is Steven Zerne and Corey Lamp and I all lived in a house at the same time. We were all artists. I'd gone to school with Corey. He actually grew up in Nashville, went to school at Western, came back, and then me and Corey and Steven had all worked on a comic project, which is how I'd actually met Steven in the first place. And then he and I were in a relationship for like seven years. We were all roommates. I was still very driven to show artwork. Steven was very supportive, and Corey was just very interested in doing anything with the arts, period. We ended up starting Haus Rotations. We looked for houses that were currently empty, between renters. We talked to landlords to get them to let us put a show on in the house, and we would help make sure that it was ready to be shown. So we did a fair amount of sweeping and spackling after the show to bring it back to how it was when we found it. We wanted the landlord to be there during the art show so that they could talk to potential renters. People could be in the house to see the house and the artwork would be up. Our landlord was like, "Well let's do this." His name was Steve Benneyworth—he was a big local sculptor. His metal-working studio was actually in the basement of the house. We'd hang out on the back porch, and we'd work on stuff together in his studio, and then have beers. He'd kvetch about Richard Sera, and his time up in New York.

JOE NOLAN: House galleries like Rule of Thirds happened because there just wasn't a space for us. And the other part of it was fostering the audience for contemporary art because there wasn't an audience for it either.

SHAUN SLIFER: I'm from Nebraska, but we moved to West Tennessee when I was fifteen or sixteen, and then I moved to Nashville to go to Watkins, basically to get out of Memphis. I went to high school with someone who went to Watkins and said, "It's cool here. It's an art school." And I'd never actually thought about going to art school, but I was not a good student in public schools. I really faltered for the last six years or so. So art school was a way that I felt like I could go to college and maybe do well. I wanted to be a scientist, actually. I wanted to be an ecologist or biologist or something like that, but I didn't think I could go to a place like UT and actually survive the college campus culture of distraction. So I moved there for Watkins, which at that time was downtown. I ended up in this kind of strange building with like mostly a lot of film students. I just started taking classes there full time.

LESLEY PATTERSON-MARX: I was in a couple of group shows at Rule of Thirds. One time Shaun Slifer challenged a bunch of people to do a Polaroid show. He challenged a group of artists to go out and take a Polaroid somewhere in their world. The picture I took was of a neighbor that was tending his garden. He had like a mini farm on Ashwood. This neighbor basically had just this beautiful garden. And I would walk every day and see him. So I said, "Can I take your picture?" And I'm so glad I did, because you know, now there's a tall skinny house there.

SHAUN SLIFER: Ally Reeves found a house to rent with two of her friends, Greg and James, and I just remember that it happened really quickly that they got this house on Bernard. They moved in there super fast and she called me and said, "Yo, I got this place in your neighborhood. We're going to do it. The landlord seems kind of crazy." Then they were just in there. So Ally was going to school at Austin Peay in Clarksville studying studio art. Her friends James and Greg were people that she knew from West Philly. She kind of had had another life when she was younger living in West Philly in the anarchist punk scene there. And those guys were from Nashville and part of a scene of people out that way. They had all moved back to Nashville independently and circled up back into this house. Those are the guys who built the skate ramp out back later, but that's where they kind of come in. We lived in these two shoebox brick duplexes that were like crappier than almost every other house on the block. That's where I learned to ride a bike again, as an adult. I would just tear around on this bike that I pulled out of a dumpster and like partially refurbished. I worked the whole time I was in college—Watkins was really kind of a working college at that time. Everybody I went to school with, it was really a lot of different age groups. And a lot of people had part-time jobs. I worked at Tower Books and then I worked for Bob at Fido for what seems like years. At that time there was a melding between work life, activist life, and Watkins life.

TERRI SMITH: Some of the people involved in the art scene were also involved in music scenes or in activism in the case of like Shaun Slifer and Ally Reeves who knew activist people all over. So there's these sort of networks, and that was one of things about Rule of Thirds, there were a lot of out-of-state artists and that's what I remember really liking. They were hosting people who weren't from Nashville. So it was like different stuff, you know? But I remember thinking the scene there felt like an indie band scene. Even though it was art, it had that feel of like small indie band coming through town.

SHAUN SLIFER: They had two living rooms and they didn't have any furniture for one of them. That is literally what the beginning of Rule of Thirds was. They moved into their bedrooms and kitchen, and then they were like, "We have this huge white space." Greg's room was maybe an attic, I think. We thought the previous tenant had been growing weed in there because it was covered in foil. James was involved for a while. He was the third in the Rule of Thirds at that time.

JOE NOLAN: James Cathcart hosted movie screenings there, and half pipe skate parties—and Bernard Street is steep like a ski slope for skaters. Now, he's an artist and producer across the film and music industries, but he started in that living room space up from the original International Market & Restaurant.

TERRI SMITH: I think it's important to create a welcoming environment where people feel like they can ask questions and it's casual and it's social. And then you can trick them into looking at things that maybe aren't easy to get. In Nashville at that time, the social aspect was the key. So people go see art and if you don't understand it immediately then people often feel stupid. And there's a misconception in my experience that they jump from feeling stupid to feeling like the artist wants them to feel stupid. But when you're in a more casual social setting people meet artists and actually have conversations with artists and they feel involved. They feel like they're a participant and that makes them more engaged, which makes them more invested, maybe even more creative themselves.

SHAUN SLIFER: I remember we bought a five-gallon bucket of white paint and painted the living room. It was either a gallery or a yoga studio. Rob McClurg became my ceramics instructor at Watkins, but he was newly in town from Chicago then. He had these track lights he dug out of the dumpster behind the Art Institute of Chicago, and he brought them with him to Nashville. He was like "Dude, I got these lights that you can use." Which is the other thing we needed to make it feel like a gallery. At this time I was good friends with Lain York, who was one of the people in front of what was happening at The Fugitive and at Zeit-geist. And Ally had done a residency at Ruby Green. You know, these spaces were kind of operating similarly. You had media contacts and you'd send them a press release. You are a space doing a thing. And usu-ally you're listed in some kind of calendar. And then, if you're lucky, a writer will like also write a summary or maybe even come and review the show. So we just started doing it like that, except that our address is a residential address and it's a house venue or whatever. We made posters. The first show we did was Bryce McCloud in the early days of Isle of Printing. And so he went like above and beyond with these fuck-ing amazing hand-printed posters for it. And that got a lot of attention.

TERRI SMITH: I remember this piece Ally did where she had this Plexi-glass box hanging on the wall, it was small. And there was this leaf, like a real leaf in it. And there was this little kinetic thing that hit against the leaf or made the leaf move. I just loved that. I think every time I see her, I still mention that piece.

SHAUN SLIFER: We had the US getting involved in another war at that point which was massively unpopular. And so we were sort of involved in varying degrees in the anti-war movement. We were doing a lot of like street-level organizing with Food Not Bombs in Nashville, which for us really became a locus of a lot of different types of activists who were looking to do something that was very hands-on. We shared food with the homeless population in Nashville at least once a week to twice a week, if we could get away with it. That was kind of our boots on the ground way of trying to get involved in something tangible while we were involved in other parts of the movement and trying to figure out where to place yourself in your early twenties in terms of like all the stuff you think is wrong with the world and what you're going to do about it. And so we had this gallery space and we were straddling the kind of work that we were doing through school and through just participating in the art scene as it was in Nashville, going to openings and talking to other artists and being friends with them. And then we were trying to find ways to integrate the activism as well, which meant at that time pulling in groups like the Beehive Design Collective or some of our other friends from the kind of lefty political street art world. So it was still really like for me, wheat pasting and stenciling political messaging of some sort, of hopeful messaging of some sort. One of the things that we did was provide a venue that was almost nonexistent in the Southeast for lefty traveling things to come through. We were relatively reliable in terms of being a venue that was a little bit different than punk venues or collective houses.

JOE NOLAN: All these alternative spaces were a response to a lack of galleries, but also a lack of galleries interested in showing challenging contemporary art, and a lack of galleries that were interested in working with local emerging artists. By the end of the 1990s that tide was turning, but projects like Rule of Thirds and the Yart Sales were necessary because lots of artists felt like selling art off your porch and programming exhibitions in your buddy's living room were the only options they had.

KATIE CONNOLLY: I was roommates with Madeline Wolf and Jonny Silva. And our apartment was like doubling in rent in Sylvan Park, so we had to move and we needed a bunch of money to move. So I said, "We need an art sale." We didn't know where we could do it. And I said, "Well, let's have a yard sale with art." And then, either me, or Jonny, or simultaneously we just said, "Yart!" We had success before doing yard sales, so I thought, "Let's just try it." We had a huge yard. It was a really big success. We moved a lot of art that day. We made these great fliers that were glittery and collaged, and we delivered them and dropped them off at different places to try to get art collectors to come. It was really exciting.

JOE NOLAN: I remember Jonny Silva telling me about the first sale. I was so knocked out at the "Yart" name and also at how kind of obvious the idea was once these artists had been smart enough to see it in the first place. My brain sort of immediately went into overdrive and I had all these ideas about how to advertise for nothing and moving to an even more accessible location.

KATIE CONNOLLY: We were just making art all the time. Madeline and Johnny were painters and would do some mixed-media pieces. But I was doing collage and integrating a lot more crafty stuff into my art. I'd come from a more arts and crafts background, and they came from a more fine art background. Art was everywhere. Art was all over the kitchen. Art was all over the living room. Art was in the bedrooms, and we just had projects going constantly. It was a really creative and exciting time.

JOE NOLAN: My friend Renee Marino had an apartment in a house on Belmont. It had a big porch and a big front yard and tons of foot traffic just down from Bongo Java, between Lipscomb and Belmont Universities. I got us into some yard sale listings and I got us in the public radio weekly calendar announcements. I got Heather Nelson from this publication *All the Rage* to do a story about Yart. Jonny and Madeline and Katie all made stuff. And then also Renee and Gadsby Creson and myself.

KATIE CONNOLLY: I remember Renee Marino got involved. And I remember her talking about "Yart Sale 2: Electric Boogaloo."

JOE NOLAN: I was really into Tom Waits at that time, and I sketched this Fellini-esque carnival scene with oil pastels. There was this big-top circus tent in the background and this weird sad clown in foreground looking out at the viewer it was basically album art for a record that didn't exist. I remember this guy was really rummaging through everybody's work, shopping really seriously. He asked me how much it was and I probably sold it for twenty bucks. I remember he said, "You should do more clown paintings." About twenty years later I got an email through my website. This woman had purchased the painting at an estate sale and tracked me down because I'd signed the back of it. She was really excited about her find. I remember thinking "Maybe that guy was right about the clown paintings."

KATIE CONNOLLY: I had been in Chattanooga for a couple of years and moved back up to Nashville, and it was so exciting hanging out with Madeline and Johnny and watching them paint. It really got me involved and they were really supportive of what I did. Even though I didn't consider it art, they told me it was. That was really welcoming.

JOE NOLAN: We did at least a couple Yart sales on Belmont, but those things lose momentum if you don't want to run it more like a business. I'd never ever heard of the word Yart before that, but then you started to see other signs and notices for sales, and Watkins College ended up doing a big annual sale in their student center that they called "yArt" or even "YART." Regardless of how people spell it I still see them pop-up now and again, and I always think about how Johnny and Madeline and Katie invented that and did it first.

KATIE CONNELLY: I was really tickled to see it resurrected, to see somebody use it. I was like, "Hey, that looks familiar." Some kid went to the Yart Sale and just kept that idea in their brain and used it later. Nashville was catering to tourists and country music, and it still had a really good underground music scene. It feels like that's how the underground art scene emerged too. It was just, "We're all kind of freaks and we need to help each other out."

JOE NOLAN: The beauty of those house spaces—still—is that it's intrinsically casual to be hanging out in somebody's living room or grabbing some wine in the kitchen. There's also something a little absurd about exhibiting in yards, or garages, or basements, and that aspect of those domestic displays is disarming. You can't be too self-conscious looking at art in somebody's backyard shed.

DAVID ONRI ANDERSON: I saw a lot of talent in Nashville and in my friends, but they didn't have spaces to show in. And then the spaces where they could show are not the right spaces for them. They're just too white and clean and pristine, and we're all trying to be wild here. So we all needed a space that feels wild still, where you can act in ways that you would want to in your home. Some of the best music shows are house shows because people feel more comfortable and you don't have to pay at the door. There might be like a jar going around or whatever, but there's just a completely different vibe. There's also this feeling of wildness and people being uninhibited. In my opinion, there's a need for that in art, and in people's experience of art, to not feel this pristine, overly precious atmosphere because of the art. So it's about trying to get an authentic experience of the art and the artist and not trying to like be too bogged down by art trappings.

JOE NOLAN: One reason we've seen various takes on the house gallery continue to pop up is because the post-internet music culture is always reinforcing DIY, cottage industry models. Computers and the internet sort of smashed the traditional music business but they've creatively empowered indie artists. The same is true for visual artists. During the pandemic lots of galleries thrived off of online sales. And lots of artists are finding ways to bypass galleries using the internet and even creating their own spaces to display their work and to curate.

DAVID ONRI ANDERSON: My art career wouldn't exist if I didn't curate, because when I make these connections with other artists, and give them a platform and a space, it kind of opens more dialogue and more opportunity between both of us. It opens up avenues for me because I never went to grad school. I never went to the meetings or schmoozed with the right people or partied or anything. I just stayed in my studio and I never really went out that much. I just tried to stick to my studio in my life. I realized that if I'm going to have a social life or a network, I need to include other networks and other people. I do that by becoming interested in people's art or what they're doing. So that's been my way of building a path in a community, and staying afloat in a social and—hopefully—a career way.

JOE NOLAN: David had a studio in his basement when he lived in Wedgewood-Houston. Then he started showing work there in this cave-like space with all this exposed rock. It was a super weird. He named the space Bijan Ferdowsi after his landlord who is this really talented calligraphy artist from Iran.

DAVID ONRI ANDERSON: I cleaned out my studio and the first show was actually my own work because I just wanted to see what it'd be like to turn my basement into a gallery space. And then once that space was inhabited and people actually came, I had this feeling that people were inspired to show in that space and to do stuff that fit the cavern vibe down there. This tiny time zone of 2014 to like 2017 is when I lived there. I could walk to Zeitgeist, to Lusk, to Dozen bakery. So it felt nice to have like this art zone close to the art district that was like this wild and more raw and DIY situation. The basement was kind of dingy. It smelled like mold, apparently. Everyone told me that and I guess they were right. So it's kind of this dingy basement with limestone jutting out everywhere. And then kind of high ceilings in the main area and uncovered insulation in the ceiling. There was painting stuff everywhere. Around the corner was my friend Zach's studio. And going down the stairs and turning right immediately is this sort of square box area with raw wood walls and insulation ceiling. That was my studio space. And that became the Bijan Ferdowsi space. There were big barn doors going outside. We had a studio rat that got an ink jar on its head and was running around, clinking around with a jar on its head for a while—that was the subject of a painting by Matt Christy. It just had a dungeon vibe. I cleaned it up and it was well lit so it had this perfect feel of an intentional clean space, but still a dungeon. It was just a really gnarly alchemical space.

JOE NOLAN: David left the We-Ho neighborhood when he got a house in South Nashville. That was the end of Bijan Ferdowsi, but the Electric Shed was a huge upgrade.

DAVID ONRI ANDERSON: So when we moved in it was supposed to be a garage and it had no insulation, it was a raw studded space and the ceiling was raw. So me and my brother and our friend, Frank—who's a good electrician and construction guy—we built out the walls and put in the electricity and built out the ceiling and put in the lights and made it climate controlled and put in an air conditioner. And that took probably eight months. It shouldn't have taken that long, but we were doing it little by little over the year. I moved into the house in April 2018 and by October it was ready and we were excited to have Earthen show there. The idea for the shed is that it kind of mimics the raw wood inside of the house. So the idea of the shed is to keep it raw wood and to always have this raw wood and concrete material as it is. So whoever shows in there, that's just what they have to play off of. There's no white walls, but it's very clean—it's probably the nicest, cleanest space I've had as a show space for art. The first show for Electric Shed was in October 2018, and that was Earthen Clay.

JOE NOLAN: You see the same kind of whimsy and energy in the stuff David makes and in the work he shows in the shed, and sometimes all over his backyard. It's not a retail space and it's not run like a commercial gallery. The schedule is driven by inspiration – it's another part of his art practice.

DAVID ONRI ANDERSON: I'm always open to my friends doing stuff at the shed. Electric Shed is my way of keeping the curatorial torch alive. I'm always open to guest curators and to swapping shows. So I've realized that working in a large group of people—it's like being in a music band—it's hard for everyone's lives and schedules and ambitions to line up all the time. I realized after a while I needed to consolidate the rent to one place, which is my backyard in my house. I curate out of there and don't do every single month, but just as things come up. That's what Electric Shed has become. I'm trying to maintain the integrity of running a curatorial space without having this intense schedule.

GRANTLAND HOUSE

JOE NOLAN: The Grantland house was in the 12 South neighborhood that's now posh as hell. Back then, my friends who lived east of 12 South had their houses broken into. That house was Terry Glispin's place and Jack Ryan lived there for awhile and then it was sort of passed-on to another generation of artists. For years it was a house where people lived, but also a studio and a kind of headquarters where lots of both parties and plans were made. I don't have any idea how many cigarettes were smoked on that porch.

JACK RYAN: And we'd have these huge parties at The Fugitive, and the street would be packed with cars for the openings, but really no one ever hung out outside on the street—everyone knew better. And there was so much room inside to have a party and then it would relocate. And then it would go to Grantland Avenue. Then the party would go on there for as late as could be. It was pretty rough over there—it was almost as bad as The Fugitive. The floors were so slanted in that house you could roll a ping pong ball from one end to the other.

LESLEY PATTERSON-MARX: I feel like those golden years of The Fugitive and the Grantland house, we weren't plugged in yet. If we had a phone, it was a flip phone. I have lots of memories of answering machine messages and we're just right on the cusp of being plugged in. And I feel like there's so many ways in which the internet brings us together, but there's so many ways in which we can all stay in our bubbles.

JACK RYAN: People used to come up to Terry and say "You're the director of a school and you live in this shit hole?" That was a real common thing, "You're a professor there and you're the director and this is where you live?" It was horrible and it didn't bother us at all. I didn't think about it. We were just starting our careers. We had an exhibition there and I don't even remember why. I remember that I hung a piece of my work in what was my bedroom, where my bedroom was cleared out. Otherwise, mostly we had a lot of parties there. I remember we had lamps out in the front yard and everyone would be out front and lighting fireworks. Terry Glispin always had fireworks. Those were always going off outside of the house.

LESLEY PATTERSON-MARX: Terry would have an end-of-the-school-year-party and invite all the students to celebrate. And I just remember that seeming normal because I went to Murray State and that was just like what the teachers did there, too. We had a big party at the end of the year. And those are some great, great memories. I just remember it would be one of those things where you start out showing up around 3 P.M. and then end up leaving around 3 A.M. because it felt like all my favorite people were always there at those parties. Jonathan, who's now my husband, lived in the neighborhood. And so I remember him riding his bike up there.

JACK RYAN: I also remember getting in that huge car that I drove Greg Pond up to Nashville in. I remember Terry saying, let's go for a drive and he just wanted to do a big loop around the whole neighborhood, like past Kurt Wagner from Lambchop's house. I remember Terry just drove like a bat out of hell, like literally sliding through intersections and about halfway through it I said like, "Can you let me out of here on the corner?" Because I was pretty sure we were going to go straight into Kurt's house or something like that. But it was so much fun, you know? So there was a car like blazing around the neighborhood, you know, just for fun. And it was that same car. That car had gone from driving Greg up to Nashville. Then it lived down in Sewanee. And then I think Greg gave it to Terry who drove it around for a long time. An enormous vehicle. But the neighbors were super tolerant. Or maybe they enjoyed the parties. You know, we got to befriend them despite the fact that we were also probably really annoying. Once a month there'd be a blowout. And it was like all over the street.

JOE NOLAN: The Grantland house was the place to go after an opening at The Fugitive. That crazy falling-down house was an important intersection for The Fugitive and Watkins.

JACK RYAN: I remember we would have critiques for Watkins students. And sometimes we'd do them at The Fugitive. All the students were there and all the teachers would show up. Like, even if I wasn't teaching the class, I would go. Barbara Yontz would go. You'd have Mark Hosford show up who had his own new position on the other side of town at Vanderbilt University. And I remember it might go on for three hours past when it was supposed to. It might go on until ten o'clock at night, then we'd all go to Grantland, and the students would come. And the students at Watkins weren't like eighteen-year-old students. They were like in their twenties and some were even older—a very nontraditional student population. They would come to the house and party.

BETH GILMORE: I remember us shooting fireworks off the porch for like New Year's or Fourth of July. I don't remember which one it was. I guess we were warm enough to be outside so maybe it was Fourth of July. Inside the house, there were tongue sculptures installed in the wall, like resin thumbs and tongues. They were on big screws and they were screwed into the wall in the kitchen. There were these permanent installations and also dance parties and food. I remember Terry and Erin [Hewgley] making some really good tacos with a molé sauce. Maybe the kitchen was painted bright green and the floor was really lumpy. It was really fun. I remember having a good time there. It was such a good group of friends and allies in art.

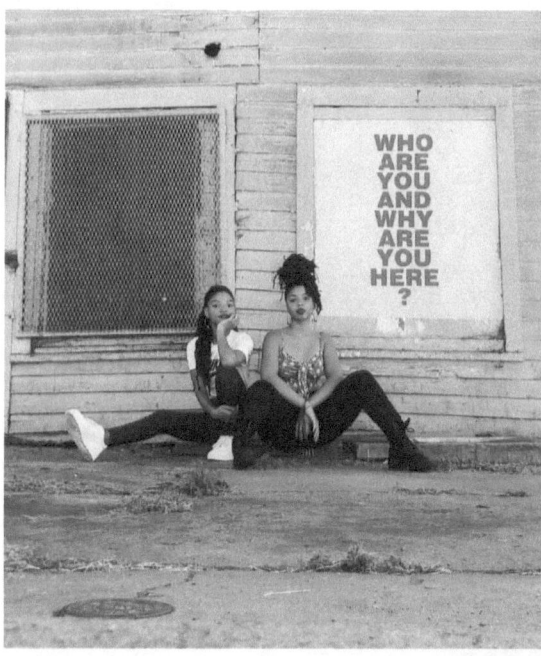

AUG. 23, 2018 Musical duo Chloe x Halle stop by 1201 Buchanan Street for a photo op in the emerging Buchanan Arts District, North Nashville. *Credit: Kelly Bonadies*

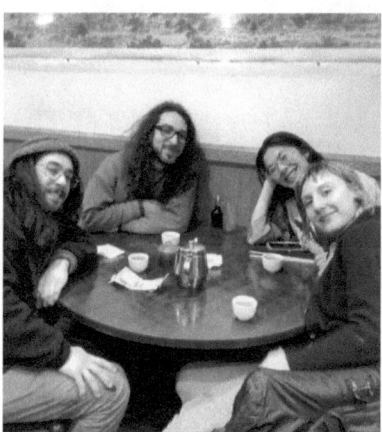

2015 The Mild Climate curatorial team meets at Vegetarian Dim Sum in Chinatown, NYC. From left to right: David Onri Anderson, Zack Rafuls, Mika Agari, and Earthen Clay. *Courtesy of David Onri Anderson.*

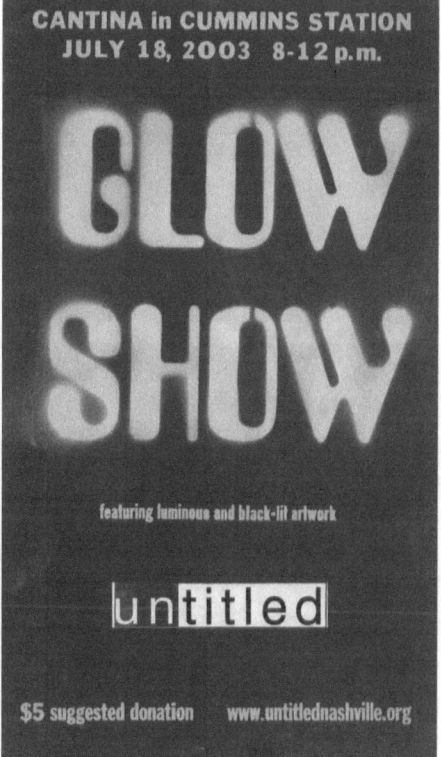

CANTINA in CUMMINS STATION
JULY 18, 2003 8-12 p.m.

GLOW
SHOW

featuring luminous and black-lit artwork

un**titled**

$5 suggested donation   www.untitlednashville.org

JULY 2003 A poster for one of Untitled Artists' annual *Glow Show* exhibitions. The irreverent displays celebrated the spectacle of fluorescent, glow-in-the-dark, and black-light art. *Credit: Landry Butler*

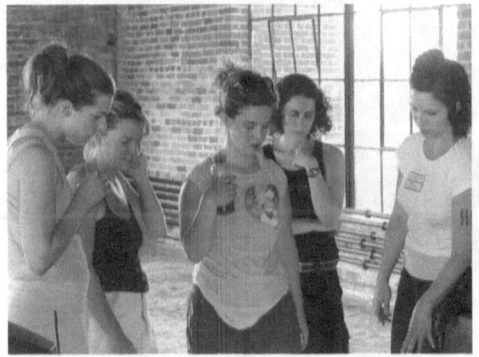

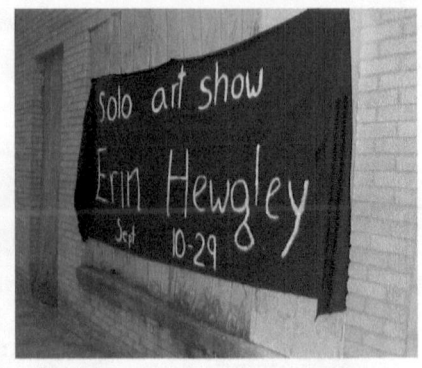

2006 Off the Wall installing a show at Marathon Village—Mahlea Jones, Janet Berkley, Quinn Dukes, Jaime Raybin, Iwonka Waskowski. *Credit: Jaime Raybin*

2005 A makeshift banner announces a solo exhibition by artist Erin Hewgley at the Secret Show Series' outpost at 310 Chestnut St. *Credit: Jaime Raybin*

MARCH 5, 2005 A postcard for the Secret Show Series' *Metrosexual Tent Revival* exhibition at the Chestnut building. *Credit: Jaime Raybin*

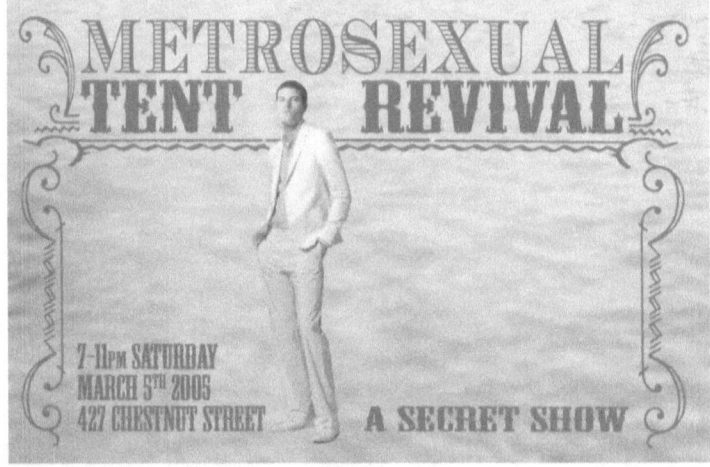

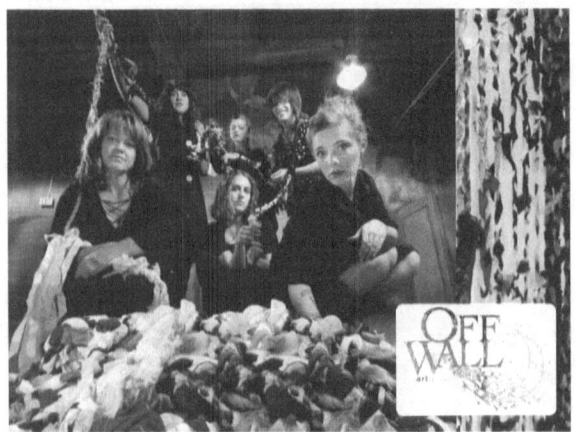

2006 Off the Wall official group picture: Front row from left: Janet Berkley, Jaime Raybin, Quinn Dukes. Back row from left: Jenny Luckett, Mahlea Jones, Iwonka Waskowski. *Credit: Jaime Raybin*

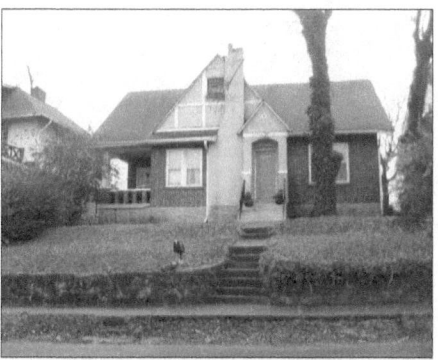

DECEMBER 18, 2009 The Rule of Thirds house at 1507 Bernard Avenue. *Credit: Shaun Slifer*

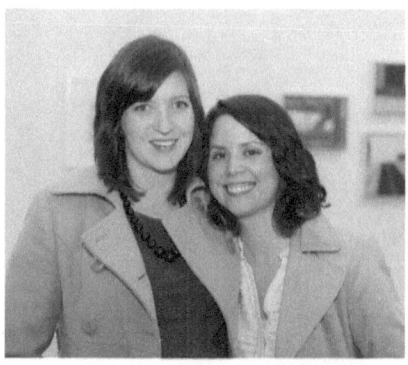

2012 Artist Jodi Hays with curator Sara Estes at the opening reception for Jodi's *Strong in the Broken Places* exhibition at Threesquared. *Credit: Dane Carder*

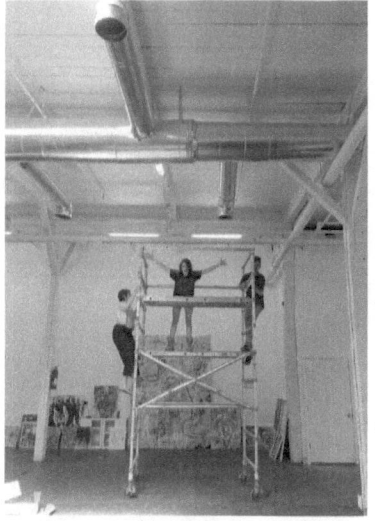

MAY 29, 2013 Annie Williams, Kelly Bonadies, and Scott Pierce (HK artist and assistant) in Harmony Korine's studio at 100 Taylor Street. *Credit: Kelly Bonadies*

2008 Dia de los Muertos exhibition at Plowhaus, poster by Eric Denton. *Credit: Ben Vitualla*

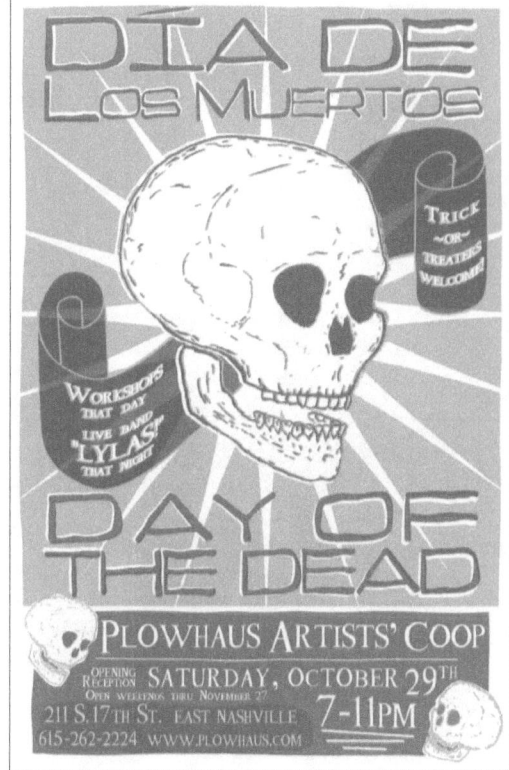

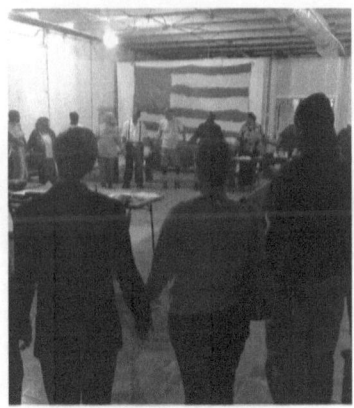

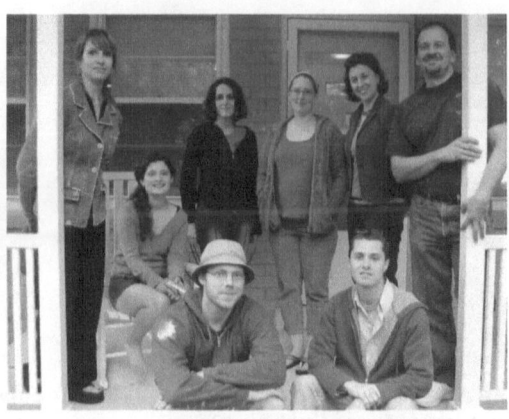

JUNE 28, 2016 North Nashville Leadership Council and the Buchanan Area Neighborhoods Alliance hold a community meeting at 2100 Buchanan Street. It brought together longtime and new residents, stakeholders, and community artists. *Credit: Kelly Bonadies*

C. 2005 The Secret Show Group from left to right: (back) Iwonka Waskowski, Amanda Dillingham, Jaime Raybin, Eve Peach, Heather Springs Thompson, Derek Gibson, (front) Will ClenDening, and Jason Driskill. *Credit: Amanda Dillingham*

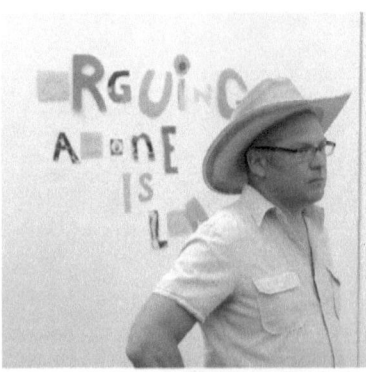

JULY 2012 Artist Brady Haston at Matt Christy's *Arguing Alone Is Lonely* show at Threesquared. *Credit: Dane Carder*

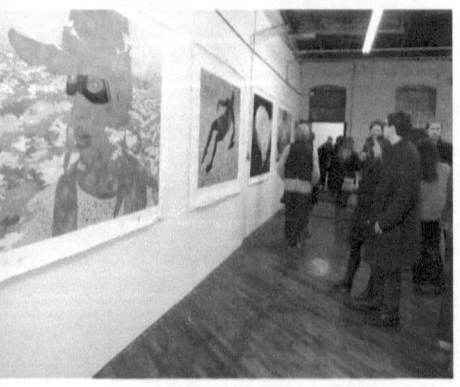

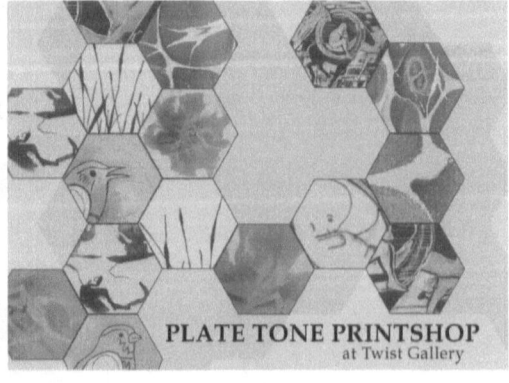

JAN. 19, 2013 The big wall at Threesquared during the opening reception for Casey Pierce's *New West* painting exhibition. *Credit: Dane Carder*

2007 Platetone Printshop at Twist Gallery exhibition postcard. *Credit: Jaime Raybin*

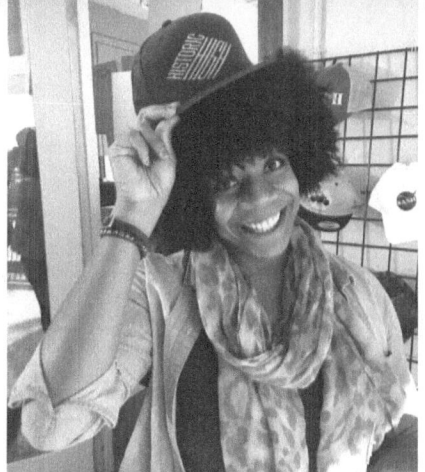

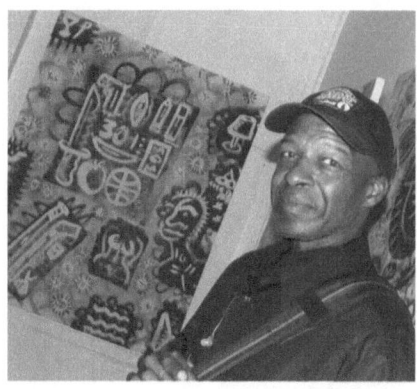

SPRING 2017 An unknown gallerygoer sports Historic High at Brikolaj. *Credit: Jared Brennan*

SPRING 2017 An unknown art crawler making the scene at Brikolaj. *Credit: Jared Brennan*

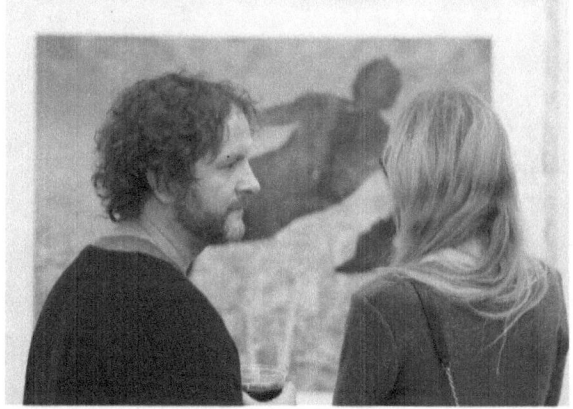

JAN. 19, 2013 The author with Antonia Oakes at the opening reception for Casey Pierce's *New West* exhibition at Threesquared. *Credit: Dane Carder*

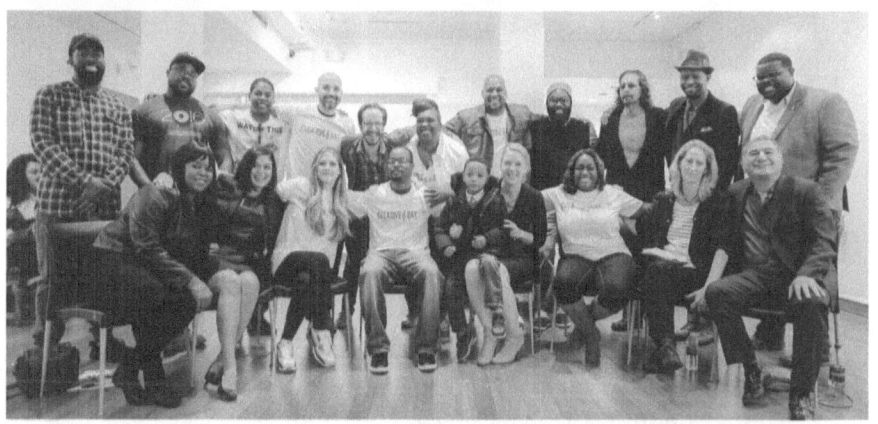

OCT. 22, 2016 Following a panel in the Fisk University Galleries during the Inaugural Creatives' Day Celebration Weekend. Seated bottom row, left to right: D'Lisha Davis, Tanisha Cobb (exit/in), Kelly Bonadies, Brian Sexton (Founder of Creatives' Day), Ahmaru Waters, Audra Ladd, Jessica Rich, Robin Paris, CEO Nashville Arts Paul Polycarpou. Top row standing, left to right: Marcus Speller, Eric Brown Jr, Dacari Middlebrooks, Aron wright, Freddie O'Connell, Anasa Troutman, Adrian Granderson, Jason Eskridge, Andy Van Roon, Thaxton Waters, Jamaal Sheats. *Credit: Kelly Bonadies*

Packing/Planting
1950–2015

THE PACKING PLANT IS a former abattoir and sausage factory known for creating a regional baloney brand. Nowadays it's a warren of art galleries along with a risograph print shop, a poetry library, and a local radio station. The Packing Plant is the headquarters of the city's longest-lived artist-lead spaces, and the Wedgewood-Houston neighborhood has become the center of Nashville's contemporary art scene.

JON SEWELL: I'm from here, but we lived in Houston when I was in middle school. In middle school there was a young Black girl named Evangeline Thomas. She was super cool. Our names were alphabetical in attendance it was "Sewell?" then "Thomas?" She turned me on to anarchist politics. And we were in seventh grade going "What is this word?" So I got into that first and then started finding punk after that. Evangeline might've turned me on to an Epitaph Records compilation or something. It was street punk that pretended to be more working class, even if it wasn't. And that was back in the day, obviously before the internet, but you would get someone's album and you would have to look at who they thanked or who they toured with and then, "All right, now I'm going to try to find that album."

JOE NOLAN: Radical politics and art don't always go together, but they can when they do. In Nashville it mostly leaks into art through the independent music scene. The Packing Plant isn't wearing an ideology on its sleeve but the whole vibe is informed by mutual aid and cooperation.

JON SEWELL: We came back to Nashville for high school. I had a punk band and we played at Lucy's a bunch. We called it Murdered Minority. That was super heavily influenced by the anarcho-punk crowd. So you have to have a very "gotcha" name. We had lots of peace symbols and anarchy symbols and stuff. We did a 10 inch. After I got my master's degree we had a band called Party Cannon and I played drums standing up. It was more performance-based. The song title is the complete lyric. You know, "Let's Eat Roadkill" you just say, "Let's eat roadkill!" a bunch. The goal was to try to get kicked out of all these places we played. The last performance of Party Cannon was like ten years ago at The Packing Plant. I remember everybody chanting "Fuck Jon Sewell!"

JOE NOLAN: The commercial galleries are a cornerstone in the We-Ho art community, but The Packing Plant, and the art and literature and music happening there, are the beating heart of the place.

JON SEWELL: The Packing Plant was caving in. It had Frankenstein roof lines. It had terrible graffiti on it—like a backward swastika. You got some devil stuff over here, some random clothes. I got a call from the building maintenance guy the first time I ever go in it. He told me, "The key is under a stone." I go and get the key and go in with my structural engineer. He falls through some stairs. There's no lights. There's no windows yet. The space is even more chopped up and the floor is all weird. There was a hallway that went nowhere. Another hallway that went nowhere. There was a vintage baby stroller with a doll sitting in it, facing the doorway. My structural engineer said, "Man, you sure do pick them."

JOE NOLAN: That place was a mess, and even when they started showing art in the front gallery it was just this place that felt like it was falling down. Seeing the transformation in that space has been like watching a large scale art project happening in real time. It's part sculpture, part found object, all DIY.

JON SEWELL: The first person I showed it to was a guy named Ben Todd. He was running a place called Glen Danzig House that was in Wedgewood-Houston. It was a house show venue—people lived there, but they also put on punk shows in their living room. And he was also running a record label called Nashville's Dead, which was also a website, which did an annual festival. They would have a curated list of shows to go see on their site. Ben and I had an interesting relationship because he was kind of the generation below me. So I got the building and I sent texts that I knew would get his attention, but it was kind of cryptic. He shows up with a couple of friends cause he didn't know what was going to happen—I just invited him to a slaughterhouse. And Ben looks at it and we were going to do a venue in the big backspace for bands to play. So people walk in through the back of the venue. It's like the perfect setup so you can load-in the back. And then in the front room he was going to do a record store up there where he'd put out his band and then also other local acts. Ben was saying, "Yes! This is exactly what I've been looking for." I thought that was awesome because I don't have a vision. There is no master plan. I was just going to finish out the space as there was demand or interest. It was around that time that Ben passed away. He died like eight years ago.

JOE NOLAN: So much of the programming at The Packing Plant is rooted in DIY ethics. It's a great match because that building is a DIY project too.

JON SEWELL: I was a union carpenter in a display shop. They did a lot of auto shows. We were building football fields of high gloss laminate for cars to drive over. It's very seasonal work, but it's high energy. You work all the goddamn time during that season of twelve-, fourteen-hour days, seven days a week. It's also high waste. I started as an apprentice then came up and I was running my own CNC department—programming woodworking equipment at a computer, but also running the machine. The guy that was training me bounced and they decided, "I guess you're in charge now." We're cutting all sorts of interesting ass shit. And then we have a ton of drop. Because I ran my own department people were working under me. I'd say, "Here's a pallet to put all the drop on. When that pallet is full, you let me know." I'd get the forklift and go hide the drop in the warehouse. Then I'm negotiating to get general foreman pay because they needed me. I'm a department head. I'm a made man. I had shit in the warehouse, and that's why The Packing Plant is blue. It's because there was a lot of blue and white signage material that was the drop from a job. That's how much waste there is. I was saving all that. I used those materials to build out The Packing Plant. If you go upstairs, there's a bunch of acrylic everywhere because I'd saved that. If it gets one scratch on it they can't use it. Volkswagen scratched acrylic. You know I can use that. The treads to get upstairs are old Volkswagen floor panels. You get upstairs in the common area, there's aluminum and high gloss floor panels that connect together—they were from an auto show. I had an economics professor that called it the "slack in rapidly moving systems." I took advantage of slack in the system to build out The Packing Plant little by little as people came up.

JOE NOLAN: Nashville was used to seeing art in nongallery spaces, but those first shows at The Packing Plant were an extreme version of that.

JON SEWELL: And the very first show I did there was when Zeitgeist had just opened across the street. So I made a display called *Culturegeist*— you know, you've got to kind of poke somebody in the eye. It was a pop-up show that Veronica Kavass curated in the front room.

JOE NOLAN: That first series was billed as *Culturegeist at The Packing Plant*. The opening show was a video installation by Mika Agari. It was a video called "Walmart." She hid cameras on Walmart shelves.

VERONICA KAVASS: There wasn't really a lot to work with. It was very rough. It wasn't painted. It was just cinder block. But I was like, "We can do cool things in here." But there was a lot of rubble. It was this really rough space. The first show I did was Mika Agari. It was just a projection in that first space to the right. That small gallery space. I liked her art work a lot. I'm always oriented more toward kind of sound and film-based work. I love working with that kind of stuff. Also, you can't really hang paintings in that space with the way it was looking. The video is of her sticking a TV in a Walmart, with her doing her weird ass artwork, some kind of choreography playing on the screen. She stuck it in there and then filmed people like either just walking right by it or suddenly seeing it and being like, "What the fuck?" She set up a camera right across from it, and it's capturing the reaction to the little TV that's in this Walmart. Mika had just graduated from Watkins.

JON SEWELL: Then Mike Callaway-Fagen was a professor at Indiana at the time. He comes down and does a student show where they're deep frying all sorts of things in the gallery. There was no place to poop and the power is all run off an extension cord coming from God knows where.

VERONICA KAVASS: They deep fried high heels and just anything. They were deep frying everything.

JON SEWELL: So then Veronica hooks up with Ann Catherine Carter and says, "She's young and interested in curating." And the younger artists are obviously more plugged in because they're going to more things, there's more energy to what was up. And at that time we were just calling the building The Packing Plant. And then Ann Catherine Carter started using that for the name of the gallery and curating some of the pop-ups. Then the first permanent tenant was the Mild Climate gallery with Ann Catherine Carter, Mika Agari, Zach Rafuls, and David

Onri Anderson. I was still not charging any rent because I don't think I'd gotten the final use and occupancy permit on the space.

DAVID ONRI ANDERSON: Company H was a collective in Watkins. I don't know who started it, but me and Zach and Mika and Kayla Saito and Earthen Clay, and a few other people were all part of that collective for several years. And we did programming and curating. People before us did stuff and handed that collective name down to us, and that was like a collective that existed beyond my time also. After our core group in company H was out of Watkins, we formed Mild Climate. I was doing Mild Climate in around 2015 before I had even graduated Watkins, I guess. Zach and Mika were ahead of me by like a year, and Earthen like two years ahead. And then I think around 2014, Zach started joining in and helping Ann Catherine. And then I was also helping out, but not officially part of the programming. I think around 2015 Ann Catherine stepped down, that's when I stepped-up more and did curating and actual planning and programming and Mika joined with me. Earthen joined at some point and then Mika moved to New York in like 2017. And then Tristan Higginbotham joined in 2017. And we did that until the end of 2018. And then we did stuff in like New York and Georgia. We did some traveling and we did lectures at RISD and Georgia State, Athens and other places. Mild Climate probably existed for about three or four years.

JON SEWELL: So we kind of work it out where they're paying a small amount of rent, and then I just keep going, fixing up one room at a time as there was demand. Then COOP moved in across the hall from Mild Climate.

JOE NOLAN: Fort Houston started as Brick Factory in the Cummins Station building downtown. They were a shared maker space and they also curated shows and hosted parties after the downtown Art Crawl. You'd drink wine and look at paintings while you wandered through all these saws and worktables. Visual art didn't become a bigger focus for them until later, but when they moved to Wedgewood-Houston the curated gallery spaces in The Arcade followed almost immediately.

JON SEWELL: Fort Houston moves into the neighborhood and I think they link up with Zeitgeist thinking, "We'll do our own crawl over here." So I decided I was going to fix up the space and then Mild Climate moved in. And then when COOP was interested in that other space, I was already talking to a barbershop, but it didn't really fit the vibe. And I ultimately want to do stuff that I'm interested in, and I wasn't interested in a barbershop. So when COOP was moving in, we did do some improvements. So then it's Mild Climate and COOP. I get COOP as a refugee from The Arcade because the original downtown Art Crawl was declining.

JOE NOLAN: The Packing Plant was coming online just as the real purge of the Chestnut building was happening.

JON SEWELL: And then the next big tenant I got was Channel to Channel. They moved from down the street at the May Hosiery building. So they're essentially like an economic refugee from May Hosiery that gets bought out by big Chicago people—their pockets are so deep they're dragging. And they were trying to jerk Dusten around and move him between units. They told him some things that they didn't honor. Dusten comes and sees it on a Friday and by Saturday we've agreed on terms.

DUSTEN HEDRICK: 2015 is when the building switched ownership. And then it took a year for them to really get a game plan on what was going to happen. And in 2016 is when they decided, "All right, second floor is being demoed." They wanted to move me downstairs and they showed me a place near Dane's studio. But I had already talked with Jon. It was really weird and serendipitous where it was almost the exact same day that I got the email that this was happening, Brian Jobe called me and asked me if I knew Jon Sewell at The Packing Plant down the street?

JON SEWELL: So I decided, "Well, now I'll bust my ass to finish out that space." That's the big space. We found the best arrangement for the pocketbook was for him to sublet those two side rooms. It's still like that today. Now that COOP's moved into that space they sublet to Risology Club and to Open Gallery, which is run by the art department of David Lipscomb University.

JOE NOLAN: COOP was started largely by faculty at Watkins. But after COOP established its Arcade presence, Watkins opened an official off-campus gallery for their students and alumni there. It's just called Watkins Art Gallery. Once COOP left The Arcade it was only a matter of time before WAG moved to We-Ho. It's great that the receptions at The Packing Plant include work by students. It's part of what makes our scene unique.

JON SEWELL: After Watkins moved in it was time to build out the upstairs. I did that in phases too: there's a kitchenette/common area, and there are two rooms off of it. At that time Jonathan Edelheuber's basement flooded and we were Instagram buddies. We weren't really friends in real life, but we'd like each other's stuff and both had an Arkansas connection. But I saw his basement flooded where he was using his studio. So I just reached out and told him I had an enormous area upstairs. It's not climate controlled. There's insulation in the walls, but not enclosed. It gets kind of dusty, but there's an area where I'm not working in and you could set up there. Since then he's worked with LA galleries, galleries in Berlin. I saw he's in a group show in Berlin and Hong Kong.

JOE NOLAN: When the Fugitive was in Wedgewood-Houston it was lots of small industry and some residential housing. But it used to be country living.

JON SEWELL: It was literally a field of cows, and the Packing Plant sets back on the lot because at the front of that lot was a house. And there were houses up and down that street. They went away as the neighborhood became more industrial. They built this little smokehouse in the backyard, and the bottom floor of the packing plant is two buildings that were each added on to before they enclosed the space between them. So they started doing a lot of sausage there. They made baloney there. So I think in the 1950s a meat packing plant appears on a Sanborn map of the neighborhood. And it's a smaller footprint than what's there now, because it kept getting added onto. Risology Club is in what used to be a walk-in refrigerator space. That was the walk-in freezer. The big COOP space was the sausage packing area. The northwest corner is the room where the pigs used to hang—you kill a pig, it was taken over there. It would hang from these joists that I've removed and saved, and a couple of them are on the side of my house because they're cedar which is pretty interesting. The front room at one point in time had a spice vat in it. Once an old lady showed up and she said, "I lived in the house at the front of this lot. My dad was plant manager. Grandma lived across the street in a trailer and I'd come every spring to pick these flowers that she planted and I'd take them to my house." She asked to see the place and I was like, "Yeah, of course!" She said her son came and worked here for a little bit during the summers. They came to one of our first pop-up shows. I have pictures of them. They said two brothers named DeFord ran the place. They fell out. They didn't like each other. So that tiny room upfront was then divided into two. You could still see there's a rough part of the floor where they broke it up. Her son said there was a spice vat in this one room. The son said he had to come in every morning and tap the side of the vat to get the rats out of it. One of the bathrooms is where they had the souse vat. That had like all the extras just boiling. He said they literally used a rowboat oar to stir that stuff up. The older woman said the two brothers had a falling out because "they was bad for women and gambling." You can imagine where the money went. They had a bologna contract with Nashville schools. Every morning a truck would pull up, they'd have a little conveyor ramp, they'd come down and they'd just load out in the morning. They sell the business, the real estate, the equipment, everything to Elm Hill Meats. Elm Hill Meats is still around. So if you're a bologna fan and you go to Kroger right now, Elm Hill Meats bologna is from The Packing Plant. But then they get the building back in some weird transaction. I think they get it back in like the 1970s then they sell it again in the early 1980s. Anyway, it becomes a distribution hub for adult entertainment items. They block up all the windows, you know, and it's just a warehouse to store these adult items. Kids used to come home and their parents would be like, "Where'd you get that video?" They'd find interesting stuff in the trash here during that period.

Art Words

1990–2022

NASHVILLE'S ART CRITICS put a spotlight on the city's contemporary art renaissance beginning in the 1990s. In alternative weeklies, regional journals, and national publications they helped to contextualize and define the emerging scene in the city limits and beyond. Nashville's contemporary art scene bubbled up from the homespun, improvised and underground, and its best art writers combine the dogged commitment of beat reporters with a broader understanding of the art conversations happening at the national level.

JONATHAN MARX: I started working at the *Nashville Scene* in the summer of 1990. I had just graduated from college and was looking for jobs and the *Scene* had just been bought out—it used to be a newspaper you would throw in people's driveways with a bunch of coupons. But Bruce Dobie and Albie Del Favero bought it out and wanted to turn it into an alternative news weekly—kind of like the *Austin Chronicle* or *Creative Loafing* in Atlanta. I came in about a year after that and I was initially just an editorial assistant. And then a few things shifted around and basically I was given kind of an entertainment editor role, and then I became de facto person who is editing all of the arts and cultural and music coverage. When I started, Susan Knowles was the art critic at the *Scene*. So she was contributing back in the very early nineties.

SUSAN KNOWLES: Dave Ribar and I worked together at Cheekwood. I started working there in '82. We were starting to do—from time to time—contemporary artists, solo exhibits. I contacted *Art Papers* in Atlanta and said, "There are some contemporary artists in Nashville. I think these would be worth covering." Xenya Zed, who was the editor there then said, "Well, send us something." So I did. And so that was my first published review for *Art Papers*. And then I was the Tennessee editor for *Art Papers* for years and years after that. This is maybe '84. Marilyn Murphy is at Vanderbilt doing this incredible work that's all these big industrial scenes and they're all the Tennessee scenes like the Norris Dam for example, those big pastel drawings. There was kind of nothing going on here except for Vanderbilt pretty much. So I pitched an article to *Nashville Magazine* and Amy Lynch was the editor there. Marilyn could get good images of her work. And so they gave us a nice spread and they gave us a cover. There was a publication called *New Art Examiner*—they were in Chicago and had an office in DC. I pitched them and started sending them an occasional piece. And then *Number* came along in Memphis. Homegrown, great people over there. And then the *Scene* comes along. I think I was the first art writer for them.

JOE NOLAN: I'd done a lot of creative writing at Michigan State University, and I'd done an internship at a newspaper. But after moving to Nashville in 1992, I was more focused on music than criticism. I'm one of those artists constantly looking for new books, new music, new art. You take it all in, and you analyze and learn from the stuff that sticks. I started blogging in 2004. I wrote about the movies I was watching and fringe culture stuff. When I started blogging, I was putting that research part of my process into writing, and that's when I realized I could be publishing this stuff in more established publications and platforms. All that old lit/journo education kicked-in. I started writing for the *Scene* in 2006. After I published my first Critics' Pick in the paper I immediately contacted Leslie Leubbers at *Number*—the regional art journal in Memphis. I told her I was an art writer for the *Scene* and she accepted my first pitch.

SARA ESTES: I was really passionate about *Number*, and I loved that *Number* was a print publication, and it was a cool print publication. It was printed on newsprint. It was a big square. So it was also kind of like a different shape. And there was a huge image on the front and cool graphics, you know—it just looked like an art publication. And it was thin, it was readable, easily digestible. It wasn't heavy on the advertising front, even though it did have ads—even the ads were all cool.

It was more of an experimental publication, and it felt like an underground magazine.

JOE NOLAN: If you were involved in the early days of Nashville's contemporary art scene, you were reading *Number* and you were reading the *Nashville Scene*.

SUSAN KNOWLES: Freelancing for the *Scene* was cool. Albie Del Favero was a publisher, and Bruce Dolby was the editor. And Bruce is a real journalist, a writer. They were high concept and snarky and it was fun. They let me, pretty much, pick out what I wanted to do. And sometimes there were columns that were like two or three different shows. When I was talking to an artist, a lot of what you're picking up is intuitive—and that's important. And that's good because that's the way artists are and work. My intention was to serve in the same way I feel like working as a museum curator, as a bridge between the artist and the artist's intention, and the public. I didn't write many scathing things.

JONATHAN MARX: David Ribar was the first person who I think really brought a keenly analytical bent to what he was doing. And he really was willing to take a stand about the aesthetic and cultural value of what was happening in our community. He wouldn't get mired in sort of analyzing the aesthetic qualities of work, just because. You know, "This has value and here's why" or "This is not good! And this is why we should actually care that it's not good." People in the community wanted criticism. They wanted people to take a stand about the value, the artistic value of what was happening in the community.

DAVID RIBAR: So I actually came to Nashville because there was a job at Cheekwood that opened up. A friend of mine had left and said, "Hey, you need to check this out." So I did. And they hired me in 1979, right in the summer. So I came down here not knowing a soul, and I was the preparator. And I think they paid me $8,600 a year. It was a real labor of love. So, I worked at Cheekwood for twelve years. Half the time I was preparator and in 1985 I was promoted to curator of exhibitions. That required me to do some writing for the shows I'd organized. So, that's kind of how I backed into doing writing about art in the first place. I left there in '91, like two weeks before I started teaching at Belmont. I had done a number of pieces for *Art Papers* and really enjoyed it. It was a complement to what I was doing at Cheekwood. I started writing for the *Scene* in '96, I think. I did it in part because I needed to develop a portfolio of things to use for tenure.

BOB DURHAM: Ribar was hilarious. He was as nasty as they come. He would excoriate people. We'd just love to get his damn reviews and we'd just laugh our asses off. You could say there wasn't much going on at that time, but there were intimations that things were going to be happening in this art scene, and Ribar was good. He was a young, angry man and he was right. He was really fun. It was well thought out and he really let people have it. Most of the shit that was showing then was shit, right?

SUSAN KNOWLES: I started doing the things for the radio, but that was Adrienne Outlaw who got that started with her WPLN stuff. And then she encouraged me. I did about thirty productions for them. The first one was Billy Renkl. I did one on Anna Jaap, and of course Sylvia Hyman, Jeff Hand, Carrie McGee. I did one of The Fugitive shows. I can remember going there and interviewing people in the space. I loved what they were doing so I would try to cover it in some way, whether it was radio or a piece for *Sculpture* or *Art Papers* or *Number* or whatever. That was a moment. That was a really exciting breakthrough time.

ADRIENNE OUTLAW: I think the first job I had that I really enjoyed was working for WPLN and the fact that they entertained my interview. I told them I wanted to do sound-rich stories on the arts, and they actually let me when I had no previous radio experience. That really opened the door to thinking that this was a city where I could do some fun things. I started out freelance at WPLN. If I remember correctly, from '96 to '97 or '98, I was just pitching projects. And then they hired me as a general assignment reporter, and I said, "That's fine as long as you guarantee that I get to do one art story per month." So I think I produced anywhere from four to six stories each month. I loved them. I was also doing the column for *In Review* newspaper—it was called "Unframed." Pretty much every publication I wrote for folded. I was the editor for the *Art Now Nashville* critical review. I've always loved writing.

SUSAN KNOWLES: We were trying to figure out a way to get funding for art writers. Because, you know, this is pitiful. You work really hard and you drive over to Memphis and you have to find a friend to spend the night with. And then you write the thing and you have a full-time job anyway. And maybe you get paid $30 in about two months or something like that, you know? So soon enough I went to work for the Metro Arts Commission. They were kind of more connected to the NEA and to what's going on. I started kind of lobbying internally to see if we couldn't free up some money, either us or the Tennessee Arts

Commission or the combination of us to start funding art writing. I was trying to make the argument that writing is fundamental to having an art scene. We have artists here who are working, we have a lot of creative people, but we're not getting coverage. And so what can we do to help?

DAVID RIBAR: As a professor I taught something called art experience or art appreciation. One of the things that becomes really clear to you is that you have to explain to people—who don't typically, normally care—why something matters. In the visual arts, artists always assume people know what they're talking about. Or can easily figure it out— "Read my statement." It doesn't cut it. You have to really break things down a lot to be able to get people interested and involved. So, it was clear to me that one of the components in the community that could have been better was "How do you explain to people why certain things matter that they wouldn't normally be attracted to?" So that was also a way that art writing got under my skin. Nashville was also a very conservative community. And that too was one of the motivations I think underneath why I wanted to write.

ADRIENNE OUTLAW: I am often not able to quickly and intellectually understand a piece of art without writing, and it was always a fascinating exercise for me to cover an artist's work. Particularly if I didn't like the art, if the art was irritating, if I had no understanding of what it was, but everyone else seemed to understand. I would just physically write out a description of it and then, "Oh, that's what it's about." Those moments of epiphany were just euphoric for me. With the WPLN radio stuff I really went into it because in addition to extending my own education in the arts—because I don't have an MFA—I really wanted to use that as a way to bring to light the art that I find to be most fascinating, raw, and gritty. I can't even tell you how many times I'd have to meet an artist at eleven o'clock at night and have beers with them so they would actually talk to me—those people who don't necessarily talk about art very well. They definitely have something to say, and you can see it through their art, but it takes them a long time to say it and you have to help them a lot. So I viewed my role as both really trying in whatever capacity I had to help them find their voice and also to connect their voice. The WPLN listenership appreciated that because they would have a better understanding of this untapped talent we had in Nashville. They just weren't going to find out otherwise. It always really bothered me when writers or reporters always go to the museum artist.

They talk to the curator, they read the statement, and it's all so canned. These people have been at it for thirty years and they know how to talk the talk and walk the walk, but it's just boring.

DAVID RIBAR: I have a hard time with statements, you know? It's propaganda on some levels. It's not devious or malicious, but the problem is that it often overexplains. It narrows the explanation to something that is unassailable or kind of airtight. But it cuts off so many other things that could happen. Part of it's about marketing and branding—now even more so. I have a real skepticism about it. If I get a statement and an idea ahead of seeing a show myself, there's no fun in that. There's no discovery and creativity. The insights come after you've been able to connect with the visual experience first, and by yourself. When I did stuff I never went to receptions. Never.

DAVID MADDOX: Now I've done a little writing of different kinds in the past. In Chicago, I'd done some writing in local publications, more obscure—not the *Reader*. And then I went to Jonathan and somehow we had some conversation about doing more of this. And the first time I came back to him with an idea, I said, "Well, there's this woman. In TAG Gallery"—it was when it was upstairs on the second floor in Hillsboro Village. "They have Lesley Patterson." And he kind of looked at me and he's like, "Lesley Patterson? Are you yanking my chain?" I didn't realize that Jonathan and Lesley were dating at that time. I know they weren't married yet because I was at their wedding, which was at the VFW on Gallatin or something. I was just reacting to Lesley's work—it was some of the books and stuff. I said, "This is really important stuff. I want to write about this."

JONATHAN MARX: David Maddox is just an incredibly, incredibly smart person, and I feel like he showed up in part because maybe he had gotten an inkling that we were looking for people to kind of step in and write really thoughtful criticism. Like I think part of it was a response to the criticism that the *Scene* was not really doing criticism, they're doing coverage. Dave was like, "You know what? I think there's things I could say and do here." He's someone who is perfectly positioned to understand and appreciate and respond to formalism, but who doesn't feel the need to apply a formalist critical lens to everything. He came to it with kind of an openness and a curiosity about "What's here and how can I contribute?" It was almost like a civic duty for him.

DAVID MADDOX: My first trip to Nashville was probably in '85, which is interesting because there were things that you remember from then—you know, Cain-Sloan still was operational and you could eat lunch in the Iris Room and stuff, all this old Nashville stuff. Then I came to town in '89 to go to business school and I've been here most of the time since then. I was away for about four years in the '90s. I went back to Chicago to work and then came back again. I was living out in White Bluff and coming into town. I was over at Downtown Pres and one of our members, Herb Williams, had an exhibit over at The Arts Company and it was his Crayon stuff. I had some thoughts about it and I wrote them up in an email to Herb or something. He said, "Wow, you should send that to the *Scene*." And I think I knew to send it to Jonathan.

JONATHAN MARX: Sometimes criticism is going to take the form of advocacy for something, and sometimes it's going to take the form of an advocacy against something. Any critical analysis should be considered a conversation starter, even if it can feel like a conversation ender. Because anybody who is approaching their critical role in a way that is designed to try to shut down any other ways of examining things, is already inviting a conversation about the integrity of their criticism.

DAVID RIBAR: I think that's the goal of writing: to be an advocate for something that needs help, especially in a place like this. And the credibility of the person making the advocacy is part of it, but also having the right forum and venue for it. And, you know, now our media landscape is so fractured and so polarized. It's hard to imagine. having something with that kind of voice out there for people to read and to respond to. Does it really matter? Maybe not. I'm a pessimist. I just think this is true of all media in general—political writing is the same way. There's too many voices and people who want information are going to gravitate to a specific source. Let's say it's Substack or it's a particular blog or a website that somebody has set up whose opinion has been built-up over time from the legacy media. But they're credible and there's enough of a scene to support that. But there's not a local framework for this in the same way there is for music. That's the 800-pound canary, the Godzilla that drives everything.

DAVID MADDOX: It was a scene that had these starts and stops for something to get going. And so in 2003, there was still a sense that a commercial gallery was a novelty. And, you know, there had been a couple of attempts at them. There was Cumberland Gallery and there had been Zimmerman Saturn. Before Nancy Saturn did the craft thing, American Artisan. You'd have kind of starting and stopping, and it was pretty clear that there really wasn't an art market here, but that people were giving it a try. You had Zeitgeist, which had the ability to be kind of sustained by an architecture practice. So they weren't depending purely on art sales. Anne Brown was going, and she was kind of being entrepreneurial about this. The pop-ups were really important. The Untitled group, things like that were really important.

DAVID RIBAR: When I moved here, I joked to people that I could lay naked in the middle of Second Avenue and nobody would see me on a Friday night. I mean, it was that dead. When Anne Brown started her gallery, she began to get super interested in the visual arts scene. I think it was one of those little pieces that helped show the community that there were visual artists here who wanted more visibility and were interested in working together to make it happen. That was one of those early movements forward.

DAVID MADDOX: There was this very strong DIY sense of "You've got people here who are making stuff." They're here for various reasons, you know. Nobody has come here to be a visual artist—with some exceptions, you know. But it was pretty organic. There was an art scene that was rising up out of people who were in a community, but they weren't there so they could be an artist. The artists were kind of a reflection from their membership in the community. In a bigger city, it might be the other way around. Somebody is in New York, not because they had any position in the New York community, but because they were artists and they knew they needed to be there. And the other thing that interested me was the possibility of people making art here for different reasons. Since, again, it seemed unlikely that you were going to be selling paintings for $10,000 a pop off the walls.

DAVID RIBAR: One of the things that comes, I think, from working in a museum, writing about art, trying to explain why it matters, is you realize your own insignificance. I remember doing the math with somebody one time over a beer. We said, "Okay, how many artists are living in the United States right now?" Maybe a million. There's probably a hundred thousand just living in the New York, Boston, Washington Corridor, Philadelphia. Let's say they make ten works of art a year. That's ten million works of art a year, times how many years? Pretty soon you realize there's never been more works of art made than there are now. The height of the Renaissance wasn't even close to making this many. But from a museum perspective, one-tenth of 1 percent of 1 percent is ultimately preserved and displayed for public view and the rest is in storage. That's if you even get in the door. We're pretending a lot of things matter that really may not in the long run. And that's okay. But, take some perspective here about what you're doing and judge what you're doing on that basis.

SARA ESTES: I'm actually from Cheatham County—good old Pleasant View, Tennessee, and Ashland City. It's beautiful. I hated it when I was younger because it felt so oppressive and just like small town nowheres-ville. I was born in Chicago, and when we moved out to Cheatham County, I started to have a really deep Southern accent. And I would go up to visit our family in Chicago and they would just ream me. I went to college at MTSU for a couple of years. I was going there for the recording industry program. I was in a punk band at the time, and so my dream was to have my own incredible punk record label that I was running out of Murfreesboro. That would've been like 2003. The music scene was actually really great back then with The Muse and other venues—there was punk shows all the time. So I had a big com-munity in that niche of music and I loved it. But then as I got through the recording industry program a little bit, I was like, "I do not think the music business is for me." So I dropped out of MTSU and moved to Memphis because I had a lot of friends in Memphis. I fell in love with Memphis. It gritty and dilapidated and beautiful and soulful, and the music was awesome.

JOE NOLAN: All punks go to Memphis.

SARA ESTES: There's something about Memphis that reminds me of New Orleans or whatever. You kind of get swept up in the culture of every-thing. It was super cool. I had a ton of fun. I was with a bunch of friends. I did the thing where I lived in a house with like seven other people and you're heathens. That was fun. I went to University of Mem-phis for a year and a half.

JOE NOLAN: *Number* is Tennessee's oldest art journal. It was founded at the University of Memphis in 1986.

SARA ESTES: *Number* seemed like a huge publication because it was all over the campus. I got to know it really well—that's how the seed got planted in my head. And at the time MCA was in Memphis, the Mem-phis College of Art, and that was incredible. There was a really, really cool art scene in Memphis at that time.

JOE NOLAN: I had a photograph in the *Art of the South* exhibition at Memphis College of Art in 2019. The *Art of the South* is *Number*'s annual fundraiser—a juried survey of Southern contemporary art. One of the reasons I applied that year was because I knew it was the last chance I'd get to hang something at MCA. By then, they had already announced that the college was closing in May 2020. An important part of the story of MCA artists and educators is the impact they made on the development of Nashville's contemporary art scene. It meant a lot to show work there. They had this gorgeous gallery space. We had one of those perfect exhibition opening receptions you go to in the evening in autumn in the South.

SARA ESTES: I made a lot of cool connections there. But Memphis was a party town and there's parts of it that are kind of depressing. When I was in Memphis, my car got broken into twice. I caught someone breaking into my house, and my illusion of safety just got shattered. I became kind of scared, and so I decided, "I need to go somewhere where I'm not feeling this way." I came back to Nashville in 2007 and I started TSU in 2008 and finished in 2009. I had Sam Dunson, Jodi Hays, and Jennifer Haston for my teachers there. That was a really cool crew to be learning from. I became really close with Jodi and a few other people on staff there. That kind of opened the gateway to the Nashville scene.

JOE NOLAN: Right around 2010, Nashville started making national headlines for its population growth, affordable housing, low unemployment, restaurant scene, and business environment. Some publications even mentioned the visual art scene. In 2013, *The New York Times* named Nashville "It City." During that era we saw a whole influx of younger people and midcareer people coming to Nashville looking for the art scene. That hadn't really happened before. We'd really only just found it ourselves.

LAURA HUTSON HUNTER: I'm from East Tennessee. I left in 1998 to move to New York. I went to NYU. I started out as a journalism major but switched to art history. And then I ended up switching majors again to contemporary art and cultural anthropology. I got really excited about street art and graffiti, and I was hanging out with graffiti kids. I loved the illegal subculture of graffiti writers. This was in like the early to mid-2000s when street art was getting a lot of traction. People were starting to recognize artists like Shepard Fairey and Barry McGee. It was exciting to write about and to be around. I was there for about eleven years and then wanted to leave and missed being in the South and closer to family. I visited Nashville and thought it was great. This was in 2009. When I moved to Nashville, I was just going to get a job waiting tables and see what happens. But I ended up getting really excited about art and writing about art after moving to Nashville, because it wasn't something that everyone was automatically into. The art world at large was a little more radical in Nashville than it was in a city where it's just sort of understood that everyone knew who Jeff Koons was, you know? It also felt like Nashville was a little bit more of an underdog, which I am always drawn to.

JOE NOLAN: Nashville's contemporary art scene was always struggling to get out of the shadow of the music industry. A lot of us are also in music and fans of Nashville's music scene. I don't think you can live here if you don't love music. But we were trying to highlight the difference between what was happening in regional and national contemporary art centers compared to guitar-centric poster art or paintings by country music celebrities.

LAURA HUTSON HUNTER: The first thing that I did when I came to Nashville was go to the Frist Art Museum where they had the *Paint Made Flesh* exhibit. I was not expecting anything of that level to be here and was so excited that it was. That show had Jenny Saville and Eric Fischl and Francis Bacon. It was just amazing. And it felt more special being in Nashville than if I had seen it in New York. Contemporary art was still radical in Nashville in ways that it couldn't be any longer in other larger cities. When I talked to people in New York about Nashville's art scene the word I used was "radical." It meant something in Nashville. There were still people that you could introduce things to, and the introduction to things is always the exciting part to me.

JOE NOLAN: By that time in Nashville we had institutions taking contemporary art seriously. We had galleries that took contemporary art seriously and were open to the emerging talent that was already here. There was a lot of chatter about developing an MFA program in Nashville. Publications and platforms about visual arts were popping up in the region.

LAURA HUTSON HUNTER: A childhood friend of mine was friends with Han Schmitt-Matzen in college. So I met with him at the Frist and that was like my first week here. He told me to get in touch with Adrienne Outlaw. I met with her and started doing work with her. She was spearheading this Nashville Cultural Arts Project. She was starting a gallery called Seed Space. She had done some reporting for public radio. She had a lot of ideas that I was able to help with.

JOE NOLAN: I met Laura when she was interning with Adrienne Outlaw.

The Seed Space gallery was just beginning at her studio in the Chestnut building. Laura was in on the early curating and curatorial writing that was happening there. It was really just the corner of Adrienne's studio, but she took it seriously and booked people from all over to do all sorts of small weird projects. Even back then you could see the start of Laura the writer/editor/curator.

LAURA HUTSON HUNTER: Casey Pierce and that group were publishing *The Rabbit* zine and Amelia Winger-Bearskin launched *Art Art Zine* [a Vanderbilt University visual arts blog]. It felt like the Wild West at the time. The Frist was still relatively new. Cheekwood was still kind of experimenting with contemporary art programming. It just sort of felt like things were possible.

JOE NOLAN: *The Rabbit*'s real stroke of genius was booking epic launch parties in great venues with multiple bands and artists on display. This was just a loose collective of young artists doing some cool projects while also insisting that art should be a party. It was like the next generation of The Fugitive exhibition/dance party scene. The core group even lived and worked out of the same house on Grantland where Terry Glispin used to live.

LAURA HUTSON HUNTER: Writing was something that I was always interested in and it was a tool I had in my toolkit. I also had family in media. My mom worked at a newspaper when I was growing up. My aunt was a reporter at CNN for years. Another aunt is an anchor at the local TV station in Chattanooga. It always sort of felt like writing and journalism was a possibility for me. The art editor position opened up at the *Nashville Scene*. I feel like I've always trusted my judgment and my taste, and I think I have skills of discernment that I've always felt confident in. Being an editor is kind of like being a curator and a writer is like being an artist. I can work in both arenas and they're both fun and fulfilling. I love working with writers and connecting writers with exhibits that I think will resonate with them. I love getting stuff and making it read more fluidly. One of the things that I think is cool about art in Nashville is that there's not as many egos. There's not as much competition. So you can really sort of feel like you want everyone to do well. It feels like there's room and space for lots of different voices and opinions. And I like being able to sort of shepherd that.

DAVID MADDOX: I was trying to be almost more interpretive than critical. There were a couple of things I was trying to do. One was to use the works I was seeing as a way to develop ideas. You know, that's something Clement Greenberg did at times. So I was trying to do that, and I was trying to articulate a specific ground for the production of the kind of art that was going on in Nashville. In other words, just kind of point out the idea that it meant something different to be making art here, and therefore the art that was being made would be different. And some of the people I wrote about were specifically for that reason. I was more interested in art criticism that was engaging with ideas. Where what you're seeing on the walls connects with other ideas that are out there in the world, whether it be something that you're reading or some set of philosophy. It's not necessarily about explaining. But it's about taking the work and using it as a way of entering into a certain world of ideas. It's what somebody like Charles Olsen would do when he consumed anything he encountered. Olsen was one of the founders of the Black Mountain school of poetry.

JONATHAN MARX: I was in my early twenties at this point, probably coming into work high some days. So I had a lot to learn about how to do what I was doing. Essentially, I learned on the job and I would get a lot of feedback from my friends about what they were seeing in the paper. I think those conversations that I had in the community—I haven't really ever thought about this—that dialogue with people in the community who were actively supporting the local arts and culture scene helped inform what kind of standards I should be setting around arts coverage in the paper. In a lot of ways I was responding to all the different kinds of criticism and applying my own critical lens—as sort of raw and punkish as it was at the time. Making sure that when we were doing analysis of art, that we were talking about the how and the why of what you're seeing and ultimately what mattered most to me was making sure that we were talking about why it mattered, you know, the why behind it.

LAURA HUTSON HUNTER: When I was working under Jim Ridley, who was a really respected film critic, what he would always say is that, "Criticism is saying in public what everyone else is saying in private." And that always gave me the sort of courage to be harsh when I needed to. Or critical, I guess. I felt like it was a service that I was doing for the art industry. Like I was standing in for everyone, and saying what everyone was thinking and what I was hearing. And having the courage to say it out loud.

VERONICA KAVASS: I was born in Nashville. I basically grew up here until I was eighteen and then I moved immediately. I've lived in Nashville a couple times and then I always leave because I get annoyed with Nashville. I wrote an article for that publication *Guernica*. I wrote just a short piece about Wedgewood-Houston back in 2013 or 2014. Basically just me describing this area. It was before the hosiery mill sold and I predicted that it would sell because, of course! People were pissed off. There were a couple people who were really pissed that I even wrote that. Someone went and put a sign in front of it a couple days after the piece came out. I think it was Dane? It said "Not for Sale" or something like that. And then it sold. It sold like a couple months later.

LAURA HUTSON HUNTER: I've really been critical of exhibits, but it was more critical of the institution and not the artist. I wrote some harsh criticisms about exhibits that were at Cheekwood or the Frist. You never want to punch down. And, you know, an emerging artist that's exhibiting in like an independent Nashville gallery? It just seems like being a bully. I don't want to be a bully.

JOE NOLAN: Established artists at major institutions are, obviously, fair game. But in a local gallery scene that's packed with emerging artists it's always been more constructive to point out exceptional examples to readers and collectors—"Look at this. We should be seeing more like this." As artists decide to stay and grow their careers here, and galleries become more permanent fixtures, the criticism will also change. This is assuming we still have outlets and platforms and other resources that can continue to make writing about visual art sustainable. The lack of professional publishing opportunities also means focusing on the few shows you're most excited about. If there are only enough opportunities to write reviews about two shows this month I'm not going to write about the show I didn't like.

DAVID RIBAR: The definition of what an artist is has changed so much. Maybe, also the idea of who and what an art critic is has changed as well? What really is your goal and value now as compared to, say twenty years ago? Even in a community like this that had, you know, a really modest art scene—you've got to be a cheerleader, I guess. Like I said, an advocate, and that's always going to be the case.

JOE NOLAN: I'm always looking at books and listening to music and podcasts, and watching movies and going to exhibitions. Lots of artists operate this way—you digest tons of stuff and then ask questions. You analyze and answer the questions and then think of ways to apply these insights to your own work. Writing about art and movies is just another part of my creative practice where I'm putting that critical analysis process down in writing and publishing it. There's a whole tradition of artist's creating culture and also writing about culture. Edgar Allen Poe was a literary writer as well as a critic. The poet Frank O'Hara was a curator at MOMA and wrote art criticism. Patti Smith wrote criticism, Chrissie Hynde wrote criticism. Mike Kelley wrote a lot of criticism about his own work. Not every artist has to write, and critics don't have to be artists. Artist/critics are part of a unique, well-established tradition. It gives us a unique perspective on both sides of the conversation.

SARA ESTES: After I graduated from TSU, I was an artist-in-residence at Gallery F and that's when I started writing. I knew I wanted to be a writer because all of my art started to turn into writing. All of my senior projects in school and everything that I was doing was literally writing words on canvas. So I came to this point where I was like, "Why don't I just write?" I was getting obsessed with words and the way that you could infuse words in art. I applied for this job right after graduation at a place called *Nashville Pix*, and it was gonna be an online news publication. *Nashville Pix* hired me as like the art and culture writer for this publication. It was my first writing job. It was like a hundred dollars an article and an unlimited amount of articles. So I just hit the ground running. I was going to make $2,000 a month. I had an editor who was super cool and he was really encouraging. So I was just out there finding anything I could, interviewing anybody I could, writing about whatever was going on. That's really the first place where they just let me run wild with whatever was interesting me. It wasn't long before the magazine just shut down. They totally ran out of money.

JOE NOLAN: A forever challenge of art writing is sustaining outlets. Sometimes editorial changes can disrupt your regular writing for a publication, but a lot of the times you publish a few pieces over a year and the next pitch goes into a black hole. Sometimes you don't even know when a publication or a platform folds. As a freelancer you're often totally in the dark when it comes to anything beyond your work on your stories, often with one particular editor.

SARA ESTES: It was a great lesson of why print publication is so powerful. Because that was my first time, I didn't save any of the articles. I didn't screenshot anything. All of that's gone. Getting something in print, like *Number*, something like that, it became like the tippy-top cool thing because that can never go away. I can put that in a closet and have it forever. That's where art writing came in. I had written for *Number* and I had written for *Nashville Arts Magazine*. I had written for *Arts Nashville*. I was kind of writing just wherever I could. The very first article that I ever did for *Number* was an interview with Harmony Korine, and Patrick DeGuira was the guest editor. That felt huge for me at the time. But he was sort of a jerk, and I was not super impressed. I wrote another piece about Vesna Pavlović. So I became a contributor, and they asked me to be a guest editor there. And then I got on the board and I was doing the editing. I loved working there. We did a couple of like in-person meetings in Memphis, which was fun. I got on the board in 2015. I stayed on there for a couple of years, I think.

JOE NOLAN: For me, the Estes-era at *Number* was the first time that the editor was based in Nashville instead of Memphis. It seems even more significant given the journal's re-locating to Nashville in 2022. Sara was great to work with—it's always better when you respect your editor as a writer first. She's a fantastic storyteller. There's a literary sensibility to her reviews and she's called artists out in really constructive ways. At that time she was lead art reporter for *The Tennessean*, a columnist at *Burnaway*, and the editor of *Number* at the same time. She was an artist who was serious about making a contribution as a writer. I understood that and recognized that and respected that.

SARA ESTES: I was so enthusiastic about what was going on in the art world, and it literally broke my heart that nothing was being discussed in the media. So my whole mission for writing about art was just to get out the word on what they were doing. That felt really purposeful for me, and it was a way to use my gifts as a writer to help people and to forward this conversation. My time working as the gallery coordinator at Fisk solidified how important the writing is to really galvanize what is going on in a particular time and place. So much of what we knew about that collection was because of the stuff that people wrote. And Stieglitz produced a magazine and stuff. What I did was just what Stieglitz did. I was just trying to take advice from what he did so that it really solidified to me that this stuff has to be in print. It's got to be in writing. It has to be able to be saved and stuffed in an attic. It's got to be memorialized. So as a writer, that's all I really wanted to do. I wanted to make some money sometimes with some of the articles I wrote, but a lot of it was just like, "These are my people."

JONATHAN MARX: Over the course of my time at the *Nashville Scene*, I worked with Susan Knowles, I worked with Nicole Pietrantoni, I worked with David Ribar, I worked with David Maddox. Angela Wibking was a longtime contributor. I worked with Brittany Conner briefly,

I worked with Lisa Donovan. I worked with a lot of different people, all of whom have gone on to different things because they were all people who are engaged in the local arts and culture scene. They saw things happening they wanted to respond to—whether positively or critically. They also saw things not happening that they felt they needed to respond to. I would hope that over time, in terms of the professional work I did at the *Nashville Scene*, that the role of criticism itself doesn't really change. It has to respond to the moment that it's in and it is a working-through of a set of considerations intended to help us understand how we might collectively respond to what's happening in our environment. There are certain trends that take place in terms of the critical frameworks that people use because those things should change because the context changes, but the fundamental value or purpose of criticism ideally should remain. It should always be designed to promote discourse.

DAVID RIBAR: The quote I read when I finally quit subscribing to *Art Forum* was: *Topicality succinctly unites the mutually contradictory demands for novel factual information.* "What? Fuck you!" I threw the magazine across the room. I said, "This is it. Cancel my subscription." I don't even remember what the show was. So there's the one side, and then on the other side you've got the Chamber of Commerce public relations release that is equally horseshit. So where's this narrow channel for people to make some authentic writing? Where can you find a place to publish it? Who is your audience? If you're lucky, like I think I was, there's a wave where there's a forum for it, and there's something of an audience. If you do it and you're lucky, it's great.

Norf

1986–2022

NASHVILLE'S MODERN ART LEGACY traces back to the city's North Nashville neighborhood during the first half of the twentieth century. The historical Black community includes a cluster of Historic Black Colleges and Universities including Fisk University (1866), Meharry Medical College (1876), and Tennessee State University (1912). Today, North Nashville—"Norf"—hosts a bustling contemporary art scene that's reflected in its vibrant wall murals, galleries, artist studios, creative shops and cultural festivals.

JOE NOLAN: When you talk to Carlton there's always a vision and even a sense of mission behind his take on contemporary art and the Nashville scene. He comes by that naturally: his mother, DeLois Wilkinson, helped to organize Nashville's lunch-counter sit-ins during the Civil Rights Movement, and she also served on the Metro Nashville Board of Education.

CARLTON WILKINSON: I'm from Nashville. Born and raised. I ended up attending Washington University in St. Louis. One of my professors took me to lunch my junior year and encouraged me to become a teacher. Because of that I applied to grad school. I had a BFA in graphic design. And I ended up going to UCLA. And that was quite an experience too because that helped me really develop my artistic sense in design. In my third year there, I had an internship with the first photo gallery in all of California called G. Ray Hawkins Gallery on Melrose.

And that experience made me realize I never wanted to open a gallery. It was boring to me. I didn't like it, but it was a good experience. And so when I graduated, I moved to the Bay Area, Oakland. Stayed there a year working at the YMCA, and then my mother tempted me with a possibility of opening a space here in Nashville. So I returned in '87, '86. I got the idea of having a gallery because I was trying to get somebody to represent me and my photography, and I couldn't get that representation. So I just opened up my own damn gallery. And twenty years I ran it.

JOE NOLAN: Carlton wasn't originally planning to start a gallery and I think that's why In the Gallery developed into an incubator, a salon, an antiques dealer, a photo studio, a contemporary art showcase, and a neighborhood art institution.

CARLTON WILKINSON: My mother found the building and bought it. She was the one who said, "Hey, if you come back to Nashville maybe we can do a gallery there?" She had a good deal on it, but it needed work. It was not renovated completely at that time.

JOE NOLAN: The historic Onyx Building in North Nashville was a real head-turner. Everyone loved that gorgeous old brick Victorian with the tower and the big storefront windows. It welcomed you to the neighborhood when you crossed the Jefferson Street bridge from East Nashville. It had a previous life as an Oddfellows Hall. That was the perfect pedigree for an art gallery that traded in both traditional Africana and rule-breaking contemporary artists.

CARLTON WILKINSON: I completed the renovations. I ended up deciding that it was going to be a photo studio and art gallery, because there was a little space for both. I was thinking about showing just photography, but the second show I had was of the yarn paintings of the Huichol Indians in central Mexico. It was by chance somebody came along and presented that work to me. So I began to open my palette in terms of who I showed, and I'm making it very clear: I was not a Black gallery. I was a gallery owned by a Black curator. And that makes a difference, because I showed work from all over the world. I eventually got into African antiquities as well as contemporary art. But I showed a Russian artist. I showed artists from Latin America—Brazil and Colombia—all over. But my focus was African diaspora.

LANDRY BUTLER: There were several new art groups started around 1990. There was Untitled, there was N4Art—Carlton Wilkinson was their first president. Carlton had a gallery up there on Jefferson Street, and a lot of African American artists got together there and that's where we were kind of doing a thing called "In the Gallery." Sam Dunson, Michael McBride, James Threalkill—a lot of them were in that group. Yeah, that was good. And there was also Visual Arts Alliance of Nashville.

MICHAEL MCBRIDE: Visual Arts Alliance of Nashville was big because all the major artists and a lot of the major collectors were members of this organization. VAAN was the beginning of changing the face of art in Nashville.

CARLTON WILKINSON: We had a little renaissance going on in Nashville. VAAN, the Visual Arts Alliance of Nashville. We were members of that and N4A, Nashville African American Arts Association. We worked together showing art and my gallery was kind of central to a lot of that. I was the founder of N4A. But the name came from a guy named Bennett Wilson, who was a young artist I met. He was a self-taught artist. I loved his work and I was able to sell quite a bit of it. He had a fan base and he thought of the name N4A. Henry Jones, who's an abstract painter here and a poet, and who's a good friend of mine, he was in it. Barbara Bullock was a major figure in our group. She was one of our founders. We had some non-artist members. Musicians like Odessa Settles, who's part of an a cappella group. Some collectors got involved. We just wanted to have activity. We wanted to expose Nashville to African American artists.

MICHAEL MCBRIDE: When Carlton came here around 1990 or something, and decided to open the first gallery on Jefferson street, I think he created more interest in contemporary art that, now, we see flourishing all over. He was showing different stuff than other galleries. He was running the gamut, you know: Black artists, white artists, Latino artists. He brought that whole different vibe—contemporary, different stuff that none of the other galleries were really doing.

CARLTON WILKINSON: Kaaren Engel, she was an Afrikaner from South Africa. Jairo Prado was one of our members—he's from Colombia. Daniel Arite, who is part Italian and part Latino Mexican. So we took everybody. Anybody who wanted to work with us, we included.

JAMES THREALKILL: Carlton Wilkinson was quite a visionary.

CARLTON WILKINSON: Cumberland Gallery was very strict, right? They had a hundred mile radius thing and Carol Stein was very hard on her artists to be loyal. But I admired Carol cause she was serious and she helped me a lot. You had The Arts Company later with Anne Brown. I was involved with the Metro Arts Commission and she was very supportive. And then, Lois Riggins-Ezell of the Tennessee State Museum—she showed a lot of interest in what I was doing. So I had all of these mentors around me who helped and advised or just let me do my thing without complaint.

JAMES THREALKILL: Carlton deserves a lot of credit because he gave Black artists a venue to show their work. A lot of the mainstream galleries were not really showing Black art at that particular time. And then another gentleman, Nate Harris at Woodcuts took an old Dairy Dip and converted it into a frame shop/gallery called Woodcuts. And so that created two venues on Jefferson Street where artists could have exhibits and we can invite people from all over the city of Nashville.

OMARI BOOKER: Woodcuts is the anchor. It's one of the longest running, Black-owned galleries in the city. And, of course, it's right there on Jefferson Street, and on Fisk's property—I worked at Woodcuts for about five years. It was incredibly invaluable. I learned so much from Nate and Ms. Jean, who's kind of productions manager—she's been there for twenty-nine-plus years herself. Woodcuts is thirty-five years old. Ms. Jean's been there for thirty-four years. I learned to improve on stuff like stretching canvas, and on the pieces that I framed. Nate still lets me use that place for framing and materials. He just lets me use his account so I can order wholesale and go straight to the supplier. In addition to teaching me how to frame, Nate also gave me a space to curate. So I learned how to hang a show. I could choose pieces that I thought were important, and find artists that I wanted to show: X Payne had a show, DoughJoe had a show. And before that generation you had James Threalkill, Michael McBride, Greg Ridley—Jamaal Sheats might have had his first show at Woodcuts. It's beyond an institution. It's earned its historical marker.

CARLTON: It was survival, basically. I had to survive. I mean, it was tough economically. And then I got an adjunct teaching position at Vanderbilt that lasted nineteen years. And it helped me in terms of diversified income. There were many shows that did not make money and it was expensive to produce a show, especially with mailings. And receptions—you're good to get some water now, but back then you'd do a whole spread. And I'd try to be creative with that as well. Luckily, I was really well-schooled in a lot of things. I knew how to sweep a floor. I knew how to do graphic design. I knew how to photograph so I didn't have to outsource it. I was everything. The only thing I refused to do was accounting, so I always got an accountant. I did all my postcards—designed them, photographed them, and mailed them.

SAM DUNSON: I was born and raised in Dayton, Ohio. And my father and my mother—but more so my father—was really adamant about me going to an HBCU. And we traveled and visited a number of HBCUs in the Southeast. We had an HBCU really close to Dayton in Ohio, but we were thinking about something outside of the state to give me an opportunity to get away from home. TSU was kind of the closest school that was still out of Ohio. We visited TSU and went to a football game and all that—I absolutely loved it. So my senior year in high school I knew I was headed to TSU. But at that point I had no idea that I was going to be in the art department. I started off studying architectural engineering and it didn't go well. I was put on probation my first semester there. I was doing a little bit too much partying the first time being away from home and all that. I met Ted Jones at a discipline fair. He saw some things that I had just drawn a little bit and said I should be studying with him in the art department. I was getting pushed out of architectural engineering anyway, so that next semester I buckled down and that's my birth into art in general at the art department at TSU.

CARLTON WILKINSON: I bought Sam's first painting that he did in college because he was in another major and I really liked it. That nurtured a relationship with him. He really took on with Barbara Bullock and then there were other artists that he saw later that he was influenced by.

SAM DUNSON: I graduated in 1992 and I didn't really prepare to be an artist. I'm not even sure how you would truly prepare to be an artist. I pretty much got a nine to five job, I worked at Werthan Packaging on 8th Avenue for about six years. Even though I was working at a place that I knew was not going to be my career, it allowed me to get out of the art department and get on my own. And it gave me the time to understand that nobody was going to be creating projects for me. I was doing a lot more sculpture at TSU and I wasn't able to do that because I just didn't have the space and materials and all of that. So I started getting interested in what was going on in the city around that time. That was a kind of a bit of a boom with all of the kind of smaller and larger galleries that were coming in. I started getting connected with N4Art, the Nashville African-American Arts Association, and literally started doing what I was supposed to do. And in 1998, I decided to get my master's degree at SCAD. I went to grad school with the idea that I wanted to teach, but I had no idea that I was going to be back here at TSU. I graduated in 2000 and James Hefner was the president of TSU at that time. He was connected with a couple artists that I knew, and my name was being bounced around by Carlton Wilkinson and a couple of other people who were telling him, "Hey, you need to bring him back." TSU was in need of a gallery director so I came back to Nashville. When they called me it felt like an opportunity for giving back to something that gave me my start. That was my biggest reason for wanting to come back. I was running the gallery and then started teaching some classes. I was just as happy as I could be.

CARLTON WILKINSON: The Black artists were doing jazz art. Everybody was doing this sort of—I call slice of life. You know, very pleasant, decorative. Everybody was influenced about what was selling. Prints were a huge thing because for so many African Americans I always say there was a threshold of a thousand dollars. And then when you got over two thousand or three thousand, you're in another elite of collectors. So most people were paying under a thousand. And the only way you get to that is the limited-edition lithographs, eventually giclée, you know, things like that. And that's where Sam shares my spirit. Sam won't do that. He paints, he's done with it, OK? And the only thing you're going to get from him is an original. I really liked his spirit in that regard. I can't do that as a photographer because of the very nature of my discipline—the only original is the digital or the negative. I really encouraged him to be honest with his work, to be honest with his thinking. And Sam came from college, a very shy guy. A very shy and very thoughtful background. He had a very loving family. And I just told him, that he really needed to just be honest about what he was thinking.

SAM DUNSON: In the Gallery was a gallery that would show everybody. A number of the other galleries were a little more streamlined toward white artists. And then you had a couple of galleries showing Latin artists. But there wasn't really a gallery focused on showing everyone together, and Carlton wanted In the Gallery to fill that gap. As the gallery evolved it became a kind of showcase for the African diaspora with a lot of African artifacts alongside artwork that was not automatically recognizable as stereotypical Black art—that art almost, like, glamorized slavery or romanticized Black love or romanticized Black music. After you see that so much, people think that that's the only thing that Black artists could produce. So Carlton literally wanted to fly in the face of that. He saw that I was right on the edge of getting out of creating works that would automatically be considered typical Black art. Because I went through that phase as well. But, when I was in Savannah I was so tired of doing works that kind of were about slavery and about music and about love and so on and so forth. I wanted to do something to really show myself. And I created this work called "Conversation with Creativity" that was like a double self portrait. It was probably around 1998. It showed me talking to myself—a realistic version of me talking to a stylized version of myself with kind of my whole makeup in the background. It was like pop surrealism with dream imagery, duality, all these other things—I was literally just throwing stuff at the canvas the whole time. Carlton had an exhibition that was coming up and he wanted me to show. I showed him that piece but said I didn't want to sell it. I was trying to kind of defend myself from any backlash for being completely different than the other works that I had done and all of that. But Carlton said it was exactly what I should be doing, and that that work wasn't something that I should be hiding. I've never been driven by selling work, but that painting created a bidding war between a couple of people. So Carlton's gallery allowed artists to actually be themselves. Carlton wanted works to sell, and he had a good clientele that was eager to buy work. But he also felt you have to be your genuine self in order to last as an artist. You're not going to be able to just do work that everybody loves, you're going to have to take some risks.

CARLTON WILKINSON: I don't use this term a lot with my gallery, but looking back retrospectively, I was an activist. There was a lot of political art that went through my gallery and not just with American issues—things all around the world. Barbara Bullock was the epitome of that. I think Sam was very much influenced by Barbara Bullock. She was amazing and very honest. She's been kicked out of shows and considered too controversial. She got in a show at the National Women's Museum in DC and one work got in and the other one they said was just too hot to handle. And then she did a show down in Memphis. She did an environmental piece using trash. Putting condoms and sanitary napkins all over—it was installation. They hung it up, but then they decided they couldn't handle it. She was really in the heart of a lot of controversy. My male nudes got rejected at Belmont University. My series called the *African Male Museum*, I used the figure as expression. I also interviewed two hundred Black males about their ideas of being young Black males. What they felt about being African and American or Black, whatever. David Ribar was at Belmont. He was a radical back then. His committee accepted my work for the Leu Gallery. Then Mrs. Leu and the president of the university got wind of it and vetoed their decision. They decided it was just a little too much for them to handle.

SAM DUNSON: There were lots of expectations on Black artists that mostly came from the Black community. In the nations in Africa, the artist is pretty much a conduit that brings spirituality and creativity together to breathe life into these physical things. But African American artists, we're almost expected to kind of stay in the past, and only deal with a couple of little ideas. I am so thrilled when I see young Black artists that are doing non-representational work or doing completely surreal works. In the Gallery was instrumental not just for me, but for just about all the other artists that I know that were connected with Carlton. They were not only allowed, but challenged to really do things outside of what the natural order of Nashville was asking of artists in general, but artists of color specifically. Plus it was in a space that was growing in Germantown. So there was a lot of traffic that was coming through that was not just specifically Black patrons.

CARLTON WILKINSON: I don't think Sam's been rejected at anything. I think people really take his work to heart. But we are the ones who just decided we're just not going to paint for people who want to buy and decorate their homes. It's worked with Sam. Just recently his work was in the gallery at the new LA stadium [SoFi Stadium].

SAM DUNSON: Before I left for grad school, my artwork was starting to blaze up a little bit. I was getting a lot of opportunities thrown my way with festival work, and Artists for Oasis—a number of different benefits. I had a pretty nice little stronghold on a number of those annual events. And when I left, I was still being asked to be part of it. I became almost like this ghost figure. I was still showing work in Nashville and people were talking about Sam Dunson, but I was in Savannah at SCAD at that time. So when I came back, it was almost like a powder keg that had been waiting to go off. It was right around the time where the galleries that survived the 1990s trend had actually grown some roots and had some staying power. A lot of opportunities came my way because everybody was seeing my work, but nobody was really seeing me at all. I was an enigma.

CARLTON WILKINSON: I think the bottom line is that I encouraged artists to be more honest about what they wanted to say and I supported them. It may not sell, you know, it may get a little friction, but I'm proud because my same work that was rejected at Belmont was considered a retrospective at the Parthenon in 2005. And we had a little controversy there, and it passed the smell test. And I was the first African American to have that big space at the Parthenon. It ended up showing for three months. It turned out to be a great success. I like to think that we were an activist gallery. And for North Nashville that was very appropriate.

SAM DUNSON: Carlton challenged me every show that I had with him. I had to bring the works in and we had to have a conversation. I'd have to basically convince him that a specific work was strong enough to go in the gallery. For me to have had that at that time was so beneficial. I needed to be taught. I needed a teacher at that time and I needed somebody to literally allow me to be creative so I could find my personal voice. And at In the Gallery it wasn't just me that Carlton challenged and taught. It was a number of other artists. I think that was so beneficial for so many artists in Nashville. And with me teaching, I was trying my best to feed those same ideas to the students. I was trying to make sure that I let my students know that there were no set ideas as to what you're supposed to be doing. You're literally creating your career, so if you're trying to do something because of other people's expectations, then it's not yours. You have to get something that's yours. I think of Brandon Donahue, I think of Omari Booker, and I think of the students that they were at the time that, they were really wanting somebody to do the same thing that Carlton did for us. That gallery holds a very prominent place in my heart.

JOE NOLAN: That lineage from Sam to Brandon Donahue feels like a royal succession. In the early 2000s, Sam's shows were crucial to the whole scene. Sam was one of the highest points on the bar for local artists, and he carried the local contemporary art culture in the direction of innovative individual expression at an important time. Brandon Donahue's *Basketball Blooms*—large, floral wall sculptures constructed from found sports balls—are the iconic signature objects of Nashville's contemporary art renaissance. Brandon is from Memphis and now he lives in Maryland, but I'm always going to claim him for Nashville because this is where those blooms blossomed.

CARLTON WILKINSON: It was meant to happen, that whole period. The economy was good. And I closed in 2007 a year before the recession. I never would've survived. The building that I had In the Gallery in was hit by the tornado in 2020. It imploded. So that doesn't exist any longer. It was built in 1898. It was a Victorian building and the structure was like six, eight bricks thick. And when that thing imploded, everything collapsed in on itself. We didn't own the building at that time, but I don't think they could save it. Right now, the building is just like Joni Mitchell's song—they're building a parking lot.

CULTURE CLUB

THAXTON WATERS: My gallery opened up 2007. It was more like a culture shop. Around that time the economy was coming to a screeching halt, so that was the perfect time to open up a store. What I discovered in the midst of that, around 2009, 2010, one of my mentor elders said, "Whenever people get scared they go back to school." So that's basically what happened to me. I went back to school around 2009, 2010 to specifically get around Sam Dunson, because I was a fan of his work. I had been going to Carlton Wilkinson's gallery since the 1990s when I was in college up at TSU. I was going to his gallery down the street in between classes and everything. And I was seeing Mr. Dunson's work then. So I had already been a fan of it for a long time. I needed more technicality to my painting. I needed to know the development of painting. So I just went back to TSU to get specifically around him, even though I had graduated in 2003 with a biology degree and everything.

ELISHEBA ISRAEL MROZIK: I'm originally from Memphis, Tennessee. I moved to Nashville in 2007. I just graduated from Memphis College of Art with a bachelors in computer arts, which I don't even use. I moved up here and just took a regular job, just trying to leave home. And I started coming around North Nashville and meeting people like Thaxton. He was one of the first people I met when I moved here. I walked into his shop and we started talking and I had to finish a painting for something. So I asked, "Do you mind if I just like pull this painting again while we're talking and work on this so I can get this done, but I can also have a conversation?" That was literally what I did. I brought the painting in, started painting on it. We was just talking and we became friends. He introduced me to more people in the neighborhood. And then in 2011 I opened up my tattoo shop on Jefferson Street—I think he was actually the one who told me about Mrs. Crutcher who had the building on Jefferson Street that allowed me to be able to open my tattoo shop. With the business I had a big reach. And I was able to help start the Jefferson Street Art Crawl with everybody in 2015.

THAXTON WATERS: I was born and raised here. I was born down there at Meharry Hospital. When I was in my late twenties, early thirties, I started peeling back all the layers. I always have this analogy of the gold rush that happened down in Georgia back in the 1800s before they went out to San Francisco. Just because everybody went to San Francisco doesn't mean that the gold is not still there in Georgia. I used that analogy as I came into the community and started doing asset mapping. It's all of this gold and treasure still all around the neighborhood. Fisk was a stone's throw from my gallery. I graduated from TSU. So I needed to just go around and start talking to all these people. I discovered this history inside of a book, but these people are living and breathing all around me. That's when I started trying to go around and make those connections.

ELISHEBA ISRAEL MROZIK: Everybody was just getting really frustrated about trying to get art shows. I had met Woke and Omari and all of them. We were all just friends in the neighborhood and artists, and we were talking about our frustrations on trying to sell our artwork and get into spaces and show. We were all talking about, "Well, how can we do it ourselves?" I had a space. We knew Woodcuts, we knew Garden Brunch restaurant. We brought them all in. And that's how the crawl was formulated. And it was started just as a place to be able to show our work and circumvent the roadblocks we were getting in the gallery world. We had no money. We just all put in work, donated our time and our own personal funds to make sure it happened. And it got us noticed. We were able to get that show at the Frist. All of us are now fully working, professional paid artists who have consistent jobs. And that just goes to show how important spaces are to artists to be able to launch and grow their careers. We made a nonprofit out of this called the North Nashville Arts Coalition.

THAXTON WATERS: So I had this culture shop and I painted murals and things inside to decorate the place. But I wasn't selling paintings, I wasn't doing it on canvas. I wasn't doing anything like that. Since my business was struggling a little bit, one of the Fisk professors came in there and suggested, "Why don't you start painting like that?" And this is something I've been doing my whole life. But I just never was comfortable with the crowd that it attracted around me when I started to make work. Because people start asking all these questions. But I had to like re-contextualize it in my mind. They're just drawn in by it. So, if they can get in on the transparency of the process, this can be a whole other audience for me.

ELISHEBA ISRAEL MROZIK: The biggest focus we have is space because we're running out of it here. A lot of artists who started doing all this stuff with us, they don't live over here anymore because the tornado, the pandemic and the prices just displaced them. Our biggest focus going forward is trying to get a building, trying to get a big space that will house artists, have studio space, education space, gallery space—it's a big dream. I've been working and running my mouth and calling on these companies who are coming in and displacing us to put their money where their mouth is. They say they don't want to do these things or they want to help or whatever, and they're throwing money at people who aren't actually providing real solutions. They're just pretending. I'm working on trying to make it an actual reality. Because if people just had studio spaces available so that they could focus on their work and have a business address—I know that once I was able to get my own separate studio space, my productivity soared. My ability to handle various types of projects I'd never been able to do before. I'm doing giant mural panels right now. I'm working on sculpture pieces right now. I couldn't have done any of that out of my house. It's just not something that's possible for artists who really are trying to move up. To making a business, that space is so important, but also for engagement with the community. We're needing space for that so that we can have classes and workshops, and things that can expose people in the neighborhood to the benefits of art as not only a personal benefit, but as a business, as a career. And find these young people out here who are talented and try to nurture their talent.

THAXTON WATERS: So I started making work. But it just so happened the work that I was making was like Emory Douglas's work for the Black Panthers. I would just basically take the images he made and I just basically put 'em on canvas. So people could see me doing the work while I was making it, and then I would sell it to people up and down Jefferson Street, like off in beauty salons and barbershops and stuff like that. I did that 2010 to 2012. So this is me just grinding, doing live shows, studying, getting around Mr. Dunson. There wasn't really that many young Black artists out there just grinding like that. I had a family, you know what I'm saying? I would get out there and have a big, huge canvas and just be painting these large faces of Marvin Gaye just to attract a crowd. And then I could sell smaller paintings. I could sell them $40, $50, $60, $70 works. So it was a performance act for me. I was just trying to make money for my family, but it was training me to basically attract the art world to look in my direction.

ELISHEBA ISRAEL MROZIK: I've been a part of many groups. Nashville Black Artist Renaissance was one of the first little group cohorts I was in here. That had me and Thaxton and McBride and Threalkill, and we had this dope amazing show at the Ha Factory downtown back in like 2011. It had all this publicity. We had the Boys and Girls Club as a sponsor, we had all this stuff happening and it all fell apart when the money thing started coming up and greed started coming up.

JOE NOLAN: The Ha brothers both had spaces in the heart of the downtown arts district. They both mixed traditional Asian subjects with hip-hop and fashion-inspired aesthetics. Very vibrant stuff with a great sense of humor. You can't really talk about the visual art heyday downtown without talking about the Ha brothers.

THAXTON WATERS: Andy Ha had a spot upstairs in The Arcade. And John Ha was down on Fifth Avenue. They did like these big huge koi fish and they both had the same kind of technique and everything. So we had a show at John's and it was called Nashville Black Artist Renaissance. It was like ten artists. It was Threalkill, McBride, Michael Mucker, Elisheba. And we did the show all in that together. I did this huge piece. I'm reading Kehinde Wiley. So then I'm getting introduced to scale. I'm getting introduced to content. I'm getting introduced to patterns and things like that. So I did this huge piece and then somebody came up to me and wanted me to do something like the painting in a mural. So that led me to doing the mural over there in Buena Vista. The one off of Monroe behind Kroger's.

JOE NOLAN: "Ol' Skool Mike" Mucker did a legendary Bruce Lee mural at the Kung Fu Coffee shop. That was years before Nashville had mural movements all over the city.

THAXTON WATERS: They approached me and said they wanted something to depict the neighborhood in a friendly way using the patterns and motifs of the neighborhood. So I went around and I saw certain churches had similar symbols—these crosses and these certain same architectural motifs. I made a pattern out of it. It's still over there behind the Kroger's on Monroe. That was my first mural. And now the ball's rolling. I'm making work to walk up and down Jefferson Street with paintings under my arm. I go off into barbershops and put them on the floor in front of an audience.

ELISHEBA ISRAEL MROZIK: A lot of what I'm doing now when people are asking about this, that, and the other, I'm just say, "Okay, but what is your purpose here? Is it really community? Are you talking community just because you think there's money for you in it? Or are you really giving a shit about community?" So I tread dangerous waters there because, I call people out on their bullshit because so many people are just pretending. And a lot of companies they come saying, "Oh we want to do these things" and they just want to dip their toe in, get the diversity pin and back out. I have to watch out for those things and decide, "Is the money that we're going to take going to benefit us more, or is it going to hurt us more and benefit them?"

THAXTON WATERS: My culture shop was transitioning at this time, from 2007 to 2009, from being a shop that sold books, clothing—from turbans to tunics to t-shirts about hip hop. I had graffiti in there. I had records in there, vinyl records, it was everything. A lot of DJ material in there. A lot of stuff for graffiti writers. And then we used to have these parties in there. So it was a lot of break dancers and writers and MCs used to come up there. But the store was transitioning from that into being a hardcore studio where I made work. I was being a gallery because I now had to display all this inventory. I was going around town, "How do you get up in these galleries?" I didn't even know. And then I started seeing people had MFAs and pedigree lineage behind them. I was like, "Okay, I don't know nothing about that. So let me just open up my own."

ELISHEBA ISRAEL MROZIK: It's got to be a collective energy and we really have to not be separate. We have to start doing stuff together because that's where the power is, that's where the voice is. Everybody just stop being grieved for attention or whatever it is that they want, and just get together for artists and for creatives in a general sense. Because that's what all these other groups do. They have lobbying groups, you know? They have unions. They have people out here fighting for them and artists don't have that. Artists don't have a unified cause. We are workers, right? It's a fucking job and we have to make money to live or it's not a job. So if we as artists and creatives could come together and make a for-real organization that is our advocate, that does the lobbying for us. It has to be collective. It has to be together. If a corporation didn't have all of its people working together on one thing, then they would be ineffective. The only thing that they have different is they have money to make people do things.

THAXTON WATERS: So now at the gallery I have all these students hanging out in there from Fisk and TSU, Meharry, American Baptist College. They're coming over here from Vanderbilt and everything. So they're just hanging out, but then they want me to show their work. I was like, "Oh. Okay!" So I start showing these students' work, but then I'm studying all this history at the same time. Booker T. Washington, all this stuff. I'm studying all this history of the neighborhood that I'm in. And then I started seeing.

ELISHEBA ISRAEL MROZIK: It's harder for organic collaboration and con-
nectivity because of greed and individuals wanting to have something
in order to give to something. Whereas we would all benefit immensely
more if we all came together without that. We could be fighting for
fair wages like musicians. We could literally have strikes and stuff. We
could make it so that they can't replace commercial artists with AI art
and things like that. Tattooers could have had a lobby happening so
that we could have shown during the pandemic that we did not pose
the risk of spreading the transmission of disease like the bars on Broadway did. We could have been open and making money. We have to take
hospital grade fucking courses and stuff to be able to do this. What if
we had a collective voice in a collective lobby? I don't know why we
haven't had that yet. It's egos to be honest.

THAXTON WATERS: I was always fascinated with the stories that my dad
told me—"This is what we did on Jefferson Street from the '60s to the
'70s." My dad always used to say that when Reagan got in office then
all his fun ended. I grew up seeing Jefferson Street in the '80s and '90s,
and it looked like a damn wasteland to me. I was always trying to make
the connection from the stories he told me to what I was seeing. So now
I'm on the street and uncovering the history, and now I'm seeing that
the history happened in Alabama, happened in South Carolina. It happened in Texas. The same history that happened in my own backyard
happened in all these other Black places. They happened around wherever these historically Black colleges were. I start getting all these light
bulb moments like oh, oh, oh. So I can show the work of the students
that are in my gallery, but I could also show the work of other students
at other HBCUs because they're telling the same story.

ELISHEBA ISRAEL MROZIK: My neighbor, he passed away. He was an older
gentleman, but he was a phenomenal wood carving sculptor. I have one
of his pieces. He was phenomenal and I asked around about him and
I could not find anybody who really knew about him. He had a couple
small shows and things, his folk art was phenomenal. Those are the
types of people that we could be reaching if we had organization and
funding. Not only bringing them to light, but giving them resources to
improve their art or just show their artwork and find somebody who
really loves it and supports it.

THAXTON WATERS: I started to tell the story of Historical Black Colleges
and Universities and the five miles surrounding them because they
all tell the same story, whether they be the four here in Nashville or

whether it be the HBCUs in Alabama or Mississippi or, you know, Arkansas or wherever they be. It's the same story around these institutions. I wanted people to be transformed by the history that their great grandparents had walked, their parents walked, their aunts and uncles and everything walked. And I wanted them to see a possible future of where it's going. So I was kind of the intermediary between the millennials and the boomers. They needed that translation.

ELISHEBA ISRAEL MROZIK: My practice is focused on Black women's identity and reclamation of our identity as Black people. Specifically Black women because our identities are being defined and put out into the world by other people. And the stereotypes surrounding people who look like myself, and other Black people, are ridiculous. It causes unconscious discrimination toward Black women and girls. So my work puts out there the identity that I wish to be known by and wish to be defined by. It's also about stopping the nonsense surrounding the identities that we have been given. But Black women in particular, we face a unique set of discrimination issues where, in popular culture, darker-skinned Black women are almost nonexistent. It's difficult because popular culture and the whole "pick me" ideas of I just want to be famous and rich and I don't care what I have to do—that mindset that's out here on the internet. People will pretty much accept anything if it will make them go viral. Even if it's destructive, even if it hurts them or their family.

DONNA WOODLEY: I'm originally from Memphis and I ended up here because I attended Tennessee State and graduated back in '95 with an accounting degree. I got into art because when I finished school in accounting and I started working in accounting, I just realized it wasn't really what I wanted to do for the rest of my life. I started doing a little bit of internal searching and self-discovery, and I came to fashion design. I ended up taking a couple of semesters at O'More College of Design in Franklin at the time. I took a drawing class and did very well in that class. I worked as an auditor for close to seven years, and then got laid off during the real-estate plunge. I decided to go back to school for art because that drawing class just stuck with me. So that was a quick decision once I got laid off, to go back to school and get an art degree.

JOE NOLAN: One of the first things that really made me more aware of this new wave of art happening in North Nashville was seeing Donna Woodley's show at Fond Object. It was curated by K. T. Wolf and Sara

Lederach, who ran Galerie Luperca in East Nashville. That show was emblematic of the creative boom in North Nashville, but it was one of the first times I saw it breaking out into the greater creative scene.

DONNA WOODLEY: The very first solo exhibition I had was the show at Fond Object. I think it was September 2016 that we did that show over at the record store. That series is called *Black Women Rock: Painting Black Female Experience*. I have a really good core group of girlfriends. We had a lot of positivity going on. We started to do these Friday happy hours where we could just kind of process really anything you want to process. By the time I got to grad school, we had developed into almost like *Sex in the City* in a way. We would meet for breakfast every Saturday morning. We'd meet for happy hour every Friday afternoon at different places. One of the things that we would talk about is our experiences as Black women within the spaces that we were in. So one of my friends is a civil engineer. Another works at Vanderbilt. At the time she was in housing education. Another was in higher ed as well. Different professional careers. And then the question of "Would you rather be feared or ignored?" We started talking about this idea of feeling invisible within American society. And we came to the conclusion of it's probably better to be feared because being ignored means you don't exist. That's the foundation of those images. I had been making paintings with granny panties in them, but they were basically dealing with body image. And no racial element came into it. And so when I decided to talk about Black culture, I was talking with my friend Christopher—a redheaded guy. Super cool and a good painter as well. And so I said, "Yeah, I want to put my girlfriends in these scenarios, but I want to include the granny panties because I like the humor in the work with that." And he said, "You should put them on their heads." And I knew, "That's it!" I wish I could say I thought of that myself, but the language and the discourse in building that work up, it developed as I asked my friends to pose for me. And then it also develops anytime I show it, really, because there are so many different perspectives on it. The underwear is basically hiding the eyes. I asked my friends to pose for me and I did photo shoots of them and I actually had clean Hanes underwear, big granny panties, and I said, "Okay, put these on your head, cover your eyes. And the goal is to show some emotion, but without seeing your eyes."

JOE NOLAN: The gallery at Fond Object was just a room in a record store with a big display window that artists would get creative with.

Nashville's art scene is built on improvised gallery spaces, and Fond was a cool store with creative owners. That space was a great example of the art and music scenes cooperating very successfully.

DONNA WOODLEY: Then the other thing, when I started thinking about naming the work, I had always grown up where I was told, you know, "If you have kids, don't name your kids like, these 'ghetto names.' You want the kid to have a foot in the door for a job. If they look at a resume and they see a certain name they're not even going to consider it." That kind of stuck with me. A lot of stuff stuck with me as a younger person because I knew it wasn't right on both sides. I knew it wasn't right for somebody to judge and close the door right away. And I knew it also wasn't right for my family or whoever that was, to support that notion. So I wanted to name the paintings those names that will be on those resumes that wouldn't get a foot in the door, and then pair it with a really prestigious career. So hence "Kaneisha, the Civil Engineer." That's Jessica. It's crazy. None of my friends have those creative names. There are like two Jessicas. There's Angela and then Tracy. The only one that has a colorful name I would say is Shana. And Shana's family is from Haiti. That's a traditional name there.

JOE NOLAN: Some of that work was part of Donna's grad school thesis, and this wasn't a lightweight show. Her work always uses humor and it was hanging in a record shop, but it was formally smart and packed with content and also conceptually rich.

DONNA WOODLEY: On one wall there was like the grid of those smaller *Black Women Rock* paintings. And then I had done seven of the thirty-by-thirty-six-inch *What's in a Name* paintings. That kind of continued that whole idea of embracing these creative names. They also had the red scarves. The red scarf was this nod to the character of Mammy. Mainly Hattie McDaniel. It was about her successful career as an actress versus the role she played in *Gone with the Wind*. And then there was a window where they put my name, and it had a little shelf there. I had done these tent cards of all these really colorful names. I did all of the presidents' last names from Washington all the way to Obama at the time. So there was a colorful name with the president's last name, and then there was like a traditional, if you will, name with the president's last name. So there were two Washingtons, two Jeffersons.

JOE NOLAN: Her exhibition was full of punchlines, and she also interrogated the portrait, and provoked conversations about race and class while celebrating contemporary Black sisterhood. What more could you ask from an art exhibition at a record shop?

DONNA WOODLEY: I'm a very solution driven person, And this carries across the board—I even teach this way. I lead with love and solution. So here's the goal. How are we going to get there? What if you do this? Then this is the consequence. If you do this, this is the result, blah, blah, blah. So my thing is that I am pretty true to my personality. My images pretty much spell out my personality. My goal is to get people to see all sides of it. To laugh about the humor in it. I like to make people laugh and I like to laugh at stuff. I mean, it could be the most serious thing, and me and my family will find a joke in it. The other thing that I've found is that it is a disarming tool, to be able to have an informed conversation and for understanding from both sides. So I believe in asking questions. Once the discussion starts, it's, "So why do you feel this is the way it is?" Or "How do you feel about this?" It's like the difference between people arguing. I don't think an argument is a really effective tool for solution. I think a discussion is a more effective tool. I haven't always felt free enough to be myself, and so I found freedom and being myself in art. I move with a bit of freedom now.

THAXTON WATERS: My dad was kind of like a country boy from out there in Wilson County. And because his dad was from Watertown, my last name's Waters. The founder was called Waters. My granddad moved into Wilson County, met my grandma, had my dad, and then they kind of moved on into Antioch. He just kind of got closer and closer to town. I come from sharecroppers and stuff like that. Back in the '50s and '60s and '70s he used to go to Club Stealaway. He used to go to Club Baron. He used to say it was like so many of them back to back to back to back. And he said they wouldn't be no bigger than probably a room. They probably had three tables. They had two chairs at each one. But, he said that's all they needed. And then I opened up my space in 2007 right next door to a spot that was called Buffalo Express at that time. And then they moved across the street and they were Knockout Wings. Inside of there it was only a space for probably two chairs. But they served all this chicken out of there. I thought about what my dad used to tell me. I saw how there'd be all of these small places up and down Jefferson street.

JOE NOLAN: The key to the contemporary art scene in North Nashville is the push-and-pull between Nashville's modernist legacy in the neighborhood's past and the gentrification that's happening as this new generation of artists are making their mark. In most of the murals and gallery shows and studio spaces you see artists who are connecting yesterday and today with their own unique styles. That neighborhood is haunted by its greatness as well as its tragedies—from Jim Crow to Jimi Hendrix.

THAXTON WATERS: Booker T. Washington, he's my patron saint. I basically collected all of his books. How he built Tuskegee is how I built Art History Class—bringing things in from the neighborhood, getting that neighborhood involved so they just don't see you as a weirdo over there. It's like, get the neighborhood involved, use things from the neighborhood. I'm extensively reading about this stuff, and I'm looking at the way they dressed. I got this book called *Booker T. Washington and the Art of Self-Representation*. It is awesome. And it just basically talked about how he was very keen on how his representation looked when it went out into newspapers, when it went out into articles, when it went out into books. When he presented himself in the neighborhood, what the image did. I lived down on D. B. Todd. I would basically walk from my gallery to the house, and I knew the effect it would have on people as I walked through the neighborhood in three-piece suits and stuff like that. They're only one generation away from seeing this. They might see it in their grandparents' pictures or their parents' pictures of guys in the neighborhood being like that. It's what I do.

JOE NOLAN: Thaxton had already been running the Art History Class space by the time I met him. And you couldn't forget him. He's tall and he's thin so he seems even taller. And he was always wearing snap-brim hats and vests and bowties—vintage verging on antique. I don't remember wild designs or anything, it was just that the styles and cuts and combinations were very yesteryear. It was almost like a costume, but always just a little too formal to laugh off—and he always looked sharp so you couldn't deny it. It was smart. He got this idea about clothes from Booker T. Washington, but it's always an artist's thing— the Ramones' leather jackets and James Brown's cape.

THAXTON WATERS: I'd sit with my table outside my gallery door. I had my two chairs, and then I had my little drink. I'd just be sitting out there, and I kind of looked unique because I'd probably be sitting out there in suspenders or something like that. Pinstriped pants and bowties, something like that. And then people walking up and down the street, they'd want to sit down and start talking to me. And a lot of the people that grew up around there, their heads are full of gray hair and everything. So it'd be wonderful to hear these stories of when they was a boy in the '60s. When they was a boy in the '70s and what the street and what the neighborhood looked like. I had one story a guy told me, and now mind you, he's blind, he grew up in the neighborhood. He remembered the place going from being a neighborhood to being how it is now. Now he *heard* the transition. So he said it was a neighborhood full of kids playing, people talking. It was just kind of alive in the neighborhood. Then he said he heard bulldozers. This is the interstate being built—bulldozers, construction. He said, now it's just basically 18-wheelers and cars, because it's the interstate right by his place now.

JOE NOLAN: Discussions of potential interstate routes across the state of Tennessee were ongoing between the 1940s and 1960s. By the late 1950s officials in Nashville had started to focus on a route that split the North Nashville community in two. No residents were notified and their approval wasn't solicited or welcomed. But by 1967 a group of mostly Black leaders had formed the I-40 Steering Committee. The committee demonstrated how the new route would isolate businesses and displace residents. The committee fought the interstate all the way to the US Supreme Court where their grievances were rejected. North Nashville lost one hundred square blocks and nearly 1,500 residents were displaced. Home values dropped by 30 percent.

THAXTON WATERS: You had these Black towns that were basically connections from after the Civil War. You had these "contraband camps": when the Union Army came in and occupied the capitol or occupied certain parts of the city, enslaved people at these plantations would run to wherever they were. But when they got there, they were considered contraband because they were somebody's property. So they were in an in-between space. After the Civil War, these contraband camps became quasi-cities. Two of them were Black Bottom in South Nashville and then you had Hell's Half Acre in North Nashville—on the north side of the Capitol. So these were little cities where there were burgeoning businesses, building up churches, leaders coming out of there. But as development went on from the 1800s to the early 1900s they started to spread out. So Jefferson Street came from a footpath from the capitol area. In the Hell's Half Acre area there was a footpath from there to the Hadley plantation. It started becoming more developed as people started stretching and spreading down that area. It was being called urban renewal in the early 1900s. These shanty areas were getting knocked down, people being relocated. With all the gentrification you just reclassified like every like forty years. So it happened in the early 1900s, happened again in the '40s, '50s, and '60s, and it's happening again now. It'll just be called different things in different cycles every thirty to forty years. It was developed specifically to cut through all of these problem areas in cities they called n***** towns or little coon towns. To divide them up and cut them up a little bit, break them up a little bit. The plans came down in the '50s, but the real development started happening in the '60s and '70s.

ELISHEBA ISRAEL MROZIK: People get these letters about sell your house for cash right now. They're doing it on purpose to find that person in that desperate situation or who wants that greed. And you tell somebody they could get $300,000 for a piece of shit house—that's more money than they've ever seen their entire life. That is life-changing money for them and they don't do the research behind it. Then they get out here and they realize that they can't buy anything for $300,000. And then they're going to realize how quickly that money goes away. And they get screwed. They don't have that knowledge.

THAXTON WATERS: What's so interesting about the HBCUs, those institutions, is the vulnerable communities that surround them. So when we start talking about urban renewal, start talking about gentrification, start talking about whatever we label it, it's so easy for those vulnerable people to be displaced because they never got rooted in the first place. And that's why I started seeing that over and over and over again. This just happens every forty to fifty years. It's because you never got rooted. It's because you always been vulnerable.

ELISHEBA ISRAEL MROZIK: So many people after that tornado and pandemic got screwed into selling their homes for nothing, and now they're building million-dollar lots. It blows my mind that anybody would pay a million dollars to stare at the projects. Because literally there's a million-dollar home and then there's projects right across the street. Greed is interesting. To me, it's the deadliest sin because it causes all the others.

THAXTON WATERS: When I start talking about history it's almost like a fire of passion coming out of me. It's almost like 100 percent I feel the ancestors are yelling at me to go do this now. It's almost like I have to figure out the best irrigation system of how I deliver it. I try to deliver it to my people this way. Okay, that didn't work. Now I gotta go back to the drawing board. Okay, now let me try to do it this way. That didn't work. Let me try to do it this way. Now the task is still on me to do it. I think in my heart of hearts I'm trying to follow a line of great scholars like James Porter—he was the department head of Howard University. And then you had David Driskell who came behind him. They was these scholars, artists, and they ran spaces. So I kind of see myself in that. I came into that. That wasn't my intention. But I see myself being a teacher at an institution, having my own space, and being a scholar that writes. So it's like this trifecta that I know I need to do, personally.

WE ARE FAMILY

COURTNEY ADAIR JOHNSON: Kelly Bonadies took me to McGruder the first time. I went and sat in on a community meeting, and they had began discussions for what the revitalized community center could look like. The community center is owned by Metro—it's a Metro Schools building. McGruder Family Resource Center is funded by United Way. Every Family Resource Center has a kind of lead partner, and, at that time, at McGruder, it was Matthew Walker. They're basically sort of in charge of the overall operation of the center. It's complicated. We've got three parties in here, and so getting into the building was interesting. I was working for Seed Space at the time. Adrienne had left town. So I came to the center and sat in this meeting, and found out more about the center. I was hanging out there and it was pretty quiet. Jeff McGruder and Kenya McGruder—who are grandchildren of Curlie McGruder—were sort of leading that first initial meeting. So I said, "Hey. My name's Courtney Adair Johnson. I'm a reuse artist." This place—as soon as you walk in, you fall in love. It's this beautiful school building and it felt like anything could happen there. Jeff McGruder asked if I'd be interested in writing an art component proposal for the center.

JOE NOLAN: Courtney's creative work is focused on reusing and recycling materials—that's a practice with a built-in social component and a built-in community creativity component. Lots of us do isolating work, but Courtney's practice was always broader and more connected to the world around her.

COURTNEY ADAIR JOHNSON: I'd just come home from a residency in Minnesota. I'd moved and lost studio space. I needed studio space, and I needed community. So those were two things I was looking for. And I had so many ideas. I was all into creative reuse centers, nonprofits that were working in community, social practice art. So this is all the stuff I was looking at at the time. I would sort of write my ideas down, start going to some meetings and I don't know how it ended up happening, but I realized I could partner with Seed Space as my nonprofit—all the services at the center are nonprofits. As long as you're offering services or resources back to the community you can sort of find a place in Magruder. My proposal was a residency, loosely. The artist would give back to the center in some way. We could have studio space and then we could do projects and bring artists around. We really had to do a little convincing.

JOE NOLAN: Magruder was a perfect place for Courtney to land because the whole building was going through a re-use and re-purpose phase. It's the right project in the right building in the right neighborhood, and her and Marlos have shown that they're the right people to be bringing those creative resources to that community.

COURTNEY ADAIR JOHNSON: Marlos had joined by the time we were creating the initial proposal. I feel like we went through all this together. I'd received a Metro Arts THRIVE award and hired Marlos. And then as soon as we started working together, we really enjoyed our collaborating.

MARLOS E'VAN: Courtney kind of commissioned me, but then we became co-builders. All of that started happening a couple months before I graduated Watkins. And I think that's a really important element for me, too. It went right with this narrative I had for a while of not wanting to graduate and then be blindly out into the world. So me and Courtney started building that before I graduated. By the time I graduated, we were both ready to step in full time. We did killer. We implemented the first projects and just kept going from there. So it's been a really beautiful experience that way. In the beginning, we did a lot of canvasing actually—not driving. We were walking neighborhoods and meeting people, trying to identify artists in the neighborhood that we didn't necessarily know about. It was not just about artists at first, just "Who is who?" And we ended-up running into a couple people that did photography or painted, but they'd never shown anybody before. Those were really cool connections and a really important part of the storyline. The further we went together at McGruder, the opportunities kept coming up for us.

KELLY BONADIES: I grew up in Raleigh, North Carolina. I actually came here to go to Lipscomb University where my mom had gone, and my sister had gone. I met my husband Aaron there. I ended up lasting about two months at Lipscomb. I left or got kicked out. I'm pretty sure I got kicked out. But I ended up just staying in Nashville. Two years later, I ended up going to Watkins. I started with the community education classes. I took a couple of those and then just loved it. And so I enrolled there. That was definitely my entrance to the art scene.

MARLOS E'VAN: I didn't have a senior thesis show at Watkins. There was a lot of politics involved and stuff. But I used my whole last year at Watkins to create a special topics class where I focused on creating my first full body of work. So I had this big body of work called *Dyin' By Tha Gun*, and me and Courtney would just brainstorm and chill in the studio. I really wanted to show this work, and I wanted to hang it in North Nashville. And that was one of the big motivations for us at McGruder. Courtney and I were brainstorming about who we knew and the spaces we could use. And then we started having conversations with all these people. Courtney helped me to reel some people in and Kelly Bonadies ended up doing my debut show, *Dyin' By The Gun*, at an abandoned bakery right behind Ed's Fish. I'd just graduated, but that showed me the power of community early.

KELLY BONADIES: I graduated from Watkins in 2010 and real-estate development started actually right before that in 2009 with the Open Lot building. That was in East Nashville off of Douglas on Jewel Street. We found that building and then started designing out the spaces surrounding a central exhibition area. The collective built it together and then shared the rent. Designing out a space into other spaces to sublet was kind of the first introduction to commercial real estate. James Perrin was there and Laura Cavaliere. There was a guy named Ekim who changed his name from Mike to Ekim which is Mike backward.

COURTNEY ADAIR JOHNSON: We officially started at McGruder in May of 2015. Soon after we actually moved into the building, we started researching asset-based mapping. We wanted to see what the community's assets were. What did everyone have? What was everyone interested in? You could sort of feel it at McGruder that there was like concentrating on our negatives. People only come to this place when they're at the very bottom of their situation and need help. We wanted to change that narrative in the building. We wanted McGruder to be this place where you come because it's fun and cool, and anything can happen. We wanted it to be a place with opportunities for everybody, not just for people who are desperate for some reason. So we did this asset-based mapping. And then we start realizing the importance of Curlie McGruder. The building's named after Curlie. She was the person in the neighborhood who you called if you were going to march. She was the mother of the freedom marchers in town—they were coming from Fisk and TSU and Vanderbilt. And so they'd call Curlie if they got in trouble or she'd even lead the march. After the Civil Rights movement she was a big voting rights advocate.

KELLY BONADIES: We had started looking for the cheapest house that we could find in Nashville. There was this vacant home we bought off of Tenth Avenue North in North Nashville in 2010. And then I started seeing Buchanan Street as a mostly vacant street that had been something, and had the potential to be something again. With all of the development that was happening in all the other areas of Nashville, knowing what was going to creep over there, I was trying to cultivate a different plan that would mitigate displacement and just have a completely different trajectory.

COURTNEY ADAIR JOHNSON: I actually started McGruder first and then landed as the gallery director at TSU. That makes me feel like even more steeped in the history of North Nashville. You know, I think that's some of my driving force: I love to share information and—if I have them—share resources. We'll find a space to produce something, and we'll brainstorm—our favorite pastime is to brainstorm. We'll get different funding and execute projects and be able to hire or pay people. We pay people. I have a full time job. Marlos is a working artist. We want people to get paid.

MARLOS E'VAN: We like to write new narratives, good narratives, around here. One of them that was driving us crazy was that whole thing, you know, with people saying "Oh, I can't pay you, but it's good exposure." Bruh, we've been there. If we can get somebody paid, let's get 'em paid. And so, from the jump, we've been doing that. It's crazy some of the projects that have come through here that we've helped facilitate. It's mind blowing. We haven't been name-dropping, but it's a lot of good stuff.

KELLY BONADIES: We left Open Lot and like a year later I walked into the warehouse at 100 Taylor Street and was looking for a space for Aaron to make a little music studio and have an art studio for myself. I got to know the owner and they were just kind of losing money. The space was just full of random stuff and junk and there was some guy that had toxic floor chemicals stored there. In 2011, people that had lived here and then moved, they were moving back. They were looking for these creative alternative spaces. Hans Schmitt-Matzen connected me to Alex Lockwood who had just moved here and he was looking for a space. And I feel like that was one of the first things that kicked it off. Brent Stewart came into this dusty warehouse and we were tripping over stuff and he looked at this window and he said, "I want to be here." And then I sketched on a piece of paper and designed all the suites around his little suite right around his window. So it just started unfolding. Several different people were looking for space for a wood shop or a recording studio. Harmony Korine was looking for a space. He got the giant middle space making all those giant paintings. Mickey Echo was a musician, and there'd be all these other musicians coming in looking for space. Annie Williams came in with her leather bags. I didn't own the building. I was just signing-up all these people, designing it out, and then the owner had their guys build it out.

COURTNEY ADAIR JOHNSON: McGruder has a cafeteria—a cafeteria/auditorium. It's an old school building. There's a stage with these old blue velvet curtains. I don't know if they're really velvet, but that's what they look like. It's got a library we've turned it into a free library. So we just had books in there, and these books were old and stale and not doing too much. And I wanted it to be a free library and take new donations because nobody was looking at these books. We worked on it for I guess maybe a year. We got donations in and put some signage up. The concept is take a book, leave a book. So we have some great kids books in there. The kids can have a little play area. We've got a couple murals up that we've done through the years. There was one mural there before we got there that was done a long time ago by the community. Now there's three. So we've added. Over the years artists have done some programming there. DoughJoe did a community project. And then we did an opportunity with Nuveen Barwari and Marlos. One year Oasis kids helped on that. If we're working on a project we look to our community members or other nonprofits that would be a good fit.

MARLOS E'VAN: The building sometimes it feels like home, where I can be a host when we have people there, sometimes we're sharing food. On the other side of things there's a lot of times when I help out at the front desk to help out with intake. So actually helping, taking-in clients to see where they need to go, what are they looking for? Sometimes if we're short-staffed, I'll step in and do that. Or sometimes I just sit there and listen to the folk's stories. Because I noticed a lot of people that come through there are definitely going through hardships. We give out food boxes, sign people up for food stamps, help people pay bills as far as light and utilities. We give out diapers, and sometimes feminine products for women. We have an entrepreneurship program. There's a commercial kitchen. There's a plumbing class. Catholic Charities does Free Hearts, which is a really cool program for incarcerated women. Catholic Charities also has a sewing academy. Judge Bell has an expungement court at the building that offers alternatives to incarceration for young adults accused of low-level crimes. But a lot of times people seem like they're just coming here for somebody to talk to. And for me, I've been thankful to be in that position where I might go downstairs and I just happened to be the ear that they're looking for. And I just listen. And some of the things I heard—it goes from good to funny to unbelievably bad. I'm just thankful to be in that position. When it comes to the studio, I'm in a laboratory where I'm able to practice and experiment, implement, carry out. It's my home base. It's a place where me and Courtney have definitely collaborated a lot. I mean, I shot my first film with funding from a grant that Courtney got. I shot *Northern Gardens* up there. That was a snapshot of North Nashville before it completely got bought up and turned around.

JOE NOLAN: I feel like I'm at school when I'm at McGruder. Part of that is that it's literally an old Metro Schools building, but it's also the idea of a resource that's accessible to the local community and focused on them. Courtney and Marlos have created a really unique model as an activator in Nashville's creative placemaking circles. It's the kind of resource only these artist-lead initiatives are able to knit and tape and glue and lash together.

MARLOS E'VAN: When we win these grants and awards we try to break them up to where it's a lot of programming. That means we're on the administrative side a lot, but it's a joy to bring in other people and let them shine. I think that's another big part of what we do.

THE BEAUTIFUL MONSTER

COURTNEY ADAIR JOHNSON: We got the Metro THRIVE award and then we were able to get a Mellon collaboration grant through Vanderbilt and TSU. We got $20,000 on that, and that was a lot of like fun to figure out the best ways to execute and bring in other artists or support our artists in Nashville. We make sure the programming resonates with the community. Thaxton Waters was doing shit on Jefferson that was the beginning of the revival wave we're dealing with right now. And Woke3's history of growing up in North Nashville, going to TSU, staying in the neighborhood, developing his career as a community practice artist—I think it's really amazing.

KELLY BONADIES: I really started looking at Buchanan Street. It was still not of interest to outside investment. There were buildings that were just completely vacant. I wanted to start the pace of a different type of development where it brings in something for the kids and for the families and for the arts, but also for the businesses. I was seeing all the different sides of it. We wanted to bring in something that was for everybody. So Alex was such a big boon to the project because I was able to find him a property where he ended up putting Elephant Gallery and had the plans for all his studios. So a lot of these people from 100 Taylor came over from there to Buchanan Street. And then that coupled with me trying to get the Black-owned businesses there, like Slim & Husky's. It all started combining together because Slim & Husky's and these other Black-owned businesses started recruiting local artists to incorporate their art into their buildings and branding.

ALEX LOCKWOOD: I moved to Nashville from New York in 2010. I'm originally from Seattle. My fiancée and I were getting close to having our first boy. After kind of settling in for a few years and working with my wife on her business, I started looking for studio space. I found 100 Taylor. And it was a similar situation to being in New York, where you're renting a space and the more time you spend in there, the more expensive it's getting. I could see what I had there wasn't going to last. I wanted to try to purchase a building where I could set up a studio for myself, and where I could rent out studios to other artists. During my time at 100 Taylor I became a member of COOP and I curated a number of their shows, and then I had an idea of opening a gallery. So this was 2014 when I bought the Elephant Gallery building and the lot next door.

KELLY BONADIES: The actual art that I enjoyed doing was really like inspired by components—parts of a whole, you know? They were like architectural renderings and these imaginary things that fit together. I feel like that's what translated to these communities. I was seeing all these parts of a whole, in the colors together, and how you're making something out of nothing. I never went out to be an artist, I just started immediately into the spaces. I just started being able to incorporate the arts into the structure of the buildings. Whether that's cheesy or not, I'd never see it as these separate things. Everything is connected.

ALEX LOCKWOOD: I remodeled the space. I put in plywood behind the sheetrock in the front space, even though I wasn't ready to open a gallery. This building was rundown. It had a lot of water leaking through. It had also been a lot of things. It was originally built in the 1960s as the Sam's general store—there's still a Sam's clothing store on Fifth Avenue right downtown. I'm told that back in my space—where the roof jumps up to about twenty feet—that's because they had carpet rolls that they stored back there. Most recently it was a church, but it had been abandoned and in disrepair for a few years when I purchased the building in 2014.

BRADY HASTON: Alex has done such a great job revitalizing that little area and, just making it visible and making it look fun. Making art fun. It's different than what you see in Wedgewood-Houston. And there's a completely different crowd that shows up to each of Elephant's openings, which I like.

ALEX LOCKWOOD: The art was here. The artists were here and working in North Nashville. I'm definitely late. I knew North Nashville was a historically Black neighborhood, and I wanted to be in this neighborhood. But, the gallery's only been open since 2017.

KELLY BONADIES: I didn't push the Buchanan Arts District out into the world, I put out a couple things and that caught on. Of course, anytime you're putting a concept out—especially if you're like a white woman in a predominantly Black neighborhood—you're going to get push-back. But it's something that definitely caught on in all these positive ways. All these art projects ultimately connected with the local schools—you can't go wrong with bringing arts access to schools. As soon as you're a developer, sometimes that's all people can see. But I'm from the art world.

ALEX LOCKWOOD: For the first number of years here I wasn't aware of the amount of work and the amount of artists who were around me. I came to this building because it was inexpensive. And because of the cost, it was an opportunity for me to build out these spaces. I've got to know Woke, who's been a tenant here. And Elisheba who I've worked with. I've worked with Buchanan Arts and Omari Booker. I feel like right now Elephant Gallery is changing as I'm changing. Instead of this gallery being "that Nashville art gallery that happens to be in North Nashville," I'm, trying to be more representative of the place I'm in and to be more aware of the huge number of artists, and the history of art making in my neighborhood.

WOKE: I'm from Nashville originally. My grandma lives in North Nashville. She's been living there since 1960. My family's from Hermitage. Back in high school I started doing graffiti with some friends and things like that. They showed me how to use spray paint, how to draw letters. That was something I was really interested in. I wanted to get

into some kind of group back then when I was in high school. Just trying to find those people that I could actually hang around and things.
And I ended up meeting some graffiti artists and we started hanging
out. We're still friends to this day. Those are some of my oldest friends.
I ended up going to TSU. I was already doing murals and stuff.

ALEX LOCKWOOD: The gallery's first tenants were ceramicists, and then
we had a flower shop in the front space. When they were leaving I met
Brett Douglas Hunter and a number of artists whose work wasn't getting shown around town. Brett became a studio tenant and we did our
first show at Elephant in February of 2017.

JOE NOLAN: Brett Hunter is a self-taught artist—he's the grandson of folk
artist Don Shull. He makes these large sculptures and furniture figures
of imaginary creatures that he paints with these really vivid cartoon
colors. His work has some of the same playfulness that Alex's sculptures
have, and Brett was the perfect artist to christen that space.

ALEX LOCKWOOD: One thing that's very important to me is that I'm there
to support the artist's vision of what they can do in this kind of little
space. I want the artist to paint on the floor. I want them to use the outdoor walls. I want them to really kind of take over as much of the space
as possible to make it a different experience for the viewers every time
they come in. And I want that difference to be directed by the artists
who are showing. I'm here to support that with material, with bringing
in outside designers to help with my posters. Paul Collins helped me
with editing a press release. Another designer helps put together other
material. I want an artist to come in with a strong vision.

WOKE: When we do murals, we're doing graffiti murals. We're going finding abandoned buildings and not really going and trying to ask for
permission. But then, when I went to TSU, Michael McBride was the
one that told me I should be an art major, because I was going to be a
computer science engineer. Or a computer science major. I don't know.
Whatever. I'm glad I didn't do that.

JOE NOLAN: The North Nashville muralists evolved out of a graffiti scene.
That's partly why you see so much of Basquiat's influence in the North
Nashville studios. A bunch of them got started as young Black graffiti
artists just like him.

WOKE: I still wasn't thinking about trying to be an artist. I was just doing
graffiti art. I thought I was going to do graphic design. So I did a concentration in graphic design and I majored in studio art, and then I
started being around a bunch of different artists. I started learning

about Basquiat. Basquiat really inspired me to just be able to be as creative as I want to. And he inspired me to grow my hair and everything. And Thaxton Waters gave me a book about murals and muralists who travel the world doing large scale murals. Some of the murals that we see downtown were those same artists. They travel all over to do that. I wasn't really thinking about it too much, to be a full-time artist doing murals. But when he showed me that book, I got really inspired. It inspired me enough to go out and get an internship at Seed Space.

JOE NOLAN: The North Nashville graffiti artists adapting into these muralist projects had a huge impact. There was a few early mural projects in Nashville, and then there were some cultural carpet bagging campaigns, bringing out of town muralists in. But it didn't feel like street art had arrived in Nashville until the North Nashville and East Nashville scenes were popping off.

WOKE: Adrienne was nice, man. I went on the Seed Space website and I looked on there and I don't know if it said internship or maybe I just went there. I saw Adrienne in there and I said, "Hey, I'm just trying to get an internship." And she said, "Oh. OK. Sure." So when I got there, she started teaching me a bit. I told her that I wanted to do at a mural festival because I wanted to bring a bunch of muralists out. We didn't really have muralists showing up. Mike McBride and James Threalkill had their mural at the Gateway to Heritage. And of course we have the history with Aaron Douglass and everything, but it wasn't really nothing going on in the neighborhood. A lot of buildings were there. So I told her about it and she taught me about grants. I didn't really know much about grants.

JOE NOLAN: Michael and James's mural is a massive, colorful part of a larger roadway beautification project on Jefferson Street where I-40 splits it in half. It celebrates the musicians and lost venues that made Jefferson Street a music hotbed in the mid-twentieth century, before the interstate project. Little Richard cut his teeth in the clubs on Jefferson Street and Jimi Hendrix played there when he was just a sideman with touring acts on the so-called Chitlin' Circuit of Black music clubs east of the Mississippi.

JAMES THREALKILL: There's an evolution of energy in North Nashville as relates to the creative arts that goes back to the days in the 1950s and 1960s when you had people like Jimi Hendrix and Stevie Wonder and Gladys Knight coming to town to perform in a lot of the clubs in Nashville when Jefferson Street was kind of the prominent hotspot in the city. That was all before the freeway came through and kind of broke-up the community.

MICHAEL MCBRIDE: When they started the renovation on Jefferson Street, James and I, we got a commission to paint the mural underneath the underpass. Then a lot of the young guys saw what we were doing. And then when they got old enough, they started this whole new art scene here. DoughJoe, Jamaal [Woke] they were all students of mine. And so with them starting what they call street art, they really got into it. And so they started their own Jefferson Street Art Crawl. You know, they just started trying to revitalize that. They just went with it, man.

WOKE: I was a junior about to become a senior at TSU. And when Adrienne told me about grants, she told me about the THRIVE award. She showed me how to apply for that. We got the full award and we were able to do the Norf Wall Fest. I showed her the location, she helped me organize it and everything like that. She helped me get all that information straight, and budgeting and things. That was my internship assignment the whole time, the whole summer.

JOE NOLAN: The creative arts attract a certain kind of person with certain kinds of skills and not every painter or dancer is also likely to have a facility with administrative skills. But those kinds of skills are crucial to making creative practices sustainable. Not everybody can do it, but you'll find those people in every scene—the people who can organize and lead and connect people. Woke is one of those.

WOKE: So then we did the Norf Wall Fest. I wanted to do a "Norf" because I'm from North Nashville and N-O-R-F, that's how I hear people say it. So I just kind of spelled it out like that. I started inviting Elisheba in, Ol' Skool, and DoughJoe and Sensei. A bunch of them came out and they painted and the turnout was good. People came out. They really loved it. They kept talking about it, about the murals down there under the Jubilee Bridge. I did a piece on Buchannan and the other muralists did their own works under the bridge. I was inspired to start like a crew or something. One of my friends, Keep3—he's the one who taught me graffiti—I told him about it. I said, "What if we did a crew called Norf?" So I ended up inviting all of those artists together and we talked, and ultimately it was me, DoughJoe, Sensei, Keep3, and a guy named Malcolm Voltaire who formed Norf. Everything got started through that Wall Fest.

JOE NOLAN: My favorite mural from the fest was Brad Wells's monochrome portrait of W. E. B. Du Bois.

WOKE: Brad died just a few months after we did that. He was a really great guy. Norf's official first thing was actually *The Gathering*. It was in that same location where Norf Wall Fest happened. We had live music, we had vendors come out. We had people helping sponsor the project. We didn't have any grants or anything like that. We had a place for kids to do paint-and-drawing things. And then we did a mural live during that time. During that whole event we started and completed that mural. People came out and they watched, and it was just a good time. It was 2016, *The Gathering*.

JOE NOLAN: One of the reasons the murals in North Nashville standout is because a lot of the artists live or work there. They're making art there. They reflect the day to day life of the community. It's a hyper-local scene and that's beyond authentic.

WOKE: My work has always been inspired by my surroundings. I want to talk about my surroundings. Norf got a grant for a project that we called *Home Invasion*—we were talking specifically about gentrification and homelessness. That was in 2016 or '17. I think that mural has actually been painted over. The murals that we're creating now, we're putting the inspiration in the work, and it inspires people. The gentrification, it's something that's just happening. But you can make work about it and talk about it, and for me, as an artist, that's what I've been doing. Trying to think of ways to liberate ourselves from the system enough to where we're able to have ownership. Right now, with how everything is moving in Nashville, it's really hard for artists or anybody to live or to own. I'm trying to shed light on it. To make work that's shedding light.

MICHAEL MCBRIDE: Anne Brown was one of the main people that got James Threalkill and I going. About 1986 she had the Greater Nashville Arts Foundation. And it was located in the old Church Street Center where the library is now. That mall had stores in it, it had nightclubs in it, it had all this, and her office was there, too. And so she came up with the idea about doing murals. So the first murals done in Nashville— before it was known as public art—was done by James and I, and some of the kids from Edgehill. Anne Brown came up with the idea because a lot of stuff was being graffiti bombed. And so she thought up the idea about organizing these kids to do these murals. Now you see murals all over East Nashville, West Nashville, North Nashville and James and I laugh about that because everybody thinks that's new. Anne Brown was the main person really moving art to where it is. She was always in the forefront of that. Anne Brown was at Texas Southern University back in the late 1960s. That's a Historical Black College with John Biggers. He was there. Debbie Allen and Felicia Rashaad's mother was there. Brown came from the theater side of the arts, and what brought her to Nashville was that she came to teach at Fisk. So she taught at Fisk before she opened up The Arts Company.

CARLTON WILKINSON: We did what we did in the 1990s and this is just a whole new generation of people who are graduating students. I think the gentrification of North Nashville is just changing the whole land-scape, and I think there's an effort to look at the history of North Nash-ville. It's very complicated. It is generally known as an area that was predominantly African American. It was a center for protests through Fisk and TSU and Meharry. So a lot of things are going on, and I think there is an effort by the young people, young artists to document that. To document that spirit, because otherwise you're going to be looking at a lot of murals about Airbnbs.

JAMES THREALKILL: And when you look at those beginnings with Carl-ton and Woodcuts, and then now see what's taking place with the Norf group—those young artists who came together and facilitated doing these outstanding murals in North Nashville, and had an exhibit at the Frist Art Museum. Right now, you've got a lot of young, talented energy that's taking place in that community. The guys with Slim & Husky's are supporting the arts with the opening of NKA Gallery on Buchanan Street next to their pizza place. And then Carl and Jennifer with Garden Brunch were big art patrons because that place was so popular. People were coming from all over the city to eat. And so when they allowed artists to hang work there, man I can't tell you how many pieces I sold out of that venue just from people going to eat there. And so they were just key players in giving artists another venue.

SAM DUNSON: I'll be honest with you. I sit back in awe about all of them. Jamaal [Woke] was a student at TSU. And he was so strongly con-nected to hip hop. I mean the entire hip hop genre—the graffiti, the whole culture in general. And growing up in Nashville he was really connected with North Nashville a lot more than I was because of the fact that I came here as a student, but hadn't really grown up in the area. When he was a young student, he was strongly into mimicry of another specific artist. So he was trying to get kind of a vibe of what that particular artist was doing in his own work. And I was trying to basically let Jay know that he should create his own line of who he is as an artist. And then bring those other artists in to enrich his path—as opposed to making his path through those artists. And it was honestly at a time where social media was really jumping and you were able to see what artists were doing and artists' lives and all of that. And one of the things that Jay did for his senior thesis was actually talk about the idea of being a muralist and a public artist that was going to create his own career. There have been a number of artists that have said "I want to be a studio artist. I want to go to grad school," and I was all on board, but Jay was thinking about doing something that would pretty much be a blueprint for other artists in the program that didn't want to go either to grad school or didn't want to go into an established creative job working for someone else. He literally had his mind set on creating his own future. And the Norf Wall Fest, when it started off, I was amazed at the idea that those artists were coming together as a group, but also finding strength as a group, enough to force art entities to come to them. They could have been literally going on their hands and knees asking and begging for money. But, instead, it was almost like they established something that was going to force art entities to find them. And it seemed like so many things were trying to swirl around North Nashville at that time to kind of bypass that as an opportunity for young Black artists. But it was almost like there was a heartbeat with the Norf group that was loud enough to force people to see that there was life there. When you think about DoughJoe, Jay, Alexander, Omari, they've created this monster. It's a beautiful monster.

CARLTON WILKINSON: So it's changing, unfortunately. Changing fast and furious. A fixer-upper in North Nashville is $400,000. I mean, a dump is $400,000. And when we had the tornado, that exacerbated things because a lot of those homes that were destroyed were rentals. And they were not owned by people in North Nashville. It almost feels like a desperation to really make sure we don't lose that spirit of what North Nashville was and is or can be. And luckily the institutions are there, but we're losing that old generation of Nashville. And so the young people, many of 'em don't live there. They live all around and so you have people coming in and reminiscing and romancing what North Nashville was.

OMARI BOOKER: Mr. Dunson is my mentor and my great friend, and it's not an accident that those influences produce special work. I spend a lot of time in other cities and I think there's something special about Nashville in general, and especially this crazy little zip code where we now have all of these crazy murals. Woke started doing those when he was a TSU student in his early twenties along with DoughJoe and Elisheba and the others. It's like when you look at the great local basketball coaches and the great teams—there's a line. We're definitely in an era where people pay so much attention to the now, but there was a whole other line that was behind them. It didn't come out of nowhere.